English Language and Literature

A LEVEL AND AS

Ruth Doyle
Angela Goddard
Raj Rana
Mario Saraceni

SERIES EDITOR:
Angela Goddard

OXFORD
UNIVERSITY PRESS

OXFORD
UNIVERSITY PRESS

Great Clarendon Street, Oxford, OX2 6DP, United Kingdom

Oxford University Press is a department of the University of Oxford. It furthers the University's objective of excellence in research, scholarship, and education by publishing worldwide. Oxford is a registered trade mark of Oxford University Press in the UK and in certain other countries

© Oxford University Press 2015

First published in 2015

British Library Cataloguing in Publication Data

Data available

ISBN 978-019-833749-2

10 9 8 7 6 5 4 3 2 1

Printed in Great Britain by Ashford Print and Publishing Services, Gosport.

Acknowledgements

The authors and publisher are grateful for copyright permission to reprint the following material:

Chimamanda Adichie: extracts from *Americanah* (Fourth Estate, 2013) copyright © Chimamanda Adichie 2013, and from 'The Headstrong Historian' in *The Thing Around Your Neck* (Fourth Estate, 2009), copyright © Chimamanda Adichie 2009, reprinted by permission of HarperCollins Publishers Ltd.

John Agard: lines from 'Listen, Mr Oxford Don', copyright © John Agard 1985, from *Mangoes and Bullets* (Serpent's Tail, 1990), reprinted by permission of John Agard c/o Caroline Sheldon Literary Agency Ltd.

Margaret Atwood: extract from *The Penelopiad* (Canongate, 2006), copyright © Margaret Atwood 2006, reprinted by permission of Canongate Books Ltd.

W H Auden: lines from 'Spain 1937' first published in *Another Time: Poems* (1940), from Collected Poems edited by E Mendelson (Faber, 2007), reprinted by permission of Curtis Brown Ltd, on behalf of the Estate of W H Auden

John Baxter: extract from *The Most Beautiful Walk in the World: a pedestrian in Paris* (Short Books, 2011), copyright © John Baxter 2011, reprinted by permission of HarperCollins Publishers, USA.

Alan Bennett: extract from 'Her Big Chance' from *Talking Heads* (BBC Books, 2007), reprinted by permission of The Random House Group Ltd and United Agents (www.unitedagents.co.uk) on behalf of Alan Bennett.

Ben Bova: 'Tips for Writers' at www.benbova.com, reprinted by permission of the author.

NoViolet Bulawayo: extracts from *We Need New Names* (Chatto & Windus, 2013), reprinted by permission of The Random House Group Ltd.

E E Cummings: lines from 'yes is a pleasant country', copyright © 1944, 1972, 1991 by the Trustees for the E E Cummings Trust, from *The Complete Poems: 1904-1962* edited by George J Firmage (Liveright, 1994) reprinted by permission of Liveright Publishing Corporation, a division of W W Norton & Company.

Rana Dasgupta: extract from 'Arrivals' in *Tokyo Cancelled* (Harper Perennial, 2006), reprinted by permission of HarperCollins Publishers Ltd.

David Eggers: extract from *What is the What? The Autobiography of Valentine Achak Deng: a Novel* (Penguin, 2008), reprinted by permission of The Wylie Agency on behalf of the author.

Ekow Eshun: extract from *Black Gold of the Sun: Searching for home in England and Africa* (Penguin, 2006), copyright © Ekow Eshun 2005, reprinted by permission of Penguin Books Ltd.

Sue Grafton: extract from *K is for Killer* (Pan Macmillan, 2011), copyright © Sue Grafton 2011, reprinted by permission of Macmillan Publishers Ltd.

Seamus Heaney: lines from 'Death of a Naturalist' from *Opened Ground: Selected Poems 1966-1996* (Faber, 2013), reprinted by permission of Faber & Faber Ltd.

Ernest Hemingway: extract from *In Our Time* (Charles Scribner, 1925), copyright © 1924, from The First Forty Nine Stories (Arrow, 2004), reprinted by permission of The Random House Group Ltd.

Rachel Khoo: introduction to *The Little Paris Kitchen: Classic Recipes with a simple and fresh approach* (Penguin, 2012), copyright © Rachel Khoo 2012, reprinted by permission of David Higham Associates.

Jhumpa Lahiri: extract from 'The Third and Final Continent' in *Interpreter of Maladies: Stories* (Flamingo, 2000), reprinted by permission of HarperCollins Publishers Ltd.

Philip Larkin: 'The Whitsun Weddings', copyright © Philip Larkin 1964, from *The Whitsun Weddings* (Faber, 2010), reprinted by permission of Faber & Faber Ltd.

Roger McGough: 'Cake' and '40-Love', from *After the Merrymaking* (Cape, 1971), copyright © Roger McGough 1971, reprinted by permission of United Agents (www.unitedagents.co.uk) on behalf of Roger McGough.

Janice MacLeod: extract from *Paris Letters: One woman's journey from the fast lane to a slow stroll in Paris* (Sourcebooks, 2014), reprinted and reproduced by permission of Sourcebooks, Inc

Arthur Miller: extract from *Act 1, All My Sons* (Penguin Modern Classics, 2009), copyright © Arthur Miller 1947, reprinted by permission of The Wylie Agency on behalf of the Arthur Miller Literary and Dramatic Property Trust. All rights reserved.

Terry Pratchett: extract from *The Colour of Magic* (Corgi Books, 1985), copyright © Terry Pratchett 1983, reprinted by permission of Colin Smythe Ltd.

Reginald Rose: extract from *Twelve Angry Men* (Methuen Modern Plays, 1996), copyright © Reginald Rose 1955, 1996, reprinted by permission of Bloomsbury Methuen Drama, an imprint of Bloomsbury Publishing Group.

Alice Sebold: extracts from *The Lovely Bones* (Picador, 2002), copyright © Alice Sebold 2002, reprinted by permission of David Higham Associates.

Alan Sillitoe: extract from 'The Loneliness of a Long Distance Runner' in *Collected Stories* (Flamingo, 1996), reprinted by permission of HarperCollins Publishers Ltd.

Joe Simpson: extract from *Touching the Void* (Vintage, 1997), reprinted by permission of The Random House Group Ltd and the author

Ali Smith: extract from *The Accidental* (Hamish Hamilton, 2006), copyright © Ali Smith 2006, reprinted by permission of Penguin Books Ltd.

Sue Townsend: extract from *Rebuilding Coventry: A Tale of Two Cities* (Penguin, 2013), copyright © Sue Townsend 1988, reprinted by permission of Penguin Books Ltd.

Timm Ulrichs: 'ordnung – unordnung' (1961), reprinted by permission of Timm Ulrichs and the Wentrup Gallery, Berlin.

Timothy White: extract from *Catch a Fire: The Life of Bob Marley* (Omnibus Press, 2000), copyright © Omnibus Press 2000, reprinted by permission of the publishers.

John Williams: extract from *Stoner* (Vintage, 2012), copyright © John Williams 1965, reprinted by permission of The Random House Group Ltd and of Frances Collin Literary Agency.

Tennessee Williams: extracts from *A Streetcar Named Desire* (Penguin Modern Classics, 2009), copyright © 1947, 1953 by The University of the South, reprinted by permission of Georges Borchardt, Inc, on behalf the Estate of Tennessee Williams, and of New Directions Publishing Corp; and from *Cat on a Hot Tin Roof* (New Directions, 1975), copyright 1954, 1983 by The University of the South, reprinted by permission of Georges Borchardt, Inc, on behalf of the Estate of Tennessee Williams, and of New Directions Publishing Corp. All rights reserved.

William Carlos Williams: 'This is Just to Say' (1934) from *The Collected Poems of William Carlos Williams, Volume 1 1909-1939* (New Directions, 1991) reprinted by permission of Carcanet Press Ltd, and of Pollinger Limited (www.pollingerltd.com) on behalf of the Estate of William Carlos Williams.

Jeanette Winterson: extract from *Oranges Are Not the Only Fruit* (Vintage 2011), copyright © Jeanette Winterson 1985, reprinted by permission of The Random House Group Ltd; extract from *Weight* (Canongate, 2005), copyright © Jeanette Winterson 2005, reprinted by permission of Canongate Books Ltd.

and to the following for their permission to reprint copyright material:

AQA for extracts from the AQA Language and Literature AS specimen paper 2014 and from the AQA Specifications.

Cancer Patients Aid Association, India (CPAA) for 'Smoking Reduces Weight' advertisement

Crown Paints Ltd for advert used in HouseBeautiful magazine, February 2014 including Crown Paints slogan

EE Ltd for advertising slogan for Orange

Express Newspapers/N & S Syndication and Licensing for headline 'Tearful Andy loses Wimbledon but wins over a nation', article by David Pilditch, Daily Express, 9 July 2012

The Gate Theatre, Notting Hill for flyer for the production of Grounded

Guardian News and Media Ltd for extracts from: 'Female rock fans shout out: I shouldn't have to like pop just because I'm a girl' by Caroline Sullivan, theguardian.com, 14 Aug 2014, copyright © Guardian News & Media Ltd 2014, and 'Freewheeling Paris. Parisians may have gone Velib mad, but cycling in the city can be scary' by Agnes Poirier, The Guardian, 28 Oct 2008, copyright © Guardian News & Media Ltd 2008

Hibü (UK) Ltd for advertising slogan for Yellow Pages

Independent Print Ltd for 'The 30 Second Briefing', Business Editor James Ashton/Jamie Oliver, The Independent, 22 June 2013, copyright © The Independent 2013

Jo Malone London for 'Rain and Angelica' from a promotional brochure for the London Rain limited edition perfume series

The Royal Exchange Theatre, Manchester for flyers for productions of *Cat on a Hot Tin Roof*, *Hamlet*, and *Crocodiles*

Telefónica/O2 Holdings Ltd for advertising slogan for O2

Telegraph Media Group Ltd for headline 'After 77 years the wait is over', article by Paul Hayward, Daily Telegraph, 7 July, 2013, copyright © Telegraph Media Group Ltd 2013

Thomas Cook UK & Ireland for advertising slogan.

Any third party use of this material, outside of this publication, is prohibited. Interested parties should apply to the copyright holders indicated in each case.

Although we have made every effort to trace and contact all copyright holders before publication this has not been possible in all cases. If notified, the publisher will rectify any errors or omissions at the earliest opportunity.

Image acknowledgements:

Cover: Brandon Bourdages/Shutterstock.com: **p14:** James Chapman; **p34:** Scott Barbour/Getty Images; **p39:** Matt Madden; **p48:** (l) Angela Goddard, (r) Laura Hol Art; **p49: (tl, tr, bl, br)** Angela Goddard, **p55: (l, r, b)** Matt Madden; **p59:** Matt Madden; **p114: (t)** © Hemis/Alamy, (b) Zvonimir Atletic/Shutterstock; **p156: (t)** Oxford University Press, Othello, The Moor of Venice, 1826 (oil on canvas), Northcote, James (1746-1831)/Manchester Art Gallery, UK/Bridgeman Images, (b) © Ben Molyneux/Alamy; **p163: (t, b)** © AF archive/Alamy

Page layout by Phoenix Photosetting.

Contents

Key

AS level and A level

AS level (but useful as skills development for A level)

A level only

Introduction to the Student Book

This book is divided into chapters, each of which covers a distinctive topic area or skill that is developed and assessed in the AQA specifications. Key features of the book include the following:

- **Chapter aims:** Each chapter has a clear statement of aims at the start.

- **Key term:** This label indicates that a term is important, because it will recur throughout the course. The first time each key term appears in the book, it has been emboldened and defined briefly in the margin. Many subsequent appearances of each key term throughout the rest of the book have also been emboldened, to emphasize that they are key terms.

- **Glossary:** A glossary at the back of the book lists all of the key terms, with their definitions, for easy reference.

- **Activity:** The book explains and teaches concepts and ideas, and the topics to be covered in each chapter should be clear from the aims listed at the start. But in order to learn thoroughly, you need to try things out for yourself and have hands-on experience. Activities are included that will allow you to develop transferable skills.

- **Feedback:** For most of the activities, feedback is available either in the main part of the Student Book, or at the back. Feedback will indicate the main points likely to arise, but is not provided for more open-ended activities.

- **Extension activity:** These activities are designed to take you further into a particular area of learning.

- **Research idea:** This is a larger-scale piece of work, such as is required for the coursework component. A research idea cannot be completed immediately: it takes time to plan and develop.

- **Link:** This feature indicates the ways in which your work on a topic may link to other chapters in the book; to ideas for further reading; or to information online.

- **Remember:** This prompt will give you advice on developing good study skills.

- **Did you know?:** This feature introduces interesting facts that will be helpful to your studies.

- **Looking ahead:** This feature explains the ways in which the skills you are developing will be relevant to the whole course and to any future career plans.

- **Review your learning:** A few short questions at the end of each chapter will remind you about what you have learned and help you to summarize it.

- **References and Further reading:** Some of the ideas referred to are related to past research work. Where this is the case, the name of the researcher is given in the text. You can read the full reference at the end of the respective chapter. The 'Further reading' section contains a list of texts that you will find useful when pursuing the subject further.

- **Index:** An alphabetical list of topics is provided at the back of the book. It enables you to find passages you want to look at again.

Weblinks are included throughout this book. Please note that Oxford University Press is not responsible for third-party content and although all links were correct at the time of publication, the content and location of this material may change over time.

A note on spelling

Certain words, for example 'specialized' and 'organized' have been spelt with 'ize' throughout this book. It is equally acceptable to spell these words and others with 'ise'.

Introduction to the AQA English Language and Literature AS level and A level specifications

Key features of the AQA specifications

The following list describes the key features of the AQA AS level and A level specifications and the ways in which this book supports them:

- **AQA's AS and A level specifications have been designed so that they can be taught together.** This book follows the AQA structure and therefore can be used by both AS and A level students. Each chapter will indicate which AS and A level papers are covered.

- **AQA's study of language and literature is integrated**, and this is also the approach of this book. There are no separate sections devoted to 'language' and 'literature'. The same methods are used to analyse literary and non-literary texts. This means that you can build up a single set of skills that you can take from one assessment to the next.

- **AQA's specifications include skills and tasks of different kinds.** There are opportunities for your own creative writing as well as for independent research. Text-analysis skills underpin all of the areas of study. All these types of work are thoroughly addressed in this book.

- **AQA's specifications offer a choice of set texts** and a choice of how to balance literary and non-literary texts. Teachers will be using their professional judgement to choose the texts that are right for you. The aim of this book is to provide you with useful approaches to any of the set texts chosen.

- **AQA's A level specification requires the study of all three of the literary genres** – prose fiction, poetry and drama. This provides good coverage for any transition into higher education. This book shows you what is distinctive about the literary genres, as well as offering approaches that will work with all three.

- **AQA's AS level specification requires the study of poetry and prose fiction.** It will be clear in this book where AS level study finishes. If you choose to take the full A level as well, you can pick up where you left off – nothing is wasted!

> This section of the book covers the:
> - key features of the AQA English Language and Literature AS level and A level specifications
> - Assessment Objectives that apply to this subject
> - different writing skills that you need to develop
> - language levels that underpin analytical methods.

The specifications at a glance

The A level specification

The A level specification has three components:

- Paper 1: Telling Stories – 3 hour exam; 40% of A level
- Paper 2: Exploring Conflict – 2½ hour exam; 40% of A level
- Non-exam assessment: Making Connections – coursework folder; 20% of A level

Paper 1: Telling Stories

This paper is divided into the following three sections:

Section A: Remembered Places

This section is based on the AQA Anthology *Paris*.

It is a closed-book assessment – meaning that you cannot take your book into the exam room – and will be based on material from the Anthology provided on the exam paper.

There is one compulsory question.

Section B: Imagined Worlds

This section is based on a prose fiction set text.

It is an open-book assessment, meaning that you will be able to consult your text.

You will answer one question from a choice of two.

Section C: Poetic Voices

This section is based on a poetry set text.

It is open book.

You will answer one question from a choice of two.

Paper 2: Exploring Conflict

This paper is divided into the following two sections:

Section A: Writing About Society

This section is based on a set text (either fiction or non-fiction).

It is open book and requires you to show your knowledge of the text by completing a re-creative writing task.

You are also required to write a critical commentary, explaining the choices you made in your writing.

Section B: Dramatic Encounters

This section is based on a drama set text.

It is open book and you will answer one question from a choice of two.

Non-exam assessment: Making Connections

This is a coursework folder. It consists of a personal investigation that explores a specific technique or theme in both literary and non-literary discourse (2,500–3,000 words).

The AS level specification

The AS level specification has two papers:

- Paper 1: Views and Voices – 1 ½ hour exam; 50% of AS level
- Paper 2: People and Places – 1 ½ hour exam; 50% of AS level

Paper 1: Views and Voices

This paper is divided into the following two sections:

Section A: Imagined Worlds

This section is based on a prose fiction set text.

There is one compulsory question.

This section is closed book, meaning that you cannot take your book into the exam room.

Section B: Poetic Voices

This section is based on a poetry set text.

There is one compulsory question.

This section is closed book.

Paper 2: People and Places

This paper is divided into the following two sections:

Section A: Remembered Places

This section is based on the AQA Anthology *Paris*.

It is closed book, and the assessment will be based on material from the Anthology provided on the exam paper.

There is one question, which is compulsory.

Section B: Re-creative Writing

This section is also closed book. It requires a re-creative writing task, based on some material provided in Section A. You are also required to write a critical commentary, explaining the choices you made in your writing.

The English Language and Literature Assessment Objectives

Assessment Objectives describe the different skills, knowledge and understanding on which you will be assessed in any subject. Each task you carry out, either on an exam paper or in your coursework folder, will be assessed through more than one of the Assessment Objectives listed below. Nowhere on either the A level or the AS level specification are you assessed through only one of the Objectives. This is because work in English requires a number of different elements in order to be successful. You should be able to see this as you read the description of the Assessment Objectives below.

Assessment Objective 1 (AO1)

Apply concepts and methods from integrated linguistic and literary study as appropriate, using associated terminology and coherent written expression.

This Assessment Objective rewards you for three things:

1 Being able to apply the ideas and approaches that are part of the subject area, for example applying some aspects of the language levels that are set out later in this chapter.

2 Being able to use the key terms that are relevant for the subject area. The key terms that are emboldened throughout the book are exactly that.

3 Being able to write coherently. This means that your writing makes sense and the points you make link together in a logical way.

Assessment Objective 2 (AO2)

Analyse ways in which meanings are shaped in texts.

This Assessment Objective credits your ability to point to the features of a text and suggest how they contribute to its meaning.

WQEIC LRC

7

This is not a cut-and-dried issue: meaning is interpretive, which means that there is not a single or simple answer to the question of what a text 'means'. The credit you are given here, therefore, is for arguing your case and for pointing to aspects of a text as evidence for what you say.

Assessment Objective 3 (AO3)

Demonstrate understanding of the significance and influence of the contexts in which texts are produced and received.

Texts can stay the same but their **contexts** change. The same text can be read by different people, at a different time in history, or in a different place, and be interpreted differently as a result. Something can be very different when in a different **mode**, because speech and writing allow us to do different things. Electronic texts are different again. You are not expected to try to be lots of different people in understanding different contexts, but you are expected to be aware of possible variations and to be able to write about them.

Assessment Objective 4 (AO4)

Explore connections across texts, informed by linguistic and literary concepts and methods.

No text exists in isolation. Sometimes, texts make explicit reference to other texts. For example, the slogan 'Keep Calm and Carry On' has frequently featured on T-shirts, mugs, bags and other accessories in some UK shops. The slogan plays on the idea of British people being stoical and resilient. Recently, a supermarket has started selling cool bags (for ice cream, cold drinks and so on) bearing the slogan 'Keep Cool and Carry'. This is an example of the way in which one text refers to another, and is termed **intertextuality**.

Even when texts do not explicitly refer to other texts, there can still be a link between them. We put texts into categories, such as 'advertisement', 'letter', 'blog' and so on, and we expect such texts to have certain features in common. This is true of the categories that form the basis of these specifications: what makes something 'literary' or 'non-literary'? This Assessment Objective is all about being aware of textual groupings and also about questioning them. The coursework component offers a unique opportunity for you to spend some time thinking about what literary texts have in common with other texts and how they might differ.

Assessment Objective 5 (AO5)

Demonstrate expertise and creativity in the use of English to communicate in different ways.

This is about your own writing skills. It involves some basic aspects such as technical accuracy, but it is also about being able to choose and control a style of writing for a particular audience and purpose, and to suit a specified format. The term 'creativity' means being able to show some flair and originality by thinking about how to do things in new ways rather than simply following familiar routines.

Writing skills develop over time, so you should be prepared to draft and re-draft your writing and make use of constructive criticism from readers of your work. This Assessment Objective stresses the idea of writing in different ways.

Key terms

Context. The circumstances of a text, such as when and where it was written, who wrote it and why, the mode and medium of communication, who is reading it now.

Intertextual / Intertextuality. The way in which one text echoes or refers to another.

Mode. Speech and writing are called different modes. Digital communication can draw on both of these modes, so is often called a hybrid form of communication.

The following section provides a summary of the different types of writing you are expected to demonstrate across both A level and AS level specifications.

Writing skills you need to develop

Assessment Objective 5 specifically rewards writing tasks, such as the re-creative work involved in Component 2 of both the A level and the AS level.

However, writing skills are important throughout the specifications because, if your writing is not clear, you won't be able to demonstrate the other Assessment Objectives: you won't be able to show that you can use specialist terminology, debate meaning, discuss **context** or explore textual connections.

You therefore need such general writing skills as clarity and accuracy. You do not need a special type of academic voice in your writing, however. Being academic is not about using as many long words as possible, or about writing very long sentences. It is about expressing yourself clearly, with each sentence you write making one main point. Specialist terms can be useful because they are a kind of shorthand used by experts in a field, so they can save time and space. But don't use terms you don't understand. It is better to show that you understand something in a non-technical way than to use technical terms without understanding.

Sometimes, students worry about how personal or objective to be – saying that they are unsure whether to use the **first person pronoun** 'I' or whether to use a passive style. This is a false choice and somewhat over-simplified. There's nothing wrong with using 'I' now and then, but if a piece of writing repeatedly uses the phrase 'I think', this can sound like a lack of confidence. At the same time, it is odd to express your own ideas in a style that implies you had nothing to do with the interpretation, such as 'the view was taken that…'.

> **Key term**
>
> **First person pronoun.** The pronouns 'I' (singular) and 'we' (plural).

The best, neutral-sounding style is a kind of statement style and you will see this exemplified in the style of writing used throughout this book. A statement style makes statements about a text or an idea, for example:

> 'this part of the text suggests that…'
>
> 'this idea is only partly true because…'

Statements can also be phrased tentatively, which is important, given that many different readings of a text are possible:

> 'this may mean that…'
>
> 'it could be the case that…'

Writing a text analysis

Writing a text analysis is all about organizing your points in a logical way. Going line by line through a text is not helpful because the same language feature might occur in lines 3, 8 and 14 of a text, so you would be repeating yourself. It is much better to find all the examples of a certain language feature or strategy and group them together in one paragraph, then move on to the next group of features. This will read as a much more thoughtful and thorough analysis.

To group features takes time, so writing a text analysis can mean you spend as much time preparing to write as doing the writing itself. But the reward will be writing that is concise and succinct. Writing more is not necessarily a good thing: it's quality that counts, not quantity.

A text analysis is your interpretation of its meanings. The language features in the text act as a form of evidence for your reading, so the more examples you can give, the better. However, remember that any text adds up to something holistic: it's not simply a collection of parts, but a complete entity. Make sure that you don't lose sight of the bigger picture – what the whole text is trying to say (including ideas about any contradictions in its messages), its context, its **genre** and so on.

Writing a discussion

A text analysis differs from a discussion in that discussions are responses to ideas or views, while a text analysis is a response to an extract or some data. A discussion essay is an opportunity to take an idea and tease it out in as much detail as you can. This might well mean setting out different arguments or at least showing that you are aware of different views while in the process of setting out your own.

Writing a discussion is not about splitting yourself in half and arguing all in one direction to start with, then arguing a different point of view. It is more about arguing a case, but with concessions to the fact that there are different views about a topic or text.

Re-creative writing

This form of writing is all about taking some source material and either recasting it into a different form, or developing an area that wasn't very prominent in the original.

If you are recasting material – which is the task at AS level – you need to change the material to suit a new audience, purpose and/or format.

If you are undertaking a re-creative task that involves developing a new area (the A level version of re-creative writing), your job is to add something to the text that wasn't there in the original. You will need to think about the perspectives of the more minor characters or things that have occurred 'behind the scenes' even though they are not spelt out in the text. What you write must be feasible within the plotline of the original text.

Writing a commentary

A commentary is a piece of reflective work where you explain the choices you made in your re-creative work. You need to be selective in the things you focus on, describing some of the major features of your new text and showing how your writing relates to the original text (called the **base text** in the specification documents).

Re-creative writing is explored in more detail in Chapters 4–6 of this book, where activities will help you become familiar with different writing tasks, including the writing of commentaries.

Writing a report

A report is an account of an activity. It looks back over time and describes a set of procedures that were followed in order to investigate an area. It offers findings and draws conclusions. The coursework component (called 'non-exam assessment' in the specification documents) is a report, and this area of the A level is described in Chapters 8 and 9 of this book.

Key terms

Base text. The original text, which in the case of this specification will be a set text (for A level) or Anthology material (for AS level).

Genre. In language study, a type of text in any mode which is defined by its purpose, its features, or both. In literary fields, genre tends to refer primarily to the literary genres of prose, poetry and drama, but it can also refer to types of content (for example, crime or romance).

Re-creative writing. An activity that provides insights about a text by recasting part of it, or by adding new perspectives to it.

Referencing

Referencing is a way of showing the source of ideas and facts, and it is used to indicate where a writer or an academic field has contributed to our knowledge of a subject. It is also used, more specifically, to show where quotations are from. Referencing is an important skill to acquire, particularly if you are thinking about going on to university and further study. If you quote from an academic's work and don't acknowledge it correctly, you can be accused of plagiarism, which is a serious issue.

Many subjects in the arts and social sciences use the Harvard referencing system and several reliable referencing guides are available online, often on university library websites such as the following:

http://www.otago.ac.nz/library/pdf/harvard_citeitright.pdf

References could be used in any of your work across the specifications. If you are referring to a literary text that you are studying, or to some non-literary material that you have collected, then you don't need to give the full reference each time you quote from it; a page reference, line reference, chapter, scene or poem title will be enough for a literary text, and a source will be enough for some non-literary data. But if you are quoting from an academic book or article, use the correct procedure for referring to this in the body of your writing and for listing full details at the end of your work.

To see referencing in action, look at page 13, where the work of a researcher called Crispin Thurlow is referenced. You will see that the reference in the main part of the book just uses his surname and gives the date of his research; if you go to the references list at the end of the chapter, you will see the full details that are needed. This is to enable readers to follow up his research and find it in a library or online.

Language levels

Both the A level and the AS level specifications for English Language and Literature require you to understand 'language levels'. This refers to the way in which language study has traditionally categorized language – including the language of literature – in order to analyse it.

When we use language we don't separate it into parts, but in order to study language we need to do so. The difference between using something and analysing it is similar in many other areas. For example, riding a bicycle certainly requires skill. But analysing how a bicycle works is a different kind of activity, involving looking in some detail at the mechanics of its parts.

Think of language levels, then, as a way to help you focus on particular parts of the mechanics of texts of all kinds, including literary ones. However, you still need to be able to see texts as a whole as well: the bicycle still needs to be something that will get you around and give you pleasure, as well as being something with an interesting history that is worth knowing about.

The English Language and Literature AS level and A level specifications will increase your appreciation of texts because you will understand more about how they are put together. Understanding how texts work will also increase your skill as a language producer, because you will have more awareness of the effects of your language choices. Although riding a bicycle and being a bike mechanic may be different activities, knowing something about mechanics means that you

Did you know?

The language levels were given their name by a Swiss linguist, Ferdinand de Saussure (1857–1913), who is often credited as the founder of the academic areas of **linguistics** and **semiotics** (at least in modern Europe).

Key terms

Linguistics. The academic study of language, including different languages.

Semiotics. The study of how signs and symbols work within human communication.

Key terms

Alliteration. The repeated use of the same consonants at the beginnings of words.

Discourse. A stretch of language (spoken, written or multimodal) considered in its context of use.

Grammar. The structural aspects of language that tie items together. Grammar includes syntax, or word order; and morphology, or the elements added to words to show their grammatical role (such as 'ed' to indicate the past tense of a verb).

Lexis and semantics. Lexis refers to the vocabulary of a language. Semantics refers to the meanings of words and expressions. Semantics can also refer to meaning in a broader sense, i.e. the overall meaning of something.

Multimodal. A multimodal text draws on more than one mode of communication – for example, by using images as well as words.

Onomatopoeia. The way in which some words appear to echo the sounds they describe, such as 'crash' and 'thud'.

Phonetics / Phonology. The study of the sound system. Phonetics refers to the physical production and reception of sound, while phonology is a more abstract idea about all the sounds of a particular language.

Pragmatics. Assumptions made about what is meant, or the inferences drawn from what is written.

Prosodics / Prosody. Prosody is the melody that our voices create via prosodic aspects such as rhythm and intonation. ▶

become a better bicycle user – more able to manage gears and suit them to the terrain, more aware of what the bike is doing and why something might be going wrong, more able to fix things when they do go wrong. In short, you develop a lot more confidence and control, as well as an ability to understand and help others.

When language levels were first proposed, there were only two main language levels – phonology and grammar. But as time has gone on, scholars have added to the levels, which is why in different textbooks and articles you might well see a different list from the one below. The list here is AQA's own, based on the national criteria for the subject of English Language and Literature. This is the list that you need to work with and the one that will be used in assessments:

- **Phonetics**, **phonology** and **prosodics** – e.g. the sounds of real speech and the patterns of **sound symbolism** (rhyme, **alliteration**, **onomatopoeia**) that some writers employ
- **Lexis and semantics** – e.g. the connotations of words and phrases, metaphor and idiomatic language
- **Grammar** – e.g. how the use of pronouns can shape narrative viewpoints
- **Pragmatics** – e.g. the assumptions made about listeners/readers by the speaker's/writer's language choices
- **Discourse** – e.g. the way in which different text types use particular features or routines, including aspects of visual design and layout.

The levels identified and exemplified above have to be understood, but not simply for their own sake. They have to be applied to texts. Before you try this out for yourself, here is some information about how the levels apply to texts of all kinds.

Phonetics, phonology and prosodics

This level is all about sound. English Language and Literature is not simply about written texts. Spoken texts and **multimodal** texts (for example those that involve mixtures of speech and writing, such as websites) feature as part of the AQA Anthology: *Paris*. Poetry doesn't just exist as writing: it is often performed. Plays may start as written texts (although some start as improvisations and are only written down later), but they soon acquire a parallel life on the stage.

Even writing that stays on the page, however, has connections with sound. We don't simply process writing in a one-dimensional way. We 'hear' words with an inner voice, even if we are reading silently. Good writing keys into this aspect of our behaviour, in order to make readers imagine how speakers might sound, just from a few written features such as altering spellings, for example.

On the next page is an example of a text re-creating a sense of spoken language by using written **symbols**. It is an extract from a chatroom dialogue between two university students and has been taken from some research on how people adapt to new forms of communication. In the chatroom there was no sound, so the participants had to try to make their writing represent the sounds they would have used in spoken language. Natalie wants to convey to Simon a certain way of saying 'yes'. To start with, she mis-spells 'yeah' as 'yeak'. Can you work out the sounds that are being described here?

Natalie and Simon were interviewed at the end of the research and their comments about what they were trying to do are in the Feedback section at the back of this book.

> Natalie>>yeak
>
> Natalie>>sorry yeah
>
> Simon>>why yeah
>
> Natalie>>i dont mean it like yeah man i mean it like yeay
>
> Simon>>what is the difference
>
> Natalie>>it's happier and less cheesy
>
> Simon>>and that is worthy of a yehah
>
> (Goddard, 2005)

Natalie and Simon were trying to use regular alphabetic symbols in order to simulate different sounds. This is the kind of approach that might be used by writers such as literary authors and advertising copywriters, who need their work to be understood by a wide range of readers. But there is a much more precise way of writing down sounds, involving methods that are used by experts in phonetics and phonology. Professionals such as speech therapists (who help individuals with pronunciation problems) and dialogue coaches (who work with actors and speechmakers to help them acquire different accents or languages) make use of a specially designed alphabet for transcribing sounds. This is called a **phonetic** or **phonemic alphabet**.

A phonetic alphabet is a detailed set of symbols referring to many languages, whereas a phonemic alphabet is simpler and covers a single language – in our case, English. There are many resources showing this alphabet online – for example at www.phonemicchart.com – with links to symbols that can be clicked on and heard. For the purposes of this specification, you do not need to become a phonetics expert to any scientific level. However, you should familiarize yourself with the phonemic alphabet, because it will help you to understand some of the differences between speech and writing. Also, understanding that there are different approaches to representing sounds will help you to understand the choices that writers make in their texts.

Writers of texts of all kinds may want to suggest a certain kind of voice or speaker, for example a specific kind of accent. This idea is exemplified in Simon's use of 'yehah', in the chatroom dialogue above. A linguist researching the nature of phone texts (Thurlow, 2003) claims that **phonological approximation** is also common in phone texting. By this he means the idea of shaping the writing to suggest spoken language. For example, some people write in a way that reflects their own accent, such as writing 'wivout' instead of 'without' in order to convey a London accent. As well as accent, writers might also want to suggest certain speech noises – for example when someone is surprised or shocked – in which case they need to use written language to help you 'hear' that expression. Natalie's use of 'yeay' in the chatroom dialogue could be called a speech noise or, more technically, a **response cry** – a cry that expresses emotion in response to a stimulus.

Key terms

Phonemic alphabet. An alphabet for transcribing general sounds, suitable for a specific language.

Phonetic alphabet. An alphabet designed for transcribing the sounds of all of the world's languages.

Phonological approximation. Writing that tries to reflect pronunciation.

Response cry. A spontaneous cry expressing emotion. For example, surprise, shock or joy.

Sound symbolism. The way in which sounds are used to represent ideas. For example, in onomatopoeia – where sounds represent noises. There is no logical connection between the sounds and the ideas they represent.

Symbol / Symbolic / Symbolism. A symbol is something that stands for something else, with no logical connection between the items. Symbolic is an adjective meaning 'like a symbol'; symbolism is the process or act of being symbolic.

Key term

Representation Something that stands in place of something else. Representation is how something *appears* to be, not how it really *is*.

Research idea

Look at some phone texts, emails and/or social media posts and collect some examples of writers shaping the language to suggest aspects of speech. See if you can classify your examples according to what the writer might be trying to suggest, for example accent, a speech 'noise' such as 'aargh', laughter and so on. You could compare your examples with some uses in a literary text for your coursework folder: see Chapters 8 and 9 for information about this aspect of the specification. ●

Activity

1. In the brief extract from *Lovely Bones* below, a child (Buckley) is looking for his mother, who is in the bathroom secretly eating macaroons. How does the writer represent the child's voice?

2. Look in any of your set texts for some examples of the **representation** of distinctive voices. Make a list of your examples and for each one, try to explain how the writer is manipulating language to create the sense of a voice.

There was a knock down low on the door.

'Momma?' She stuffed the macaroons back in the medicine cabinet, swallowing what was already in her mouth.

'Momma?' Buckley repeated. His voice was sleepy.

'*Mommmmm-maaa!*'

Some aspects of sound patterning are less about changing the alphabetic appearance of words and more about exploiting the conventions, or habitual ways, of thinking about certain sounds. For example, **onomatopoeia** refers to the way in which some words appear to echo the noises they describe. There is nothing universal about this – each language will have its own conventions for describing noises. The culturally specific nature of representing sounds can be seen in James Chapman's illustration below, where 'woof' is translated into 13 other languages.

The fact that language use is **arbitrary** or **symbolic** in this way doesn't stop us from making strong associations between the names of sounds and the noises or ideas that they refer to. Our associations can go beyond individual words to include the whole area of sound patterning in, for example, **alliteration**, (where the same consonants are repeated), and **assonance**.

Although it is argued that there is no real connection between sounds and their **referents**, the physical way by which we produce sounds might have an effect on how we perceive their likely meanings. For example, **plosive** sounds (in English these are p, b, t, d, k and g) involve obstructing the airflow through the mouth and releasing it quickly, causing an 'explosion'. It follows that these sounds might be used more often to suggest a sudden impact than **fricative** sounds (such as s and z, where there is a continuous airflow).

It also seems to be the case that once a group of sounds have established a particular association, new examples can join their ranks and strengthen that association. For example, many English words beginning with 'sl' suggest unpleasant sensations, particularly of wetness, while many words beginning with 'gl' suggest reflections of light on hard surfaces:

slime	glass
slush	glimmer
slather	glitzy
slick	glitter
sloppy	glaze
slug	glare
slippery	glow
slobber	glacier

Key terms

Arbitrary. Having no real connection beyond that of social convention.

Assonance. The repetition of vowel sounds in the stressed syllables of different words.

Fricative. A sound that is made by creating a continuous airflow. For example, in the sounds /s/ and /z/. You can see that this term is connected to the word 'friction'.

Plosive. A sound that is made by obstructing the airflow and then producing a sudden release of air. For example, in the sounds /b/ and /g/. You can see that this term is connected to the word 'explosion'.

Referent. The thing or person being referred to.

Activity

Seamus Heaney, one of the poets set for study on the AQA specification, uses different aspects of sound patterning in his poem 'Death of a Naturalist'.

Read the lines below and find some examples of **onomatopoeia**, **alliteration** and **assonance**. Try to explain for each example how the **sound symbolism** is being used. What is being suggested?

There is some feedback on this activity at the back of the book.

Death of a Naturalist

Then one hot day when fields were rank
With cowdung in the grass and angry frogs
Invaded the flax-dam; I ducked through hedges
To a coarse croaking that I had not heard
Before. The air was thick with a bass chorus.
Right down the dam gross-bellied frogs were cocked
On sods; their loose necks pulsed like sails. Some hopped:
The slap and plop were obscene threats.

Research idea

Find some examples of sound patterning in other types of texts, for example advertising, rap lyrics, nursery rhymes, greetings cards, epitaphs. You could compare your examples with some uses in a literary text for your coursework folder: see Chapters 8 and 9 for information about this aspect of the specification. ●

So far, quite a lot has been said about sounds as individual items but much less about sound in general. **Prosodics** (or **prosody**) refers not to sounds but to the backdrop to the sounds that we make. If the sounds we produce go towards making words, then prosodics is a bit like the soundtrack that sits behind our voices. Areas such as rhythm, pitch, volume and intonation are part of this soundtrack and are powerful contributors to meaning. You will know from your own experiences of digital communication in phone texting, in social media and in emails, how easy it is to misunderstand a writer's intention if you can't hear his or her voice. Natalie (in the chatroom dialogue on page 13) wouldn't have had to go to such trouble explaining her meaning if she had been able to use the subtleties of her own voice. Humour, sarcasm and irony are particularly hard to convey in digital environments, which is why users developed emoticons such as 'smileys' to suggest playfulness.

Writers of prose fiction use a mixture of strategies to suggest prosody, including punctuation marks and aspects of word processing such as typeface and font. For example, looking back at the brief excerpt from *Lovely Bones* (page 14), you can see how the writer uses italics and an exclamation mark to suggest the raised volume of the child's voice:

'Momma?' Buckley repeated. His voice was sleepy.

'Mommmmm-maaa!'

The duplication of letters also suggests the length of the utterance, indicating that the child held the cry for longer than usual.

As well as manipulating the writing system, literary authors also tell us directly how characters are feeling. Given that the writing system offers limited resources for expressing prosody, this means that readers can themselves create an appropriate soundtrack to back the words that are said. In the example below, again from *Lovely Bones*, note how important the terms 'resolute' and 'pleaded' are to how you 'hear' the dialogue in your head. Notice also the **onomatopoeic** terms used at the beginning:

My father listened to Lindsey in her room. Bang, the door was slammed shut. Thump, her books were thrown down. Squeak, she fell onto her bed. Her clogs, boom, boom, were kicked off onto the floor. A few minutes later he stood outside her door.

'Lindsey,' he said upon knocking.

There was no answer.

'Lindsey, can I come in?'

'Go away,' came her resolute answer.

'Come on now, honey,' he pleaded.

'Go away!'

Activity

Focusing on any of your set texts, find examples of the use of punctuation to indicate **prosody** (e.g. speech volume, intonation, speed, rhythm, pitch, speech fluency). To start you off, here are some examples of punctuation to look for:

- … (repeated dots)
- CAPITALS
- Exclamation marks!!!
- Question marks???
- *Italics*
- Dashes – with words between the dashes –
- Hyphens between l-l-letters
- Dashes where one speaker appears to be cut short by another
- Brackets of various kinds
- Inverted commas around a word or phrase.

Research idea

Collect some non-literary texts in order to look for features similar to those discussed in the activity. For example, you could look at emails, SMS, social media posts, advertising, information texts and newspapers. You could compare your examples with some uses in a literary text for your coursework folder: see Chapters 8 and 9 for information about this aspect of the specification ●

Writers of texts that are designed to be performed will not only need to pay detailed attention to how something should be said, but also to the **non-verbal communication** that should accompany the spoken language. This covers all the physical aspects of communication, such as facial expression, body posture and movement (the latter is sometimes called **kinesics**). You will also sometimes see the term **paralanguage** used about certain aspects of language that relate to a speaker's voice quality, such as laughter, a breathy voice or whispering. These differ from prosody in being less about the language system and more about an individual speaker's use of particular sound effects.

Key terms

Kinesics. Body movements involved in communication.

Non-verbal communication. Communication that takes place via means that are not language based (such as gesture and facial expression).

Paralanguage. Aspects of an individual's vocal expression such as whispering, laughter, breathiness.

Activity

Below are two brief extracts from drama set texts – both indicating aspects of non-verbal communication and paralanguage. Read the extracts and then explain how these aspects work alongside the words spoken, and how they contribute to the overall meaning of the communication.

You don't need to be studying these texts in order to be able to interpret the features used.

There is some feedback on this activity at the back of the book.

All My Sons

Act I

FRANK [*noticing tree*]: Hey, what happened to your tree?

KELLER: Ain't that awful? The wind must've got it last night. You heard the wind, didn't you?

FRANK: Yeah, I got a mess in my yard, too. [*Goes to tree*] What a pity. [*Turns to KELLER*] What'd Kate say?

KELLER: They're all asleep yet. I'm just waiting for her to see it.

FRANK [*struck*]: You know? – It's funny.

KELLER: What?

FRANK: Larry was born in August. He'd been twenty-seven this month. And his tree blows down.

KELLER [*touched*]: I'm surprised you remember his birthday, Frank. That's nice.

A Streetcar Named Desire

Scene 1

BLANCHE [*faintly to herself*]: I've got to keep hold of myself!

[*STELLA comes quickly around the corner of the building and runs to the door of the downstairs flat.*]

STELLA [*calling out joyfully*]: Blanche!

[*For a moment they stare at each other. Then BLANCHE springs up and runs to her with a wild cry.*]

BLANCHE: Stella, oh, Stella, Stella! Stella for Star!

[*She begins to speak with feverish vivacity as if she feared for either of them to stop and think. They catch each other in a spasmodic embrace.*]

Lexis and semantics

This level of language is all about vocabulary (lexis) and the different phrases and expressions (semantics) that help to shape meanings in texts of all kinds.

Some words have a grammatical function, which means that they help with the structure of a sentence or utterance. Other words have more content and direct meaning in the sense that they refer to something in the world. In the text on the next page, which is taken from a fold-out booklet advertising a new perfume range called *London Rain*, the words 'of', 'a', 'at', 'with', 'on', 'an' and 'and' are all doing structural work, while the other words in the text have more obvious content.

Although some words have a core of meaning that might be seen as factual (termed **denotation** or **denotative meaning**), a great deal of meaning is based on our associations (termed **connotation** or **connotative meaning**). Our associations can be based on many things – on the culture we live in, the region of the world we inhabit, the historical time we are part of, the influence of our more immediate social groups and, of course, our specific individual experiences.

An example of the difference between denotation and connotation can be seen in the term 'rain'. Here is a factual definition from Wikipedia:

Rain is liquid water in the form of droplets that have condensed from atmospheric water vapour and then precipitated – that is, become heavy enough to fall under gravity.

But this is probably not what comes to mind when you think about your associations for 'rain'. And your associations might well be very different from those of people who live in a different climate.

Key terms

Connotation or connotative meaning. The associations that we have for a word or phrase.

Denotation or denotative meaning. Literal meaning, dictionary meaning in its most basic, factual sense.

Activity

1. What are your associations – the ideas, the feelings, the memories, the pictures in your mind – connected with the word 'rain'?

2. How do your ideas compare with how rain is described in the advertisement below?

RAIN & ANGELICA

Glassy beads of dew, awakening
a London park at dawn. A revitalising scent,
enlivened with herbaceous angelica
and juicy lime on an earthy base of vetiver.
Aqueous and clear.

◀ **An advertisement for one of the perfumes in the *London Rain* perfume range from Jo Malone London**

Key terms

Synonym / Synonymous. Synonyms are words that have a similar meaning, such as 'help' and 'assist'. If something is synonymous with something else, it has a similar meaning to it.

Thesaurus. A type of dictionary that groups words together on the basis of similar meaning.

One of the ways in which the above advertising text works is to build up its own pictures, partly through a visual image – but also by creating a kind of word-based painting. To understand some of the connotations of words and phrases, it is often useful to think of **synonyms** – alternative words and phrases that could have been chosen, but were not. Doing this can help you to recognize the particular qualities of a word or expression that made it attractive to the writer.

Activity

1. The *London Rain* advertising text mentions a 'revitalising scent'. What other terms could have been chosen instead of 'scent' and what would the result have been?

2. Synonyms are easy to find on any dictionary website or a dictionary phone app. A collection of synonyms is called a **thesaurus**. On the right are ten synonyms for 'scent' from the Chambers dictionary website (www.Chambers.co.uk). Which of these terms would not have altered the meaning of 'scent' very much and which would have altered it drastically? For each alternative, try to explain what the difference would have been.

There is some feedback on this activity at the back of the book.

perfume

essence   aroma

fragrance   bouquet

A revitalising... scent

aura   whiff

redolence   odour

smell

It should be clear from the activity you have just completed that there are very few, if any, precise synonyms in English. This makes sense because language users try to achieve economy, so why bother to have many terms that all mean exactly the same thing?

Key terms

Formal. Designed for use on serious or public occasions where people pay attention to behaviour and appearance.

Narrator. A fictional 'teller'; the apparent voice of a fictional narrative created by the author.

Register. A form of specialist language. For example, the language of sport or science.

Semantic field. A group of terms from the same domain. For example, names for food or aspects of computer communication.

Looking ahead

The ability to choose the right level of formality and the right kind of register is a key skill throughout the specification and in any career that involves communication.

Style and register

As well as suggesting more positive or negative connotations, terms can be part of more or less **formal** styles of English. You may have been aware, looking at the list on page 19, that the term 'redolence' is more formal sounding than the term 'smell'. Formality is an important part of meaning, because it suggests different contexts for language use. Formal language tends to occur when people are in public situations, where they feel they need to monitor their own language use and be careful about what they say. It may be that they are speaking to relative strangers, in settings that are serious and/or ceremonial. Informal language is more common between people who know each other well and are using language unselfconsciously in relaxed settings.

Many formal words in English have come from Latin or French, while many informal ones date back to Anglo-Saxon or Viking eras. This can lead to equivalents where a term of French origin sounds more sophisticated than a Germanic one, for example 'cuisine' compared with 'cookery' or, from the list above, 'perfume' compared with 'smell'.

Formality in written language can make us associate an overall message with something serious and important. The *London Rain* advertisement as a whole is a mixture of more formal terms, such as 'herbaceous' and 'aqueous', with more informal or ordinary terms, such as 'juicy' and 'clear'. You need to be prepared for texts of all kinds to have these sorts of variations and patterns, because writers are often engaged in a balancing act between the danger of sounding too formal and unfriendly, and that of sounding too flippant and trivial.

As you saw previously, literary authors also have to think about how to use different styles in order to distinguish one character from another, including any **narrator**.

Formality can also attach to some words that are not commonly recognized because they are from specialist fields. Specialist terms are called **registers** or **semantic fields** and are part of the way in which groups establish their identities. There are occupational registers, such as those of medicine or law, and registers to do with common interests, such as skateboarding or fishing. This book is using an academic register, with specialist terms from linguistic and literary studies. The *London Rain* perfume advertisement uses specialist terms from herbalism in its reference to ingredients, such as 'angelica' and 'vetiver'. But notice that, as a non-specialist audience, we are given some tips about what these things are: angelica is described as 'herbaceous', which tells us that it's something to do with herbs, and vetiver is described as 'earthy', which again suggests that it's a form of plant life. Writers might want to suggest that there are things we can learn, but it's not in their interest to baffle us completely.

Metaphor

Another core area of lexis and semantics is that of **metaphor**. Metaphor is a language strategy for bringing two unrelated ideas together in order to suggest a new way of looking at something. The perfume text uses metaphor by suggesting that the dew is alive: it 'awakens' the park at dawn. Referring to an object or thing as if it were a human agent, as here, is termed **personification.** In the case of the dew, seeing it as an agent waking up the park suggests the nourishing quality of water to support life.

Below is another example of personification. This text was printed on notepads at a conference venue. The notepad 'speaks' to us and seems rather easily pleased.

I'm a notepad.
Write on me and make me smile.

Because metaphor can allow writers to suggest meanings in a very concentrated way, it is a language strategy that frequently occurs in poetry. For example, in her poem 'Valentine', Carol Ann Duffy rejects 'a red rose' and 'a satin heart' as **symbols** of love, preferring instead a metaphor of an onion to represent the emotion. Onions, like love, can make us cry, have a strong effect on us and they even have rings – another frequent symbol of love.

Although metaphor is often found in literary texts, it is certainly not exclusive to them. Metaphor is an aspect of everyday language that is so common that some analysts (e.g. Lakoff and Johnson, 1980) claim that it is a fundamental part of how we think and behave, as well as what we say. Their book *Metaphors We Live By* shows how metaphors can be grouped and how they reinforce each other in conditioning us to think in certain ways. The following activity will help you to explore this area further.

> **Key terms**
>
> **Metaphor / Metaphorical.** A language strategy for bringing two unrelated ideas together in order to suggest a new way of looking at something. Metaphors are common where something is difficult to understand because it is complex or abstract, so it is compared with something simpler or more concrete.
>
> **Personification.** Treating an object as if it were a person.

Activity

1. Below are some very common expressions that are **metaphorical**. You can see that they are metaphorical because they can't be literally true. They all use aspects of our bodies in metaphorical ways. Try to explain them in a non-metaphorical way (imagine that you are explaining them to someone who is learning English as a foreign language).

   - He broke my heart.
   - I cried my eyes out.
   - I'm going out of my mind.
   - Her eyes were glued to the TV.
   - Our eyes met across a crowded room.
   - He laughed his head off.
   - Keep your nose out of my business.
   - She just blew up at me.
   - I'm in a hurry – must fly!

2. Lakoff and Johnson suggest a number of categories for everyday metaphors. Some of these are listed below, along with an example for each. Can you add to the examples with further expressions?

   - Love is a journey

   Example: We've come to the end of the road in this relationship.
   - Time is money

   Example: Don't spend time on that.
   - Argument is warfare

   Example: He shot my argument down in flames.
   - The body is a container for emotions

   Example: I was boiling with rage.

3. Focusing on the poet chosen as your set text, identify some of the metaphors in the poems and explain why you think the poet has chosen those particular metaphors.

Key terms

Cohesion. The way sentences or utterances join together to form a whole text.

Declarative. A clause or sentence that has a statement function.

Imperative. A clause or sentence that has a command function.

Grammar

Grammar goes beyond the idea of single words or phrases and refers to the structural aspects of language, especially how sentences and utterances work and how they join together to form texts (termed **cohesion**). The notepad text (page 21) consists of only two sentences, but it is clear that they relate to each other. The notepad uses the **first person pronoun** 'I' to address us in the first sentence and 'I' becomes 'me' in the second, where it suggests that it won't be a 'happy' notepad until we have written on it. The first sentence, which is a **declarative**, or statement, is followed by an instruction or **imperative**, telling us to do something. The role of grammar, then, is to indicate how language items are connected and how they are ordered.

Grammar has already been referred to when discussing the *London Rain* perfume advertisement. At the beginning of the section on lexis and semantics, the following words were described as having a grammatical function: 'of', 'a', 'at', 'with', 'on', 'an', 'and'. These words do not all have the same function: 'a' and 'an' tell us that we are talking about a single item – that a noun is singular; 'of', 'at', 'with' and 'on' are all **prepositions**, which are words that usually introduce phrases and denote position, direction or relationship ('at the school'; 'with a friend', 'on the bus', 'of a subject'); 'and' is a **connective**, joining elements together ('apples and oranges', 'she went out and got in a taxi'). All these varied functions are grammatical, because they tell us about how different language items relate to each other.

An aspect of grammar that it is important to know about is **modification**, which is all about adding information, often to nouns and verbs. In the previous section, it was noted that the noun 'angelica' was described as 'herbaceous' so, in this case, 'herbaceous' gives us more information about this thing called 'angelica'. Similarly, we have 'glassy' beads, a 'London' park, a 'revitalising' scent, 'juicy' lime, an 'earthy' base, plus two modifiers at the end of the text, 'aqueous' and 'clear', which don't appear to describe anything specific but could refer to the dew, to rain and/or to the perfume itself. All of these words are modifiers, because they modify (add to, help to shape) the information provided.

The notepad text was described as being made up of two sentences. If a sentence is defined as having to have a **finite verb**, then technically the perfume advertisement has no sentences at all. That may surprise you, because the text certainly looks as though it is written in sentences – in the sense that it has capital letters and full stops. But the verb elements in the text are termed **non-finite**, because they don't indicate tense, which is all about when any action happened.

Here is the first sentence of the *London Rain* advertising text again, with the non-finite verb in bold italic:

> Glassy beads of dew, ***awakening***
>
> a London park at dawn

If a finite verb structure had been chosen, there would have been several options. The verb 'to be' could have been used – 'are awakening', or 'were awakening'. Each of these options would have given an indication of when the action occurred. Further alternatives would have been 'awaken' (which indicates action happening now), or 'awakened' (indicating action that happened in the past). But the term that was chosen – awakening – does not indicate either present or past time, when used on its own. However, the 'ing' form does suggest something ongoing. So in terms of meaning, the grammar suggests something timeless but ongoing – not a bad quality for what is being advertised in this case.

Sometimes, sentences without main verbs are called **minor sentences**. By this definition, all the sentences in the perfume text are minor sentences. When parts of sentences appear to be missed out, this is termed **ellipsis**. This can make texts appear note-like. You will be able to see ellipsis in action if you look at your text messages. You are likely to have messages such as 'just going to' and 'am busy will phone later', where 'I am' or 'I' is missed out. So in the perfume text, 'Aqueous and clear' is a minor sentence showing ellipsis.

So far, the discussion has been about sentences, but the idea of a sentence only really applies to written text. The term doesn't really work for speech, because we don't speak in sentences very much. Even the most carefully planned and

Key terms

Connective. A word that joins elements together, such as 'and' and 'or'. These are also called conjunctions.

Ellipsis. The omission of elements in a sentence or utterance. For example, 'going to', instead of 'I am going to', when written in a text message.

Finite verb. A form of the verb that indicates when an action occurred (called 'tense'). For example, she *helps* me (present tense), she *helped* me (past tense).

Minor sentence. A sentence without a main verb.

Modification. Modifiers add information. For example, adverbs add information to verbs (run *quickly*), and adjectives add information to nouns (a *lovely* day).

Non-finite verb. A form of the verb that doesn't indicate when an action occurred (called 'tense'). For example, in 'exploring the city', the verb element 'exploring' doesn't indicate when the exploration occurred.

Preposition. A word that typically indicates direction, position, or relationship, such as 'into', 'on', or 'of'.

> ! **REMEMBER**
>
> Spoken grammar differs considerably from written grammar, but grammar books have historically been very writing-oriented. We are only just learning about the distinctive patterns of spoken language, through large searchable collections of language called corpora (singular: **corpus**), held on computers.

Key terms

Collocation. The regular occurrence of a word or phrase alongside others.

Corpus. A collection of searchable language data stored on a computer.

Informality. The opposite of formality. An informal context is a relaxed one in which people feel unselfconscious. An informal language style could include slang, regional dialect or other forms of colloquial language that are used within personal relationships and in private settings.

Research idea

Visit the British National Corpus (at http://www.natcorp.ox.ac.uk) and search some of the examples of features you identified in the activity above. Can you identify some distinctive patterns of use in spoken and/or written texts? The results page will offer you a clickable index of sources, showing where the examples are from. ●

delivered speech will not be constructed entirely of sentences, because that would make the speaker sound unnatural. Ellipsis is a normal and expected part of spoken language – we don't say things that we don't need to, especially if we are in a shared physical space.

You could therefore argue that in writing the perfume advertisement in minor sentences, the copywriter is choosing to move away from the more **formal** structures of written English and to simulate a speech-like effect. This would suit an idea of intimacy and the personal nature of the product, which purchasers will want to feel is relevant to them as an individual. The idea of sounding like a speaker rather than a writer is therefore no bad thing.

Activity

1. If it sometimes suits advertisers to sound more like a speaker than a writer, then the same could be said of poetry, which is often about recounting personal experiences and can involve representing someone's thoughts and feelings. Focusing on your poetry set text, identify some examples where the language of the poem's **narrator** sounds speech-like. This may be because of a number of different features: ellipsis; the use of particular pronouns or other address terms; a certain level of lexical **informality**; expressions and interjections which are more often heard spoken than seen in written form.

2. Play texts have their own, distinctive reasons for wanting to sound speech-like. While poetry is not always written with performance in mind, drama texts only exist on the page as a precursor to performance, or as a record of what was performed. The written lines have to come to life. Focusing on your chosen set text, identify some examples of speakers using any of the features listed in activity 1 above, plus any further features that you think contribute to a spoken, rather than written, effect.

You can test out your intuitions about grammatical constructions, about speech and writing, and also about the connotations of different words and expressions by going to a **corpus** and doing a search. Many corpora are free to use for up to 50 examples, which is often enough to see some patterns. Enter your word or phrase in the box and search the database. One of the biggest collections is called the British National Corpus, which totals 100 million words.

A search will show you something of the habitual occurrences of words in particular environments, which is called **collocation**. Collocations are grammatical in that they are about the places in sentences or utterances where words occur. But they are also lexical and semantic, because the repeated occurrences of words alongside others creates connotations for those words.

As an example of the above, a search of the British National Corpus on 26 April 2014 for the terms 'scent', 'perfume' and 'fragrance', which could be thought to be closely **synonymous**, revealed some differences in contexts. While 'scent' was often connected with flowers, 'perfume' was noticeably linked with brand names. 'Fragrance' appeared to describe products for men as well as women, and also could be applied to food flavours such as spices.

Pragmatics

The term 'pragmatics' refers to the idea of shared or assumed knowledge. Because language is a social construct, its meanings always reflect the values of the society or the group that dominate, or have dominated, over the years. This doesn't mean that language is fixed or can't change. Look at the two words below. The second is a more-recent addition to the lexicon, devised to challenge the assumption encoded in the first – that everyone thinks having children is a good idea:

- childless

- childfree

Different cultures can have different assumptions about the correct way to do things and this can be shown in language use. For example, the Acoma (Native American) people in Arizona, USA, don't talk about 'burying' people when they die. Instead they talk about 'planting' them, because they hold the land to be sacred and believe that human beings are part of a cycle of renewal. So people are planted upright, not buried lying down. As you can see, pragmatics is closely connected with **representation**, or how people, things and events are talked about.

To understand pragmatics, you need to be able to stand back from language and from the society around you and to see it as if from a complete stranger's eyes. Asking the question 'What do I need to know in order to understand this text?' is a good starting point for gaining some pragmatic insights.

The *London Rain* text (page 19) is an example of the type of text we see around us on a daily basis – a piece of product advertising. But what if you had never heard of the idea of advertising or the idea of wearing perfume? What would you make of this text? What if you had never been to London, as most people in the world haven't? What shared knowledge about London does the text rely on?

The Notepad text (page 21) is also interesting from a pragmatic perspective. How can you explain the assumption that a notepad can talk to us? This example illustrates the fact that breaking pragmatic rules can carry a message in its own right.

Trading on assumed knowledge has advantages and disadvantages for any writer (or speaker). If readers and listeners have that knowledge, then it can be a way to express a strong connection. But if they do not, it is potentially problematic – although sometimes a lack of understanding can function as an interesting challenge. For example, advertisements can sometimes be difficult to understand if they target particular groups. However, if puzzlement leads us to take notice and to ask others about the message, then the advertisement has succeeded in getting our attention.

Pragmatic skills are all about being aware of what we are taking for granted in any interaction. But routines and practices change over time, as well as varying from place to place. The following activity will highlight those variations, especially if you can work with others in a group or pair. You will see how pragmatics and politeness, especially in interactions, are closely related.

Activity

1. What are the pragmatics of the following situations? Give an outline of the language routines that you and/or others follow in each of the following contexts:
   - Greetings and sign-offs in email use or texting.
   - Introductions and farewells in face-to-face contexts: Do you shake hands, kiss, smile, wave?
   - Buying items at a shop counter: How many times (and when) do you say 'thank you'?
   - Routines at the hairdresser's: What are the different stages that the hairdresser and customer go through?

2. Discuss any experiences you have had where you were conscious of having to learn new routines, for example in moving schools, going abroad or coming to the UK.

Key term

Speech event. A spoken interaction of a recognisable type. For example, a lecture or a phone call.

The examples above feature a range of contexts and settings. As is the case with written language, spoken language can exist in many different **genres**. You will also see spoken genres called **speech events**, which highlight the fact that spoken language is often embedded in action. Different speech events often have distinctive forms of language associated with them. The activity below will explore this idea in more detail.

Activity

Below are 20 examples of speech taken from different contexts. The trailing dots indicate that the utterances continued. Can you decide what the contexts were?

1. You do not have to say anything, but it may harm your defence…
2. I name this ship…
3. We are sorry to announce that the 12.31 train to London Paddington is delayed by 17 minutes…
4. Lords, ladies and gentlemen…
5. Have you heard the one about…
6. I'm unable to take your call at the moment…
7. Prepare to turn left in a quarter of a mile and continue to follow the A34…
8. Dearly beloved, we are gathered together here…
9. I should like to ask my honourable friend whether he…
10. Right everyone, settle down quickly now and turn to page 10…
11. Thanks for taking the time to download this *5 Live* podcast…
12. Oranges and lemons say the bells of St Clements…
13. Good morning, accounts department, this is Ian. Can I take your name please…
14. And so, my fellow Americans: ask not what your country can do for you, ask what you can do for your country…

15. Hello Chris this is Mike, um not to worry I'll try you on your mobile…

16. This amazing thing happened to me yesterday…

17. Compare the Market dot com simples…

18. Lot 231 a very nice piece of troika pottery: who will give me £100 to start…

19. Lights out away we go. Is it Hamilton or Rosberg – Rosberg got a good start – Hamilton has to slot in behind…

20. Knock at the door number four, legs 11…

Answers are at the back of the book.

Spontaneous speech

Some of the speech genres illustrated above are much more predictable than others. This is to do with the extent to which they accompany a set ritual or procedure. The least predictable genre is probably spontaneous conversation: as the word 'spontaneous' suggests, conversation can involve spur-of-the-moment contributions. Also, because conversation is interactive, it is co-produced and, the more people involved in an interaction, the less any single individual is able to influence the show.

However, even spontaneous conversation has some rules and patterns. The conversation below is between three strangers on a city bus. They are all facing each other as the conversation proceeds. In such contexts, only certain questions are acceptable as opening remarks between strangers, and one of them is to enquire about another person's journey – as here.

A: are you going far?

B: just up to the high street (.) how about you?

A: I'm off to the hospital (1.0) they're hav they're having a very bad time at the hospital at the moment they haven't got enough money or people (1.0) over there you know the cost of | **keep**ing the place

B: | yeah

A: and I went in the wrong door one day and I found out that half one chunk of it has been sold off to **Dev**on (1.0) so the **Dev**on is at **one** end and **Ex**eter (1.0) is at the **oth**er end

B: I thought Exeter was **in** Devon [laughter]

A: I know but the thing is they've sold off half that place to Branson isn't he the air | airman?

B: | oh really?

C: yeah Virgin yeah

A: yeah so well he's bought one end of it and it's been made into the hospital for (1.0) Devon and we got Exeter at the other end and all the Exeter people all their records are down that end and I went in the wrong end so they didn't know who I was or anything [laughter]

B: oh right

A: no it's change you know you never know what's going on [laughter] oh well there we are (1.0) no I like it in there the people are very very good

Transcription key:

(.) normal pause

(1.0) numbers in brackets indicate length of pauses in seconds

bold indicates stressed syllable

| vertical lines show simultaneous speech

[ ] square brackets indicate contextual information

Key terms

Adjacency. The positioning of elements in an interaction, so that one follows on from another. For example, greetings are nearly always reciprocated.

Adjacency pair. Two elements that are dependent on each other and exist in a pair. For example, a question and an answer.

Closing. Closing items conclude an interaction. For example, 'bye' or 'see you'.

False start. Beginning an utterance then stopping and beginning it again.

Filler. A word or speech noise produced by a speaker to create some thinking time. For example, 'um' and 'er'.

Framing. The idea that speakers mark their understanding of the context they are in. For example, by smiling or laughing to show that they are being playful.

Monitoring feature. An element produced by a speaker to check the attention level of the listener. For example, 'you know what I mean?', 'are you with me?'

Narrative. A social activity in which a teller addresses a listener or a reader and produces a piece of discourse about a story.

Narrative structure. The stages which a teller would generally follow when telling a story. These typically include *abstract, orientation, complication, resolution* and *coda.* ▶

The bus conversation illustrates the idea of co-production, but one speaker here is more dominant than the others. This is because she begins a **narrative** about her hospital experience, which takes up a large part of the interaction. Narrative, or storytelling, will be explored further in this book (in Chapter 1) because understanding **narrative structure** is a fundamental part of the specification. But for now, it is important to note that telling a **story** during a conversation suspends the normal rules of turn-taking – allowing one speaker to keep the floor and turning others into an audience. The main listener, B, indicates listenership by using **reinforcements**, which signal that it's acceptable for the speaker to continue: 'yeah' and 'oh really?' But there are requirements on the storyteller: the narrative has to have a shape, with a beginning and a conclusion, as well as an overall point or message.

Despite the differences in the number of speaker turns, aspects of **adjacency** and of **cohesion** are adhered to. Adjacency refers to the way in which, in interactions, some language features link together to form a unit or **adjacency pair** (Sacks, 1995). An example of an adjacency pair is a question-and-answer routine, as in the beginning of the bus conversation that you have just looked at:

> A: are you going far?
> B: just up to the high street (.) how about you?
> A: I'm off to the hospital

Other examples include openings and greetings, **pre-closings** and **closings** (Schlegoff and Sacks, 1973), the use of terms of address, mutual exclamations, requests or orders, and compliant responses or resistance. An utterance doesn't have to be next to its adjacency partner in order to be connected with it. For example, in the bus conversation, C answers A's question and so is part of that pairing, but it occurs after B's utterance:

> A: I know but the thing is they've sold off half that place to Branson isn't he the air | airman?
> B: | oh really?
> C: yeah Virgin yeah

A pre-closing is an utterance that prepares the ground for the end of the interaction. Researchers have found that the term 'right' often does this job and you can see it in action in B's final turn.

Cohesion refers to connectedness in a more general sense, for example a mirroring of words and phrases, or a set of connected contrasts, or terms all from a similar semantic field or level of formality. In the bus conversation, there are terms to do with the hospital building and its function; there are also several phrases that indicate informality, such as 'the thing is', 'one chunk' and the **vague completer** 'or anything'. There is also a **filler** ('well'), some **false starts** ('they're hav they're having') and a **monitoring feature** ('you know'), all of which are characteristic of spontaneous speech, as opposed to rehearsed or scripted speech. Another way of describing how speakers align their subject matter or style is **framing** (Goffman, 1974). Speakers who build on each other's topics or styles would be seen as sharing a frame, while a speaker who changes the subject or style of speaking would be said to be adopting a new or alternative frame. At the end of the bus conversation, it is noticeable that speaker A laughs while B does not, suggesting that A is trying for a frame of humour, but this frame is not reciprocated.

Any interaction involves speakers in **positioning** themselves – seeking **common ground** (Clark, 1996) with others or putting forward contrasting views and refusing to share an offered perspective. Every time someone speaks, they are expressing themselves – expressing an **identity**. But positioning doesn't have to mean argument in any aggressive sense. It is simply a part of our day-to-day negotiations with people about who we are and what we think of others.

Read through the conversation below, which took place between three strangers on a train. B began the conversation by commenting on the weather in Britain, which was poor at the time. The topic then moved on to what the weather is like in other countries.

> A: my granddaughters are in Australia and of course being young they love it you know on Bondi beach (.) they've just got there (.) got a flight
>
> B: my niece is over there yeah (.) she's just outside Sydney
>
> A: yeah Sydney is apparently lovely (.) for the youngsters
>
> B: she doesn't like the hot weather my niece (.) they stay in (.) they've got this air conditioning (.) the boys come home from school and then they go out at night
>
> A: I don't like air conditioning (.) I'd rather have fans I think
>
> B: I wouldn't like it red hot all the while (.) it depends how much you like the heat
>
> A: yes yes it is but you do get used to it you see
>
> A: I suppose so
>
> A: and less wear (.) you know (.) no jumpers no coats
>
> B: no woollies
>
> A: and that's what's so lovely as well
>
> B: but I haven't got the energy with it
>
> A: I lived in Zambia (.) and the Zambian weather was not too hot (1.0) just mid twenties most of the time
>
> C: sounds lovely
>
> A: it is (.) it's one of the best climates in the world really (.) I expect there are other places (.) but it was never like the Middle East
>
> C: mm
>
> A: that can be in the forties
>
> B: in India they have a rainy season
>
> A: they have a monsoon
>
> B: yeah monsoon (.) I don't think I'd like that

Activity

Analyse the conversation above, paying close attention to aspects of **cohesion** and to how the speakers align with each other or offer contrasting views.

There is some feedback on this activity at the back of the book.

Key terms

Common ground. The idea of sharing a perspective with others in an interaction.

Identity. Appearing as a certain kind of person or group member.

Positioning. Setting up and maintaining a perspective in an interaction.

Pre-closing. An item that a speaker will produce to show that he or she wants to close the conversation, for example 'right', 'so', or 'anyway'.

Reinforcement. A word or speech noise produced by a listener to encourage a speaker to continue. For example, 'really?' or 'mm'.

Story. A sequence of events that someone considers interesting enough to be the subject of narrative.

Vague completer. A way of completing an utterance that stops it from sounding too abrupt. For example, 'I did the shopping *and stuff*'.

Transcription key:

(.) normal pause

(1.0) numbers in brackets indicate length of pauses in seconds

Planned speech

In the two spontaneous conversations that you have just been studying, the participants hadn't planned beforehand what they were going to say, so they weren't consciously putting forward an argument. However, there are situations where people do just that: in courtrooms and at political gatherings, on radio phone-ins and TV panel discussions, in news presentations and interviews, people are much more consciously presenting the world as they see it.

There is a difference, of course, between a political or courtroom speech and an interview, the former being much more of a one-way communication – although if speaker and audience are in a shared physical space, the audience is bound to have an effect on how any speech unfolds. Interviews are somewhere between spontaneous conversation and a speech, in terms of the planning and rehearsal involved. But even the most pre-planned interaction can get derailed – which is why spoken language, evolving as it does in real time, is always interesting to study.

Planned spoken **genres**, such as speeches, have their own kinds of distinctive patterning and cohesion. In fact, the study of speech-making has a long history, going back as far as ancient Greece. The art of persuasion, or **rhetoric**, which once focused only on speeches, has now evolved into a wider field of study – encompassing persuasive texts of all kinds. However, speeches can often be useful sources of study for illustrating certain key patterns that are used time and time again.

The text below is from a speech given by Susan B. Anthony, who was a 19th-century American pioneer of women's rights. She made this speech in 1872, after being arrested for casting an illegal vote in the presidential election of that year. Women at that time had few legal rights and they did not have the right to vote. She begins the speech by saying that she hopes to convince people that what she did was not wrong. She then goes on to outline some key aspects of the American Constitution.

> The preamble of the Federal Constitution says:
>
> 'We, the people of the United States, in order to form a more perfect union, establish justice, ensure domestic tranquillity, provide for the common defense, promote the general welfare, and secure the blessings of liberty to ourselves and our posterity, do ordain and establish this Constitution for the United States of America.'
>
> It was we, the people; not we, the white male citizens; nor yet we, the male citizens; but we, the whole people, who formed the Union. And we formed it, not to give the blessings of liberty, but to secure them; not to the half of ourselves and the half of our posterity, but to the whole people – women as well as men. And it is a downright mockery to talk to women of their enjoyment of the blessings of liberty while they are denied the use of the only means of securing them provided by this democratic-republican government – the ballot.

Susan B. Anthony's speech above contains some classic rhetorical patterns:

- Repetition (e.g. we, formed, half, people)
- Listing, particularly lists of three (e.g. 'It was we, the people; not we, the white male citizens; nor yet we, the male citizens')
- Contrasting structures (e.g. after the list of three above, 'but we, the whole people')

Key term

Rhetoric / Rhetorical.
Rhetoric is the study of persuasive language, an area of study dating back to ancient Greece.

- Lexical contrasts or oppositions (e.g. give/secure; men/women; half/whole)
- Word order that throws certain elements into prominence (e.g. delaying the phrase 'the ballot' to the end of the utterance).

The speech below was given in a US courtroom in about 1855, by a lawyer called George Graham Vest (who later became a senator for Missouri). He was representing a man who was suing another man for killing his dog. The speech below was part of Vest's summing up to the jury. He won the case.

> Gentlemen of the Jury: The best friend a man has in the world may turn against him and become his enemy. His son or daughter that he has reared with loving care may prove ungrateful. Those who are nearest and dearest to us, those whom we trust with our happiness and our good name may become traitors to their faith. The money that a man has, he may lose. It flies away from him, perhaps when he needs it most. A man's reputation may be sacrificed in a moment of ill-considered action. The people who are prone to fall on their knees to do us honor when success is with us, may be the first to throw the stone of malice when failure settles its cloud upon our heads.
>
> The one absolutely unselfish friend that man can have in this selfish world, the one that never deserts him, the one that never proves ungrateful or treacherous is his dog. A man's dog stands by him in prosperity and in poverty, in health and in sickness. He will sleep on the cold ground, where the wintry winds blow and the snow drives fiercely, if only he may be near his master's side. He will kiss the hand that has no food to offer. He will lick the wounds and sores that come in encounters with the roughness of the world. He guards the sleep of his pauper master as if he were a prince. When all other friends desert, he remains. When riches take wings, and reputation falls to pieces, he is as constant in his love as the sun in its journey through the heavens.
>
> If fortune drives the master forth, an outcast in the world, friendless and homeless, the faithful dog asks no higher privilege than that of accompanying him, to guard him against danger, to fight against his enemies. And when the last scene of all comes, and death takes his master in its embrace and his body is laid away in the cold ground, no matter if all other friends pursue their way, there by the graveside will the noble dog be found, his head between his paws, his eyes sad, but open in alert watchfulness, faithful and true even in death.

Activity

Can you see why Vest's summing up speech had such a powerful effect? Analyse some of the patterning in the speech and think about any of the other aspects of language that you have learned about so far.

For more examples of speeches, go to:

http://www.historyplace.com/speeches/previous.htm

Later in this book, you will look specifically at how spoken language is represented in drama texts, with a particular focus on how characters engage with each other as part of the way in which the dramatic story is told. You will be involved in looking at how people take up positions in interactions, with a big difference, however: the characters are not simply talking to each other in order to connect with each other, as we do in real life (and as was illustrated in the bus and train dialogues). The characters are in interactions, and often in direct conflict, because they have been written that way – in order to move the dramatic action along. However, the more you know about how we talk in real life, the more you will be able to develop an understanding of the pragmatics of drama texts. This will enhance your analysis considerably.

Discourse

Discourse is quite a complex term because it can mean different things. In some books and articles, you will see it referring just to spoken language, but that is an older meaning of the word. Nowadays, both 'text' and 'discourse' can refer to all forms of communication – spoken, written and multimodal.

Both 'text' and 'discourse' refer not just to single words or phrases, but to whole pieces of communication. From that perspective, a discourse analysis or text analysis is an analysis of how the whole sample of language works. This includes all the **graphological** elements of textual design, layout, typeface, use of colour and so on.

> **Key term**
>
> **Graphological.** Relating to the design features of a text.

In the *London Rain* perfume advertisement (page 19), the image is clearly an important part of the overall message – working alongside the language. As readers, we are unlikely to read the words and then look at the image, not least because the words are printed across the image. Even if that had not been the case, images and words are interrelated in the way we read: we flick back and forth between the two, coming to an understanding of one aspect through the lens of the other. In the perfume advertisement, the perspective of the image is important. Students of English Language and Literature are not expected to be technical experts in camera angles and lens filters, but there are still analytical insights that you can draw from the way in which an image is framed. Here, for example, the view is from the ground, between blades of grass, fitting the focus on dew and parkland.

In the Notepad text (page 21), the notepad addresses us from the top left-hand corner of the page, with its statement about itself printed in a large font size and coloured red. The top left of the page would be a focal point in cultures whose language is written and read from top to bottom and from left to right. This strategy wouldn't work in Arabic, which is written right to left, nor in Chinese, which goes vertically down the page.

The area of discourse also includes that of **genre**, or text type. Genres are not easy to classify, so no one expects students to be able to come up with watertight definitions. For one thing, genres are constantly changing. For example, new text types such as SMS, email, social media posts and tweets have all been devised within the past 30 years, and, as a society, we had to find names for them and work out how to use them – their **pragmatics**.

In studies of literature, literary texts are traditionally divided into prose fiction, poetry and drama, and all three of these genres are included for study on your English Language and Literature A level specification. But the idea of genre can be taken further than this, because divisions can occur within those headings. Fiction can be sub-divided into further genres, for example crime, romance or – as is the case with this specification – 'Imaginary Worlds'. The fiction texts set for Paper 1 of both the A level and the AS level are linked thematically by the way the stories are told, involving unnatural or fantasy elements such as a futuristic society, monstrous creatures or a **narrator** who has died. A similar sub-division gathers together prose texts and plays within the theme of 'Conflict' for Paper 2 of the A level. In short, the term 'genre' within the literary field is a flexible idea that can cover structure and theme as well as the more traditional distinctions between different literary formats.

Genre is not restricted to literary texts, however, as there are many more text types in the world than those labelled 'literary'. Although we might think of 'literary' texts and 'everyday' texts as distinctively different, this is an idea that can and should be challenged, especially by students of English Language and Literature. In fact, the rationale for the coursework element of the A level specification is precisely to enable you to ask questions about the labels 'literary' and 'non-literary' or 'literary' and 'everyday'.

Whatever convenience is served by our labels, in reality texts of all kinds are interconnected, sometimes through quite specific **intertextual** strategies. A straightforward example of this is where a newspaper or magazine includes something that looks like an informative, factual article but which turns out to be an advertisement. The resulting text – sometimes called an 'advertorial' – is intertextual because it has features of two different genres.

Activity

Look back at the perfume advert (page 19), focusing particularly on the way in which it is laid out and also on its language use.

Would you say that the text is intertextual in any way? For example, does it suggest any of the following other text types?

- Poetry
- A set of notes or jottings
- An annotated photograph album
- A tagged photograph on a social media site
- Another advertisement

If it is intertextual, why might a connection with other text types be useful?

Discourse and discourses

The term 'discourse' has a plural, 'discourses', which has a further meaning. Discourses occur when we repeatedly talk and think in certain ways about things, such as ideas, experiences, events, places and people. Repeated ways of talking and thinking lead to a sense of 'that's how things are'. But we have this sense because of the ways in which we have constantly represented the idea in question, so we are in a circle of language and thought that is hard to escape.

The idea of discourses can be explored by thinking about the perfume advertisement on page 19. If you research the way perfume is marketed, you will encounter discourses that are shared by luxury items – focusing on the senses and on pleasure, because that's what luxury is all about. Within this, you will certainly find that the idea of luxury is marketed differently to men and to women, because of our prevalent discourses about gender and sexuality.

Did you know?

Our understanding of the nature of discourses is based on the work of an influential French philosopher, Michel Foucault. His work has been particularly important in encouraging people to examine the way in which they deal with ideas of 'difference', and in understanding how power and resistance work in societies.

Activity

Now that you have an idea of what the language levels are about, see how far you can apply them by analysing some new texts.

1. The text below is an example of a regular feature in the *Independent* newspaper. It is part of the paper's business pages and has been written by the business editor, James Ashton. The idea of the text is to give a rapid and light-hearted account of a business figure or organization that has hit the news – in this case, the chef and businessman Jamie Oliver. The text always features an image of the person or company and two voices, in a written dialogue, talking about the person or company featured.

   Analyse how this text works, drawing on as many aspects of the language levels as are relevant. Keep in mind that your task is to explain:

   - what the writer of the text is trying to do
   - how you think the business editor uses language for this purpose
   - your interpretation – your 'reading' – of the text.

The 30 Second Briefing

Can I have a word in your shell-like?
Sure.

What's that geezer Jamie Oliver doing in the business pages?
Well, it turns out he's an excellent businessman as well as a chef.

You 'avin' a larf?
Not at all. His Jamie Oliver Holdings more than tripled its profits. And yesterday he told this newspaper that he's about to expand.

Wicked! Where? Italy, I expect
Actually, no. He is taking his Jamie's Italian restaurant chain to Russia, Istanbul and Singapore, then Brazil, Scandinavia, Canada and Chile.

That's mustard. Anywhere else?
He's looking at Hungary, Indonesia, Thailand, Malaysia and India.

Lovely jubbly. Can I buy shares?
No, but he might bring in an investor, but they'd have to be "well minted", as I believe Mr Oliver might say.

Sounds like he's on a nice little earner himself
About £150m worth.

Bish bash bosh!
Quite.

2. Find a poem about rain by searching in book collections or online, e.g. using the following websites:

www.poemhunter.com   www.allpoetry.com

Compare your chosen poem with the perfume advertisement on page 19, in order to assess how each text **represents** the idea of rain.

Is one text more 'literary' in its language use than the other? Or are literary judgments less about language and more about other factors?

REVIEW YOUR LEARNING

- Have you understood the key features of the AQA English Language and Literature AS level and A level specifications?

- Do you understand the different Assessment Objectives?

- Are you aware of the different writing skills that you need to develop?

- Do you understand the language levels that underpin text analysis?

If you have understood the aspects above, then you are ready to learn how to apply the analytical methods that underpin the specifications. The first area you will learn more about is **narrative**.

Link

Thinking about what we mean by 'literary' and 'non-literary' language is an important aspect of A level coursework. See Chapters 8 and 9 for more information.

References

Clark, H. (1996). *Using Language*. Cambridge: CUP.

Goddard, A. (2005). *Being Online*. University of Nottingham PhD thesis.

Goffman, E. (1974). *Frame Analysis*. Harmondsworth: Penguin.

Lakoff, G, and Johnson, M. (1980). *Metaphors We Live By*. Chicago, USA: University of Chicago Press.

Sacks, H. (1995). (Vols I & II, ed. G. Jefferson) *Lectures on Conversation*. Oxford: Blackwell.

Schegloff, E. and Sacks, H. (1973). 'Opening up closings.' *Semiotica* 7: 289-327.

Thurlow, C. (2003). 'Generation Txt? The sociolinguistics of young people's text-messaging', in *Discourse Analysis Online*. Sheffield Hallam University. Available at http://extra.shu.ac.uk/daol/articles/v1/n1/a3/thurlow2002003-paper. html [Accessed 5.12.14]

Further reading

Do some further exploration of the online sites you have been pointed to in this introductory section of the book (for example, the BNC language corpus, the phonetics site, the poetry collections). Search for some more online resources yourself, and set up a way to organize the links you find – for example, you could use delicious.com to create your own database.

There are many further online resources, particularly on university sites. For example, University College London has a grammar page at the following link: http://www.ucl.ac.uk/internet-grammar/home. htm. It is primarily for their own students, but they don't assume any prior knowledge.

Part 1: Telling Stories

You will be able to apply all of the skills you learn in this chapter to the AQA Anthology *Paris*, as well as to other parts of the specification. For example, in the coursework component, 'Making Connections', you are required to compare a literary text with some non-literary material. Understanding how texts of all kinds work is therefore a key skill for this subject area.

> **This chapter will:**
> - help you understand how to go about analysing real-world narratives
> - give you useful frameworks for analysis and opportunities to practise your skills
> - show you how to apply what you learn to your set texts.

Relevant Assessment Objectives

The ability to analyse real narratives is tested in exam conditions in Section A of A level Paper 1 and Section A of AS level Paper 2, where you will be given material from the AQA Anthology *Paris* to analyse.

For A level and AS level analysis of this material, AO1, AO3 and AO4 are tested.

- AO1 rewards your ability to take a language approach to the texts that you study, to write coherently and to use terminology appropriately.
- AO3 rewards your understanding of **context** – the effects produced by variations of such aspects as audience, purpose, **genre** and **mode**.
- AO4 rewards your ability to compare and contrast the material given. There are obvious links with AO3 factors above, but you are free to discuss any ideas about similarity and difference.

If you are studying at AS level, you will also be asked to complete a writing task, transforming a given extract by changing aspects such as its audience, purpose, genre or mode. Obviously, your ability to do the writing task depends crucially upon your analytical understanding of the Anthology items.

For the AS writing task (and commentary), the Assessment Objectives are AO2, AO3 and AO5. See Chapter 4 for further details.

About the Anthology

All the extracts in the Anthology are non-literary. Although the labels of 'literary' and 'non-literary' are open to interpretation and challenge, the starting point for the AQA English Language and Literature course is that 'literary' encompasses the three main literary genres of poetry, prose fiction and drama. 'Non-literary' is a very broad category that includes non-fiction (such as autobiography, historical accounts, travel writing, journalism) but also texts and data that are part of our everyday experiences and communicative practices, such as information texts, letters, advertising, blogs, songs and spontaneous conversation. All the texts in the Anthology are thematically linked by being about Paris and Parisians, but each text has its own perspective, function, audience, layout, mode and **genre**.

Your task is to understand and be able to analyse all the variations within this overall collection.

Introduction

We tell and hear stories all the time. We always like to tell other people what has happened to us, what we have seen happen to other people, or even stories that we've heard from others. We also like to *be told* stories, especially if they are interesting, entertaining, surprising and unusual.

We tell and hear stories when we are face to face with friends or family, and are chatting together. A lot of what we say to one another in those situations is stories. But people also tell and hear (or read) stories when they are apart from one other. If you've gone on a trip with your family, for example, you're very likely to want to tell your friends what happens during the trip. You might do that on Facebook, with text messages, or by speaking on the phone. Or you might even keep a diary that you may or may not share with others. Again, what you'll want to tell is something that you think is *worth* telling and that you imagine (and hope!) your friends will find equally interesting.

All of this can be called 'storytelling', but a more technical name is **narrative**. Narrative always involves three elements:

- Some events, which form a **story**.
- Someone who tells about those events: the **teller**.
- The teller's representation of those events: **discourse**.

Understanding how narrative works is a fundamental aspect of the study of English Language and Literature, both at A level and at AS level. All the literary genres you are required to study – prose fiction, poetry and drama – have narrative at their heart. Also, AQA's non-literary Anthology *Paris* is a collection of narratives of different kinds. Each of the texts in the compilation adopts a particular perspective, with different writers and speakers capturing different aspects of Paris, both as it is now and how it was in the past. In addition, the non-fiction options for A level Component 2 are also strong narratives – in one case about an adventure and in another case about a crime.

What is a story?

To begin to think about this question, let's start with an activity.

> ### Key term
>
> **Teller.** The person who produces a piece of discourse about a story.

> ### Looking ahead
>
> The study of narrative is a crucial area that underpins the whole English Language and Literature specification, linking language and literature together.

> ### Activity
>
> Make a list of anything that you think counts as a story. Don't worry about being 'right' – try to include as many items as you can. You'll go back to this list at various points during this chapter. To get you started, consider the following five types of item and see if you can decide whether or not they count as stories, and why:
>
> - Jokes
> - Newspaper articles
> - Facebook status updates
> - Fairy tales
> - Travelogues
>
> Now add your own items.

The list you've just made will contain a number of different items. The key question is: Why are they (not) stories? In making your decisions, you will have used some criteria. These will be *your* criteria, but if we want to talk about stories in general, we'll need some criteria that we can agree on. In the rest of this section we'll do exactly that: we'll try to set some criteria that we can agree on and can use to define what a story is.

First, we need to decide what the essential components of a story are. Before you read on, think about this for a moment and make a few notes to help organize your thoughts.

Events

At the most basic level, we can say that a story is made up of a sequence of events ordered through time. You can think of an event as an individual unit of a story, involving:

● actors (people, animals, objects);   ● some action;   ● circumstances.

For each event, you can ask the questions:

Actors	*Who* was involved?
Action	*What* did they do?
Circumstances	*When* did they do it?
	Where did they do it?
	How did they do it?

At the very least, a story will be a string of events: 'this event happened, and then this other event happened, and then this other event happened, and then...'. In order to get to grips with the concept of events and begin to think of stories as strings of events, comic strips can be useful.

Activity

Look at the comic strip, where each of the eight panels can be considered as an event. For each event, specify the actor(s), the action(s) and the circumstances. The first panel has been completed below as a guide.

Remember that while actors and actions must always be there, circumstances are optional. For the purpose of this activity, the main character's name will be Matt.

Event (panel) 1	Actors	Matt
	Actions	typing at the computer
	Circumstances	at Matt's desk, in his study
Event (panel) 2	Actors	
	Actions	
	Circumstances	

Key term

Clause. A clause gives information about people or things (nouns and pronouns) and their states or actions (verbs). Additional information may also be given about the circumstances of the people and their activities.

You are now familiar with the concept of an event and its components: actors, actions and circumstances. In language, events are expressed through **clauses**. A clause is exactly the linguistic equivalent of a panel in a comic strip: it has information about actors, actions and, optionally, circumstances. In fact, you could easily 'translate' the comic strip overleaf by turning it into a series of clauses.

Activity

Translate the comic strip into a language-only text, making sure that each event you described in your previous activity corresponds to a clause. In each clause, identify the actors, the actions and the circumstances (if any).

The first clause in the text would be something like 'Matt was working at the computer in his study', where 'Matt' is the actor, 'was working at the computer' is the action, and 'in his study' the circumstance.

The key question at this point is: What makes a string of events a story? Think again about the comic strip example: Is it a story? It is a string of events involving actors and actions, but does it qualify as a story? In other words, is it worth telling? Is it interesting enough?

Of course, there is no precise answer here: what is interesting for one person may be boring for another, and the other way around. We can't measure the level of interest of a story in an objective way. We all respond to stories as individuals, subjectively. This is because we all have different experiences and backgrounds, and the way we relate to specific stories is bound to be different too.

However, research has found that there are some common patterns in the ways in which stories are structured. One of the most important scholars in this field is American linguist William Labov. Towards the end of the 1960s, Labov was mainly interested in studying how people of different social classes, geographical regions, genders and ethnic groups used language differently. For this purpose, he collected a great number of stories told by a wide range of people. When he analysed those stories he began to notice that they seemed to follow regular patterns.

Narrative structure

The patterns in the stories he examined were so regular that Labov was able to identify six stages in the **narrative structure** of stories:

Stage	Description
Abstract	What's the story about?
Orientation	Who was involved? Where did it take place? When?
Complication	What happened that was unexpected?
Evaluation	How bad / good / shocking / amazing, etc. was it?
Resolution	What was done in order to resolve the problem?
Coda	How is the story connected to the present?

Let's look at the stages in more detail. In order to understand how Labov's narrative structure works, we're going to take a story and build it bit by bit. We'll call it 'Charlotte's Story', imagining a situation where Charlotte and some friends are talking about how it can be annoying sometimes to receive text messages.

Abstract

First of all, when we tell stories, we generally begin by giving some clues about the main event. This is the **abstract**. We use it to get other people interested in the story and sometimes we also check that we haven't already told them the same story. A typical abstract may take the form of a question, like:

> Did I tell you about the time when...?

Sometimes, in a conversation, a topic comes up and you think of a story related to it that you want to share, so you may say something like:

> Oh, I have a great story about that!

To understand and remember what an abstract is, think of the titles of the episodes in the classic TV sitcom *Friends*. For example:

> The One with Ross's Tan
>
> The One where Rachel's Sister Babysits

These are all abstracts.

Let's imagine that Charlotte begins her story with a short abstract:

> oh yeah (.) **tell** me about it!

Before you go on, notice how this simple sentence may have very different meanings according to the **context**. In the introductory chapter of this book you learned how **pragmatics** relates to the way we understand words, phrases and even entire texts according to the context in which they are produced.

We tend to assume that words 'have' meanings. We are used to thinking of language as a list of words, each one with its own meaning, as in a dictionary. In reality, language is more complex – and much more interesting – than that. Instead of thinking of meaning as something that is fixed and 'belongs' to words, it's more accurate to think of it as something that we *construct* and *negotiate* together every time we use language, according to the context we are in and our shared knowledge. Remember that language is not a stand-alone object!

Taken in isolation, the phrase 'oh yeah, tell me about it!' doesn't mean very much. We may interpret it as someone wanting to hear a story about a particular topic, maybe. But the phrase becomes meaningful in context – that is, in the actual situation in which someone uses it. So, in this case, a group of friends are discussing how annoying it is sometimes to receive text messages when we're doing something else. So when Charlotte says 'oh yeah, tell me about it!' that's a way for her to say that she fully agrees and maybe has a story connected to it. That's why we can consider it to be the abstract of her story.

Orientation

After the abstract, we normally say where and when the story happened and who (else) was involved. This helps the listener or the reader to visualize the scene of the story. This stage is called the **orientation** because it is similar to a situation when you use a map to work out where you are and orient yourself.

In Charlotte's story below, the orientation has been underlined. This contains information about when, who and where.

> oh yeah (.) **tell** me about it!
>
> last Friday (.) right? (.) I was with Jo and Chloe in this new café in (1.0)
> Albert Road

Key terms

Abstract. In Labov's model of narrative structure, the abstract, like the trailer of a film, gives clues to what will follow.

Orientation. The setting of a narrative.

Transcription key:

(.) normal pause

(1.0) numbers in brackets indicate length of pauses in seconds

bold indicates stressed syllable

! REMEMBER

Language use is always part of some activity. Whether you're writing a personal diary, texting a friend, making a shopping list or chatting online, you're always *doing* something with the language you use. So when you do all these things with language, you produce meanings. And since these activities are often social – that is, they involve other people – meanings are also interpreted by them and sometimes constructed together *with* them.

Key terms

Complication. The twist, or complication that occurs in a narrative.

Evaluation. In Labov's model of storytelling, an assessment of the impact of the narrative events.

Complication

The main event in the story is usually something that happened unexpectedly. This is normally the reason why we tell a story in the first place. Consider how Charlotte's story could develop (underlined below):

> oh yeah (.) **tell** me about it!
>
> last Friday (.) right? (.) I was with Jo and Chloe in this new café in (1.0) Albert Road
>
> we're like (.) just sitting and chatting (.) <u>when all of a sudden I get this text from my mum (.) saying I had to go home to feed Georgie because she was going to be late.</u>

An event like this is called a **complication**, because it's something unexpected that must be dealt with: it complicates the normal course of events. In fact, it doesn't even have to be a problem; it can just be something that a speaker thinks is worthy of note. Consider the alternative underlined below:

> oh yeah (.) **tell** me about it!
>
> last Friday (.) right? (.) I was with Jo and Chloe in this new café in (1.0) Albert Road
>
> we're like (.) just sitting and chatting (.) <u>when all of a sudden this small dinosaur walks in and orders a **milk**shake!</u>

This is a complication just like the text message example.

Evaluation

A complication in a story always comes with some kind of comment. This is called an **evaluation**. It is during this stage that whoever is telling the story puts their individual mark on it, so to speak. The storyteller makes it clear that they're telling an interesting story by evaluating the complication. Expressions like the following are all examples of evaluation:

> It was amazing!
>
> I couldn't believe it!
>
> I was devastated!
>
> That was so funny!

Of course, an evaluation can be longer than a single sentence. The important point is that the evaluation involves the storyteller's personal take on the story. Look at the evaluation underlined below.

> oh yeah (.) **tell** me about it!
>
> last Friday (.) right? (.) I was with Jo and Chloe in this new café in (1.0) Albert Road
>
> we're like (.) just sitting and chatting (.) when all of a sudden I get this text from my mum (.) saying I had to go home to feed Georgie because she was going to be late.
>
> <u>it was **so** annoying! (1.0) I hadn't seen Jo and Chloe for (.) like (.) ages (.) and we were having a really good time (.) and now I had to go home and feed the dog! It's **al**ways the same (.) I'm having fun and suddenly (.) bing! (.) a text (.) and everything has to stop!</u>

Resolution

The next stage in the pattern is the **resolution**, which is where something is done, or something just happens, that brings the course of events back to normal.

> oh yeah (.) **tell** me about it!
>
> last Friday (.) right? (.) I was with Jo and Chloe in this new café in (1.0) Albert Road
>
> we're like (.) just sitting and chatting (.) when all of a sudden I get this text from my mum (.) saying I had to go home to feed Georgie because she was going to be late.
>
> it was **so** annoying! (1.0) I hadn't seen Jo and Chloe for (.) like (.) ages (.) and we were having a really good time (.) and now I had to go home and feed the dog! It's **al**ways the same (.) I'm having fun and suddenly (.) bing! (.) a text (.) and everything has to stop!
>
> <u>my friends noticed I was upset and said they'd go with me. (1.0) so we all went to my house (.) fed the dog (.) and even took her for a walk to the park! Jo and Chloe are amazing (.) they didn't mind at all (1.0) in the end we had a good laugh just watching Georgie rolling on the grass like crazy.</u>

In this example, the friends' decision to go with Charlotte is the resolution that brings things back to normal.

Coda

Sometimes, there might be one extra stage, which connects the story to the present. Charlotte, for example, ends her story by saying:

> <u>this is why I've decided (.) from now on I'm going to keep my mobile on silent every time I'm out with my friends!</u>

This is called a **coda**. The coda wraps the story up and is often linked to the **abstract**:

Abstract	This story is about X.
Coda	This is why something is now the case as a result of X.

Both the abstract and the coda are optional. This means that sometimes people include them in their stories and sometimes they don't.

Activity

Read Rebecca's story on the right and identify the stages in its **narrative structure**. The story is taken from a blog. ('Belaying' refers to securing a rope.)

At this point, it's important to remember that Labov's **narrative structure** is not a 'rule' but simply the result of his observations and analysis of a great number of stories. He was able to establish that this particular sequence of stages – abstract, orientation, complication, evaluation, resolution, coda – was a pretty regular pattern, so he drew the conclusion that this is how people *generally* tell stories.

Key terms

Coda. The 'wrap up' stage of a narrative, often linking back to the abstract.

Resolution. How the complication in the narrative gets resolved.

Rebecca's blog

On a Saturday in October, I was in the gym, doing some wall climbing. Being so clumsy, I actually managed to miss a hold. My mate Hannah who was belaying me got a bit distracted, so I held tight to the rope as I fell. The rope pulled tight and crunched my ring finger. So Hannah took me to A & E. I had X-rays done, and the doctor shows me the X-rays, he's like 'you're probably going to need surgery soon'.

I just couldn't believe my bad luck!

So the next day I had the surgery and three little screws put in. Healing was pretty straightforward. I went to physiotherapy for a few weeks. Now it's pretty much 100%. I can't quite straighten it completely on my own, but I don't really mind, so it's all good.

Of course, sometimes this pattern doesn't fit very neatly. For example, some stories may not have a **resolution** at all. Charlotte's story, for example, could have ended with her simply having to go home:

> Oh yeah, tell me about it! Last Friday I was with Jo and Chloe in this new café in Albert Road. We're just sitting and chatting when all of a sudden I get a text from my mum saying I had to go home to feed Georgie as she was going to be late home. It was so annoying! I hadn't seen Jo and Chloe for ages and we were having a really good time. And now I had to go home and feed the dog! It's always the same: I'm having fun and suddenly... bing! A text – and everything has to stop! This is why I've decided: from now on I'm going to keep my mobile on silent every time I'm out with my friends!

The **evaluation** is something that is not always found in one precise place. Take Charlotte's story again. When she says 'Jo and Chloe are amazing' she's evaluating part of the resolution. In fact, the evaluation is the most distinctive and the most pervasive aspect of many forms of **narrative**. It's better to consider it not just as an individual stage in the narrative but something that can be scattered all over the narrative, with more concentration around the **complication**.

So, when we analyse stories, we can use Labov's narrative structure as a model, but we must be prepared to be flexible with it.

Activity

Now go back to Matt's comic strip (page 39) and see if you can break it down into stages. What are the main differences between this and Charlotte's story or Rebecca's story?

Recounts

In the above activity you may have struggled to identify all (or any!) stages in Matt's comic strip. The key question, at this point, is this: Does Matt's comic strip qualify as a story? While there is no absolutely right or wrong answer to this question, we can at least notice that while Charlotte's and Rebecca's stories have all the stages of Labov's narrative structure, Matt's comic strip doesn't really seem to follow the same pattern in any obvious way. It is more a series of events ending with something that might be a (slight) complication: Matt couldn't remember what he was looking for.

This doesn't mean that we have to reject Matt's comic strip as a story, but certainly we can say that it is a different type of story. Some people would say that it is more like a **recount** – just a sequence of events, where the **teller** stands back and doesn't interfere. The structure of a recount is very simple and looks like this:

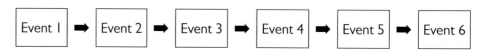

None of the events really counts as a complication or a resolution and the teller doesn't make any comments on any aspect of the story.

Key term

Recount. A kind of narrative where the teller attempts to be as neutral as possible.

In more conventional narrative, tellers do more work. They summarize the story in a nutshell in the **abstract**, they say how it's connected to the present in the **coda** and, especially, they make their own comments in the **evaluation**. Of course, the amount of work (or interference) done by the teller can vary, so the term 'recount' is not about an absolute category but sits at the end of an imaginary scale that might look like this:

Conventional narrative (obvious structure, presence of teller's comments) Recount (obvious structure, absence of teller's comments)

Go back to your initial list from the activity on page 38. Which items are more like conventional narrative and which are more like recounts? Which stages in Labov's narrative structure do they (not) have? Can you place the items on a scale like the one above?

 Activity

Now go to your AQA Anthology *Paris*. Can you put any of the texts on a scale like the one above, where some are more like recounts and some have more comments from a teller?

The role of the teller

In the previous activities, you considered how much the teller intervenes in different kinds of stories and you probably found quite a bit of variation. That's because some types of story are meant to be more neutral than others. News stories, for example, are expected to offer readers a realistic account of what happened. But what does this mean? To what extent do tellers stay faithful to the events as they unfold in reality? This is an interesting and important question.

 Activity

To get you started thinking about this, write down a very short recount about something that really happened to you, in no more than 100 words. Try to be as realistic and detached as possible: report facts and nothing else. You'll go back to this story later on.

> **! REMEMBER**
>
> Students of English Language and Literature need to develop particular expertise in how language choices construct 'realities', both in literature and in other texts of all kinds.

Now have a look at the extract from a short news story below.

An adventurer has become the first person to cross the English Channel, from Dungeness in Kent, on a solar boat powered directly by the sun.

Simon Milward, 38, single-handedly navigated more than 30 miles using no energy source other than the sun.

His 15ft catamaran, equipped with six AKT solar panels – which fed directly to power two electric motors – reached Boulogne-sur-Mer after more than six hours.

There were no batteries on the boat, which travelled at a speed of up to five knots, and the panels also produced electricity in shadows and cloudy conditions.

How neutral is the piece of news about the Channel crossing? Does the teller interfere at all? If so, how? One good way to approach this question is to try to strip the story down to its bare bones by thinking of a short title for it.

Activity

Write a title of no more than six words for the news story about the Channel crossing. You might want to compare your title with those of your friends. How different or similar is it?

At the most basic level, we could say that this story is about a man who crossed the English Channel on a solar-powered boat. That's the fact that the news story reports. But the point is: Why is this interesting? What is surprising about it? Part of the answer to these questions depends on your background knowledge. If you know the approximate width of the English Channel and how it is normally crossed – as well as some basic information about solar power – you're likely to find this event newsworthy. But not everybody shares the same information, so the teller of this story, the news reporter, has to do some work to ensure that the article is both factual *and* interesting. Indeed, we can feel that the teller is trying to impress readers in some way. If we take a close look at the language, we can see where this feeling comes from.

First of all, the actor is called an 'adventurer', which is not the same as 'man' or 'person'. It is a word that comes with a different set of **connotations** and conjures up images of explorations, unknown territories, dangerous situations and so on. This choice of word at the very beginning of the article is meant to stimulate interest, making readers want to continue.

Moving on to the second sentence, the teller tells us the name and the age of the actor in the story. So, that's very straightforward and factual. However, the adverb 'single-handedly' does something different – it expresses the teller's own personal assessment of the event. Similarly, 'more than 30 miles' is not just a simple measurement of distance – again, there's an element of evaluation in this expression. Finally, still in the same sentence, 'using no energy source other than the sun' is not completely neutral, either. Now compare the original sentence with a more impersonal one:

- 'Simon Milward, 38, single-handedly navigated more than 30 miles using no energy source other than the sun.'
- Simon Milward, 38, navigated 30.7 miles using solar power.

The two sentences relate the same event. The difference is that in the first one the teller is keen to make sure that the reader understands that this is a remarkable achievement, while in the second sentence the teller doesn't offer any evaluation and it's left completely up to the reader whether they are impressed or not.

The other two sentences in the text are similar: they are mostly factual but include elements of subjective evaluation.

Extension activity

Write more impersonal and objective versions of the final two sentences in the news story. What have you changed? Why?

So, even when the teller appears to be fairly detached, he or she always makes pretty important decisions about how to tell the story and make it interesting. This is not just at the level of language – through evaluation – but also at the level of structure: which aspects of the story to focus on, which ones to pay less attention to and which ones to leave out completely. In this case, the teller focuses a lot on how the boat engine was powered and gives some details about speed, distance and the duration of the trip, but many other details of what happened during those six hours are completely omitted.

So, the teller always has an active role in the narrative, even when his or her voice seems to be silent. Now go back to the story you wrote in the activity on page 45 and see whether you can analyse it in this way. In other words, see if you can recognize and reflect on the interventions that you, as the teller, made in the way you told the story.

Story and discourse

Now that we've established that the teller *always* intervenes, in one way or another, in relating events, the term 'story' begins to be insufficient. That's because it could refer to one of two things: the events as they 'really' happened or the events as they are told by the teller. This is a very important distinction.

Imagine, for example, that you witness a car accident as you're walking in the town centre and you then tell your friends about it, hours or even days later, in another place, maybe while chatting online. The car accident is the pure fact, the thing that happened, but what you actually say to your friends is your **representation** of it. It is a representation that you create by using language – something like 'I was walking down Elm Grove when I heard this car…'

The diagram below shows these three elements: the **story**, the **teller** and the **discourse**.

Link

Ideas about how you can explore 'gaps' in the stories you study are focused on again in Chapters 4–6, where you adopt a creative-writing approach to texts, called 're-writing'. The work in this chapter lays some important groundwork for those later chapters.

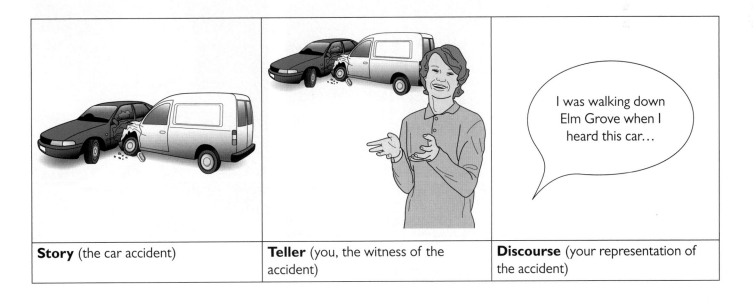

| **Story** (the car accident) | **Teller** (you, the witness of the accident) | **Discourse** (your representation of the accident) |

The position of the teller in the middle between story and discourse is important.

Media such as newspapers, for example, are 'in the middle' – between facts (story) and how they represent them (discourse). It's important to understand that being in the middle isn't just *being* somewhere but it is *doing* something. The role of the teller is always active. The teller represents facts by turning them into words and phrases, and that's an active process.

Of course, representation could be made in other ways. Images can be quite powerful, too. Matt's comic strip (page 39), for example, is made up of words *and* pictures. There are many ways of representing a story: it could be done by talking to someone face to face, by drawing images, by sending text messages, by posting on your Facebook wall and so on. These options are all variations of **mode**.

Now look at the two images below. One is a photograph and the other a painting, and both are representations of the Spinnaker Tower in Portsmouth. Although the two representations are different, the actual tower standing by the sea in Portsmouth is, of course, one and the same – that's the story. The difference between the two images is one of mode.

Different modes allow tellers to do different things. In a painting, the painter or teller can be very creative in the way he or she interprets and represents a subject. A photograph is a more-realistic representation compared to the painting. The role of photographers/tellers is less obvious. However, even then, they still make crucial decisions when they choose the positions from which to take their photographs. This is discussed in detail in the next section.

Point of view

In the photograph above you can see the Spinnaker Tower from one particular **point of view**. But of course the photographer could choose to stand in a totally different place, so the resulting image would be quite different. The photographs opposite are just four of the many different points of view from which the Spinnaker Tower could be represented.

What is really interesting here is that the four photographs can produce very different sensations in the viewer.

Activity

For each of the four photographs, write a description of between 25 and 50 words. Make sure that your descriptions are based only on what you see in each photograph and not on any factual information that you may already know about the Spinnaker Tower.

Then compare your descriptions with those of other students. Are there any common patterns in the ways in which each image has been described?

Each photograph has been taken from a different point of view. So each one shows a subjective representation of the tower and generates subjective interpretations in the viewers. This is true for every single image, not only those representing the Spinnaker Tower.

It is also true for language-based representations. The following activities will help you begin to appreciate this.

Activity

Think again of the example of the car crash on page 47. Different people, who experienced the event from different points of view, will give different accounts of the incident. In a group of four, devise some basic facts about an accident, then each choose one person from the list below and write a 50-word report from his or her point of view:

- the driver of one of the two vehicles
- a passenger in one of the two vehicles
- a passer-by who witnessed the accident from a short distance
- someone who heard about the accident from someone else.

Now compare the individual reports. How different are they? Discuss and make notes of any linguistic differences that you notice.

The previous activity highlights the fact that the role somebody played in the events of a story makes an important difference to the way in which they then tell that story. If you played a central role, you would have experienced the events directly and would be able to offer an insider's perspective. The driver of one of the two vehicles, for example, would have experienced the accident in the most direct way. A passenger would also have been a participant, but with a slightly less central role. If you were standing by the side of the road, your perception of what happened would be quite different and more detached. Finally, you could have heard about the accident from someone else and in that case you would be at an even greater distance from it.

Your position in relation to the story varies in each case along a scale from internal perspective to external perspective. The diagrams below illustrate this.

a

Protagonist. You were the main active participant in the story.

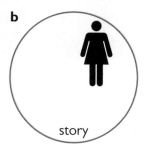

b

Secondary role. You participated in the events of the story but did not play a central role.

Key term

Protagonist. The main character in a story.

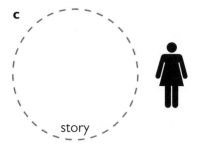

c

Witness. You did not participate in the events but witnessed them directly.

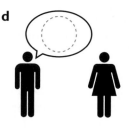

d

Second-hand. You heard about the story from somebody else.

Internal perspective   External perspective

Protagonist   Secondary role   Witness   Second-hand

Now we can begin to see what difference this makes in terms of language.

Activity

In one of the two semi-finals in the 2014 football World Cup, Germany beat Brazil by 7 goals to 1. The German press and the Brazilian press reported the story from different perspectives. Below is the English translation of the headlines and first sentences of two articles, one from a German newspaper, the other from a Brazilian newspaper.

7–1 Triumph over Brazil

The German football team has reached the final at the World Cup. Coach Loew's team outclassed hosts Brazil 7–1.

Brazil humiliated by Germany in the greatest embarrassment in football history

The dream of a sixth World Cup came to an end on Tuesday afternoon, when the Brazilian team was humiliated in a 7–1 defeat in the Mineirão stadium in Belo Horizonte.

How do the two points of view emerge in the language used?

One noticeable difference between the two extracts is that the one from the German newspaper seems less emotional and almost cold, with only the word 'outclassed' showing an element of evaluation, contrasting with the stronger and more emphatic language in the Brazilian newspaper, containing phrases like 'humiliated', 'greatest embarrassment' and 'dream'. This is similar to what we saw earlier when we discussed **recounts**, and seems to confirm stereotypical depictions of northern Europeans being rather unemotional and Latin people being somewhat melodramatic.

However, there is also a possibly more interesting linguistic difference, which relates to what the two articles are really about. This is discussed in the next section.

Theme

The German extract in the activity above is really about Germany's victory, while the Brazilian extract is about Brazil's defeat. We know this because of what the two journalists have chosen to put at the beginning of each clause. In the German extract:

> ***7–1 Triumph*** over Brazil
>
> ***The German football team*** has reached the final at the World Cup.
>
> ***Coach Loew's team*** outclassed hosts Brazil 7–1.

All the elements in bold italic relate to the German team.

> **Key term**
>
> **Theme.** This has two, related, meanings. In grammar, the theme is the first element in a clause. It says what the clause is about. In more general usage, theme can refers to the topic or subject matter of an entire text.

In the Brazilian extract:

> ***Brazil*** humiliated by Germany in the greatest embarrassment in football history
>
> ***The dream of a sixth World Cup*** came to an end on Tuesday afternoon
>
> ***the Brazilian team*** was humiliated in a 7–1 defeat in the Mineirão stadium in Belo Horizonte.

All the elements in bold italic relate to the Brazilian team.

The first element in a **clause**, like those above, is called the **theme** and indicates what the clause is about.

> **Activity**
>
> Go back to the reports you wrote in the activity on page 50. Are there any interesting choices that you made with regard to theme? Can you relate those choices to **point of view**?

No matter how objective we may attempt to be, every time we represent a story or even a single event in any **mode**, we always adopt a particular point of view, which comes across through the language choices we make.

Deixis

In general, we can say that in narrative we tend to focus on aspects of the story that are more interesting and relevant to us. Even when we try to be neutral and unbiased, this still shows up in a number of ways in the language choices we make. Consider these very factual and almost identical statements:

- Millions of tourists come to Thailand each year.
- Millions of tourists go to Thailand each year.

The only words that are different are the verbs 'come' and 'go'. But it's an important difference. The choice of the verb 'come' makes us realize that the first statement was written from the point of view of someone who was in Thailand. And, from his or her point of view, the millions of tourists come towards him or her. By contrast, the use of 'go' tells us that the second statement was written from the point of view of someone who was outside Thailand. In this case, the teller is perhaps one of the potential tourists who might visit Thailand. The two diagrams below illustrate this difference.

a   Tourists come to Thailand

Thailand

b

Tourists go to Thailand

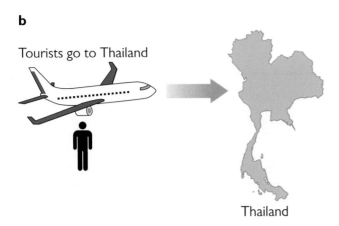

Thailand

In the English language, 'come' and 'go' are only two of the words that have the power of clarifying where the teller is in relation to the **context**. There are many more words and phrases that point to places in the teller's context. Consider, for example, 'up', 'down', 'over there', 'in the back', 'to my left', 'in front', 'behind' and so on. If somebody says 'I'm going up to Yorkshire tomorrow', the word 'up' indicates that the person is somewhere south of Yorkshire. If somebody else says 'I'm taking the train down to London', that means he or she is currently somewhere north of London.

What is special about these is that they can only be interpreted by reference to the actual location in which the teller uses them.

The ways in which language refers to places in somebody's context is called **deixis**, a term that comes from an ancient Greek word meaning to indicate. Exactly the same principle applies when we refer to points in time. So, words and phrases like 'later', 'two days ago', 'next month', 'yesterday' and so on refer to various points in time, again from the teller's point of view.

The ability of language to refer to physical places is called **space (or spatial) deixis**, while when we refer to points in time through language, we use **time (or temporal) deixis**. The two diagrams below illustrate these two concepts.

> ### Did you know?
> **Prepositions** can be used idiomatically as well as literally and, as a result, they can be hard for foreign learners of English to understand. For example, think about the difference between 'getting up to' something and 'getting down to' something.

> ### Key term
> **Deixis.** The act of pointing to something by using certain language items. Deictic expressions refer to aspects of space (spatial deixis, for example 'over there'), time (temporal deixis, for example 'yesterday') and person deixis (who is being referred to, for example 'they').

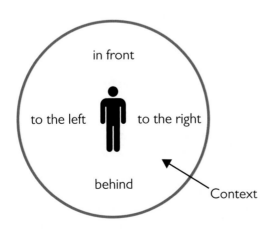

Space deixis

Time deixis

The position of the teller in the centre represents the fact that all references to space or time that he or she makes must be interpreted from his or her point of view. The word 'tomorrow' refers to a particular day depending on when 'now' is. If the teller is speaking on 11 June 2014, 'tomorrow' is 12 June 2014, and so on.

In addition to space and time, deictic expressions can also refer to people. Pronouns such as 'I', 'you', 'she' and 'he' point at different participants in a particular context and their roles. This type of deixis is called **person deixis**. In a situation where Richard is telling Amir about something that Lucy has done, the pronoun 'I' will refer to Richard, 'you' will refer to Amir and 'she' to Lucy.

Whose story is it?

Deixis, and **point of view** in general, are important aspects of narrative because they establish the perspective from which a story is put into **discourse**.

Activity

Consider the following Facebook status update, by someone called Becky:

> The house I'm the keeper for totally flooded out, the tide just came right in!!! What a mess! And the owners are away on holiday... so it's just me and a mop trying not to electrocute myself. Hope you have a great weekend!

There are three participants involved: Becky, the owners of the house and Becky's friends on Facebook. But whose story is it?

The centre of the narrative is clearly Becky. The pronouns 'I', 'me' and 'myself' refer to Becky, the phrase 'came right in' indicates that her position is inside the house. The owners of the house are part of the story but the narrative doesn't follow their perspective, while Becky's friends are not really directly involved, even though she refers to them through the pronoun 'you'. This, therefore, is a very subjective narrative, where the teller is also the **protagonist** (main character). Because she establishes this personal point of view in the narrative, Becky invites her friends to see things from her own perspective. This includes her feelings too. Her **evaluation** 'What a mess!' tells everybody the way she feels about the event and the readers of her post are induced to share that feeling.

Now, let's go back to Matt's comic strip on page 39. The comic strip comes from a book entitled *99 Ways to Tell a Story*, where cartoonist Matt Madden created 99 different narratives of the same story. Some of the ways in which he decided to do that involve changes in point of view. The following comic strips are a few examples.

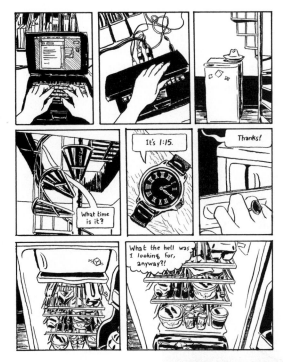

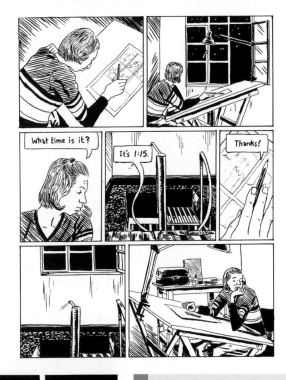

The first one follows a subjective point of view, so the reader sees things through the eyes of the protagonist. It's almost as if there were a micro-camera right between his eyes. In the second one, the narrative focuses on Matt's girlfriend Jessica and, although the perspective is not as subjective as the previous one, Jessica is most definitely the protagonist, whereas Matt is very much in the background as we can only 'hear' his voice. In the third comic strip, quite imaginatively, the reader sees things from a perspective inside the fridge. What these comic strips demonstrate is how different these narratives are, even though they are based on the same story, and that this difference depends entirely on shifts in **point of view**.

Notice also how different the information is in each narrative. In the very first comic strip (on page 39), we see what Matt is doing but have no idea who asks the question from upstairs. The opposite is true in the comic strip focusing on Jessica: it is only in this one that we know that she was trying to draw something but was clearly feeling 'stuck' at that particular point. In the 'fridge' example we know very little, except that there are some muffled voices at one point, and then there is the very last bit of the story. So, a shift in point of view doesn't simply mean looking at the same thing from a different angle – it means constructing a radically different narrative.

Activity

Read this other very short narrative:

> Today, I went out to lunch with my girlfriend. I asked if she was going to finish her meal, hoping to steal a bite or two. She somehow took this as me saying she was overweight, threw her drink at me, and stormed off. I just wanted some steak.

Now write two more narratives based on the same story. One from the girlfriend's point of view and another from your own point of view as a witness. It is very important that you consider the changing points of view very carefully. When you write the narrative from the girlfriend's perspective, try to imagine what she sees, thinks and feels. This means that not all of the information in the original story may be relevant. Also take this into consideration when you write the narrative from your external point of view.

You now have three narratives based on the same story. Like the comic strips, these are likely to be very different. The girl, for example, may have a totally different take on the event, whereas your perspective will be more external to the story, since you were not an active participant in it. Again, we can represent these three situations with diagrams:

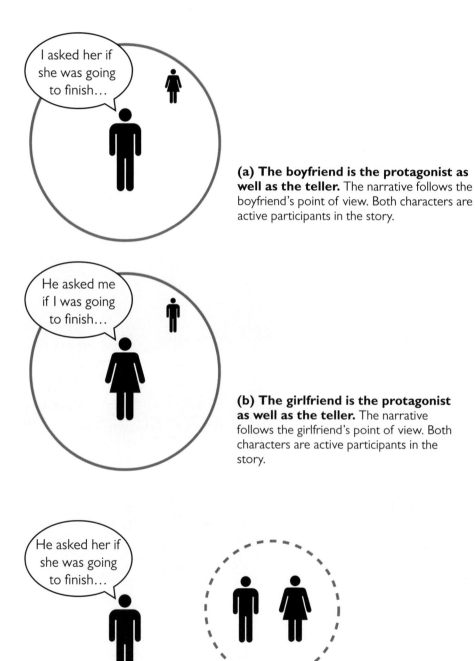

> I asked her if she was going to finish…

(a) The boyfriend is the protagonist as well as the teller. The narrative follows the boyfriend's point of view. Both characters are active participants in the story.

> He asked me if I was going to finish…

(b) The girlfriend is the protagonist as well as the teller. The narrative follows the girlfriend's point of view. Both characters are active participants in the story.

> He asked her if she was going to finish…

(c) The narrative follows an external perspective. The teller is not an active participant in the story. The boyfriend and the girlfriend have equal importance, although the teller can choose to focus more on one or the other.

A speech balloon is a way of representing somebody's utterances. As speech is a key element in most stories, it is also an important component of narrative. In the next section we'll see how speech is presented in narrative.

Activity

Now go to your AQA Anthology *Paris*. How far can you apply the ideas that you have learned so far in this chapter, and in the introductory chapter, to the texts in the Anthology? Try to answer the following questions:

- Who are the actors and what are the actions and circumstances in each text?
- What is the **narrative structure** of the texts? Bear in mind that each text is an extract and you will not be expected to know the whole book that the extract has been taken from. However, the extract itself will be structured in some way.
- Who are the storytellers in the extracts?
- Whose stories are being told?
- What is the position of the **narrator** in each extract? Are they part of the story, or not?
- Who is the text aimed at?

In your answers, give as many examples of language features as you can from the texts and try to use accurate labels to describe the features.

The presentation of speech

At the beginning of this chapter we saw what an 'event' was. When someone says something to somebody else, that's an event too. It's called a **speech event**. Like all other events, speech events involve some action (speaking), participants (the speaker and the listener) and some circumstances (a time and a place). Of course, speech events are very frequent in stories and play an important role in narrative. There are two main ways of reporting speech: directly and indirectly.

Direct speech

In **direct speech** (DS), the teller reproduces the exact words that were uttered in the story. In Matt's comic strips, for example, the speech balloons represent the characters' utterances. When we tell a story, we can choose to do the same thing. Instead of speech balloons, we would use **reporting clauses**, such as 'she said…', 'he replied' and so on. One type of reporting clause that has become very common in recent years among teenagers is 'he/she was like…'. Although it tends to be disapproved of by parents and teachers, and you probably wouldn't use it in **formal** circumstances, this is a reporting clause just like 'he/she said…'.

Now consider this short extract:

> I asked 'How old is she?' and he was like 'Fifteen'. So I thought 'Yeah, right'.

There are three instances of reported speech here, all of them direct. The third is a bit special, since it reports speech that took place in the teller's mind, and this is normally called **reported thought**.

Key terms

Direct speech. A form of speech presentation in which the narrator reports some speech by reproducing the exact words uttered by a character, usually enclosed in quotation marks and introduced by a reporting clause.

Reported thought. A form of thought presentation in which the narrator reports the thoughts of a character as if it was speech occurring inside the character's mind and not said aloud.

Reporting clause. A clause used by the narrator when introducing speech. For example, 'she said', 'he murmured'.

Direct speech (or thought) is pretty straightforward. Since the teller reports words as they were uttered, all that can change is the reporting clause. The structure is however always the same: there is a reporting clause and the actual utterance enclosed in quotation marks:

Reporting clause	Utterance
I asked	'How old is she?'
he was like	'Fifteen'
I thought	'Yeah, right'

As a little practice, you can use Matt's comic strip on page 39 in the following activity.

 Activity

Considering Matt's comic strip, write a reporting clause for each instance of reported speech or thought. The first example has been done for you.

Reporting clause	Utterance
Jessica asked Matt	'What time is it?'
	'It's 1:15'
	'Thanks'
	'What the hell was I looking for anyway?'

Indirect speech

Key term

Indirect speech. A form of speech presentation in which the narrator reports a speech event by integrating the words uttered by a character within the narrative.

Reporting exactly what was said can be laborious sometimes. A long series of utterances reported directly can break the flow of the narrative. So tellers can choose to take greater control in the way they report speech and incorporate it more tightly within the **discourse**. When this happens, tellers use **indirect speech** (IS). Quite simply, what happens in these cases is that somebody's utterances are integrated within the narrative.

If we take the first speech event from the previous activity, one way of reporting it indirectly would be:

Jessica asked Matt what time it was.

Notice that the quotation marks have disappeared, since the speech isn't reported exactly as it was uttered by Jessica. Notice also the shift in tense. The present tense in the original utterance has become past tense here. This is because Jessica's words have now become part of the teller's narrative, which, like most narratives, reports events that happened in the past.

One more thing to pay attention to is that this works well if the teller is an external witness to the event. If the teller is Matt, then the reported speech would look like this:

Jessica asked me what time it was.

Or, if the teller is Jessica, the same speech event could be reported indirectly as:

I asked Matt what time it was.

This means that pronouns – 'I', 'me', 'he', 'she' – change according to who it is that reports a speech event. In the following activity you'll be able to practise with indirect speech.

Activity

In Matt's first comic strip (on page 39) there are three speech balloons and one thought balloon. Convert them into indirect speech and thought. Do this twice: the first time you are the teller from the point of view of a witness. The second time Matt is the teller. The first one has already been done for you, as a guide.

Direct speech/ thought	You are the teller	Matt is the teller
'What time is it?'	Jessica asked Matt what time it was	Jessica asked me what time it was
'It's 1:15'		
'Thanks'		
'What the hell was I looking for anyway?'		

When you turn direct speech into indirect speech, there is more than one way of doing it. Just to give you an idea, you can see below how Matt himself has done it.

From up in the studio, Jessica asked me what time it was.

I told her it was around one...

I heard her say thanks from upstairs.

I couldn't for the life of me remember what I had come looking for!

Your version may be slightly different from Matt's. That's entirely normal. Remember: in indirect speech, tellers take control of the reported speech and it's up to them how much of the original utterance they wish to report and in what form. Notice that Matt doesn't always quite reproduce the original words. This is perfectly normal.

You could, for example, narrate the final event as:

> And I just stood there, staring into the fridge, not knowing what I wanted any more.

When tellers report speech (or thought) events, they can be more or less intrusive, just as when they report any other type of event. Tellers are in charge of their narratives and it is up to them how much they want to – or can – stay close to the actual story. For example, if we now consider the comic strip where the focal point is inside the fridge, and take into account that the first two speech events were muffled (the door was closed) and couldn't be heard well, we could report those speech events as:

> She said something. It sounded like a question, and he said something back.

In this case, the teller reports that there were some speech events but doesn't really reveal what was said. The distance between this and the original speech events is even greater. In fact, in this case this isn't quite indirect speech, but rather a **narrative report of a speech act** (NRSA). In terms of distance from the original speech event, DS, IS and NRSA can be placed along a **cline**:

Speech event

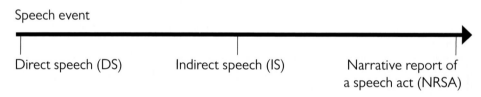

Direct speech (DS)   Indirect speech (IS)   Narrative report of
                                                           a speech act (NRSA)

Activity

To familiarize yourself further with these concepts, do the following:

1. Focus on a spoken narrative from the Anthology where there is a substantial passage of direct speech. Turn this into a new text where you are the teller and you are reporting what has been said. You're in charge now, so report things from your point of view. How has your new version changed the nature of the original text?

2. List all the texts in the Anthology that involve speech. Include all types of spoken language – spontaneous speech; speech that was planned and scripted, to be spoken aloud; **representations** of spoken language in various formats, such as prose texts and comics; interactive hybrids of the spoken and written **modes**, in the form of online conversations. Think about how these different spoken or speech-like texts vary and write some notes to help you in an analysis. Think about their language features and why they occur; also think about any prosodic (**prosody**) and paralinguistic (**paralanguage**) elements that would have been part of their original **context**. For those texts that can be viewed and/or listened to in their original format, make some notes on the differences between the original texts and how they are represented in the paper-based version of the Anthology. You will be doing more work on this area in Chapter 4.

Research idea

Here's an idea for a small research project. Follow these steps:

1. Go back to the list you made at the beginning of the chapter (on page 38) and select two of the items in the list.

2. Collect 10 texts for each of the two categories you have chosen.

3. Analyse the texts and try to answer the following research questions about the two types:

   ● Does the narrative follow an evident structure?

   ● In which one does the teller adopt a more subjective point of view?

   ● What kind of reported speech is used in the two types of text?

REVIEW YOUR LEARNING

It is important that you understand the main elements of narrative. As a revision exercise, answer these questions:

● What are the main components of a story?

● What is a recount?

● What is the difference between story and discourse?

● How does point of view affect narrative?

● What does it mean to say that we can place direct speech, indirect speech and narrative report of a speech act along a scale according to their distance from the original speech event?

References

Labov, W. (1972). *Language in the inner city: studies in the Black English vernacular.* Philadelphia: University of Pennsylvania Press.

Madden, M. (2006). *99 Ways to Tell a Story.* Jonathan Cape.

Further reading

Porter Abbot, H. (2008). *The Cambridge Introduction to Narrative (2nd edn.).* Cambridge: Cambridge University Press.

The work of William Labov is extensive and you can read more of it by going to his own website at: http://www.ling.upenn.edu/~wlabov/

Read 'Oral Narratives of Personal Experience' on his site at: http://www.ling.upenn.edu/~wlabov/Papers/FebOralNarPE.pdf

Toolan, M. J. (2001) *Narrative: A Critical Linguistic Introduction.* London: Routledge

This chapter will:

- help you understand how to go about analysing stories in fiction
- give you useful frameworks for analysis and opportunities to practise your skills
- show you how to apply what you learn to your set texts.

In the previous chapter you learned about **narrative** in 'the real world' – that is, storytelling that we all do every day. In this chapter you will explore and understand how narrative works in fiction and how it is different from real-world storytelling. You will be able to apply the skills you learn to the prose fiction texts set for study (called 'Imagined Worlds') as well as to other parts of the specification. For example, in the coursework component 'Making Connections' you are required to compare a literary text with some non-literary material. Understanding how texts of all kinds work is therefore a key skill for this subject area.

This chapter builds on the work you did in Chapter 1 and takes it further in looking at literary texts. It does contain some technical detail that may be new to you if you have not taken a language approach before. So be prepared to go over some of the aspects more than once in order to understand things fully. If you can grasp the ideas here, you will be in a good position to analyse any extract you are given on an exam paper. Details of the relevant exam papers are given below.

Relevant Assessment Objectives

For A level analysis, AO1, AO2 and AO3 are tested.

For AS level analysis, AO1 and AO2 are tested.

- AO1 rewards your ability to take a language approach to the texts that you study, to write coherently and to use terminology appropriately.
- AO2 rewards your ability to explain what texts mean, by showing how meanings are built from the language choices that writers and speakers make.
- AO3 rewards your understanding of **context** – the effects produced by variations of such aspects as audience, purpose, **genre** and **mode**.

The ability to analyse fictional narratives is tested in exam conditions in Section B of A level Paper 1 and Section A of AS level Paper 1. There are some differences between the A level and AS level exams, as follows:

- Section B of the A level exam is open book, while the AS level exam is closed book.
- The AS level exam involves the analysis of an extract.
- The A level paper asks you to analyse an extract as a starting point, but you also need to go beyond the extract and ultimately beyond the book itself, in order to talk about the type of novel you are studying – that is, its genre.

Introduction

In fiction, the fundamental elements of narrative are the same: **story**, **teller** and **discourse**. The main differences between real-world narrative and fiction narrative are connected to:

- the nature of the story
- the roles of the teller
- the possibilities of discourse.

The first thing to consider is the concept of fiction and how it relates to what you learned in Chapter 1.

What is fiction?

When you walk into a bookshop, you will notice that the shelves are labelled with the names of categories: Travel, Cookery, Reference, History and so on. These names can vary from shop to shop but one label that is in virtually every single bookshop is 'Fiction'. Like many common words, 'fiction' is not easy to define.

Activity

1. Without consulting any reference material, think about the word 'fiction'. What does it mean to you? It might be useful to make a list of items that you feel count as fiction. In drawing up your list, try to include as many items as you can. Then compare your definition and list with those of your fellow students.

2. Now look at the **concordance lines** from the British National **Corpus** below and make any adjustments to your definition, if necessary.

of one hundred and fifty publications –	fiction	and non-fiction, scientific and socio-political
'organic produce is better for you' is a	fiction.	The study has argued that naturally
the possibility of using various 'science	fiction'	techniques to counter climate change,
cattle. Their lives are ruled by improbable	fictions:	lines, flags and whistles; a thirty-two-legged
at children. If it is your first work of	fiction	of any great length, I think you are doing
and it was a long time ago. He moved into	Fiction,	checking his favourite thriller author
and how much will have to be some kind of	fiction,	or simulation, where the risks are too
where is the wash-hoos?' That might be pure	fiction	but nevertheless it was a very amusing
of life. This might make a good science	fiction	story – The White Cloud, it could be called
something that was much more likely to happen in	fiction	than in real life. Unfortunately there

One thing that seems to be common in the way people use the word 'fiction' is that it relates to something that is not true, that is just an invention. Fiction, therefore, involves creativity, in a way that real-world storytelling normally doesn't – although, of course, the word 'creativity' itself is debatable. If we now take our basic components of **narrative – story**, **teller** and **discourse** – the question is: Which of these can be the product of someone's imagination? How, and to what extent?

Key term

Concordance line. A line of text from a corpus, showing where the searched item occurred within a sentence or utterance.

Between reality and imagination

In Chapter 1, our basic definition of a story was that it is composed of a series of events. In fiction, this is exactly the same. So one easy conclusion we could draw is that stories in fiction are composed of invented events. This sounds logical, but we should go a little deeper. We saw that an event is made up of actors, action and circumstances, so we can ask: What exactly is invented within an event?

Link

A comparison between the opening sections of some literary and non-literary material could form the basis for a good coursework task. See Chapters 8–9.

The best way to begin to answer this question is by considering passages from different narratives. The following are the opening paragraphs of five books.

Princeton

Princeton, in the summer, smelled of nothing, and although Ifemelu liked the tranquil greenness of the many trees, the clean streets and stately homes, the delicately overpriced shops and the quiet, abiding air of earned grace, it was this, the lack of a smell, that most appealed to her, perhaps because the other American cities she knew well had all smelled distinctly. Philadelphia had the musty scent of history. New Haven smelled of neglect. Baltimore smelled of brine, and Brooklyn of sun-warmed garbage. But Princeton had no smell. She liked taking deep breaths here.

Ghana

'Where are you from'? he said. 'No, where are you *really* from?'

It was the businessman who wanted to know. He'd been slumped beside me with his eyes shut and his mouth open since we'd left London. As the Boeing 777 dipped towards Accra he heaved himself up straight.

'Where are you from?' he repeated.

The overhead light glistened off the darkness of his skin. He wiped the film of sweat from his forehead.

I gave him the usual line.

'My parents are from Ghana, but I was born in Britain.'

Tent

I was lying in my sleeping bag, staring at the light filtering through the red and green fabric of the dome tent. Simon was snoring loudly, occasionally twitching in his dream world. We could have been anywhere. There is a peculiar anonymity about being in tents. Once the zip is closed and the outside world barred from sight, all sense of location disappears. Scotland, the French Alps, the Karakoram, it was always the same. The sounds of rustling, of fabric flapping in the wind, or of rainfall, the feel of hard lumps under the ground sheet, the smell of rancid socks and sweat – these are universals, as comforting as the warmth of the down sleeping bag.

Budapest

We are on our way to Budapest: Bastard and Chipo and Godknows and Sbho and Stina and me. We are going even though we are not allowed to cross Mzilikazi Road, even though Bastard is supposed to be watching his little sister Fraction, even though Mother would kill me dead if she found out; we are just going. There are guavas to steal in Budapest, and right now I'd rather die for guavas. We didn't eat this morning and my stomach feels like somebody just took a shovel and dug everything out.

Turtle

In a distant and second-hand set of dimensions, in an astral plane that was never meant to fly, the curling star-mists waver and part...

See...

Great A'Tuin the Turtle comes, swimming slowly through the interstellar gulf, hydrogen frost on his ponderous limbs, his huge and ancient shell pocked with meteor craters. Through sea-sized eyes that are crusted with rheum and asteroid dust He stares fixedly at the Destination.

In a brain bigger than a city, with geological slowness, He thinks only of the Weight.

Most of the weight is of course accounted for by Berilia, Tubul, Great T'Phon and Jerakeen, the four giant elephants upon whose broad and star-tanned shoulders the disc of the World rests.

Activity

After you've read the five passages above, decide which aspects of the events narrated seem real (R) and which seem invented (I), and tick your answers in a copy of the grid below.

Remember that the point of this activity is not so much to try to guess the 'right' answers, but to reflect on the reasons that led you to choose your answers. So, for example, avoid doing Internet searches on these passages, because that would defeat the object of the activity.

	Princeton		Ghana		Tent		Budapest		Turtle	
	R	I	R	I	R	I	R	I	R	I
Actors										
Action										
Circumstances										

The way you chose your answers in the above activity depends very much on your background knowledge – not so much about the actual books, but about the world in general and the way you have experienced it so far. When you read narrative, your background knowledge is important, because it allows you to make hypotheses about the world you read about in the text. You begin reading equipped with your existing knowledge of the world, and that knowledge is gradually increased as you read on. As you read, your idea of who is involved, what they do and the circumstances they are in becomes clearer and makes more sense.

Read the accounts below of the five passages and see whether these explanations match the experience you had as a reader.

In 'Princeton', the **protagonist**'s name is Ifemelu. This is a name you may not have come across before. This *could* mean that it is a totally invented name. But it could also mean that it is a name that is common in a different place, perhaps far away from Britain. It's not easy to decide if Ifemelu is a real person or not, just based on her name. But there are other elements that can help to make sense of the story. The passage also mentions a few places. At least some of them will sound familiar to you. You have probably heard of Philadelphia and Brooklyn. So you can begin to establish that Ifemelu is in the United States, and you can be pretty confident that the circumstance of this opening passage, the actual locations where things are taking place, is real.

Still, Ifemelu doesn't sound like a typically American name. So it's possible that she, or perhaps her family, was originally from somewhere else. This seems to be confirmed when the teller mentions 'the other American cities she knew well': this only really makes sense with reference to someone who is *not* American. So, another thing you can infer just by reading this passage is that Ifemelu, the protagonist, is not American. This is, of course, a very common situation. There are millions of people in the United States who live there but were born somewhere else. So is Ifemelu a real person, or is she the product of the teller's imagination? There's nothing obvious that suggests one way or the other. If she's a real person, are her actions and feelings real, too? We will leave these questions unanswered for now. What is important is to notice that we accept Ifemelu as a possible person because we recognize the context she is in.

In 'Ghana', you can see very clearly how your understanding of what is going on increases gradually, sentence by sentence. First, someone is asking someone else where they 'really' come from, suggesting that the initial answer wasn't convincing enough. At this point we don't know why that was. Then we realize that the two characters are travelling from London and are sitting together. We then know that they are travelling by plane and the destination of the journey is Accra. Here we begin to rely more on our background knowledge. It is our knowledge of what a Boeing 777 is that tells us the two characters are travelling by plane. What about Accra? We may or may not know where this place is.

As we keep reading, we discover a further detail: the colour of the other passenger's skin. Then the protagonist's answer to the initial question reveals to us some information about that person's origin (which is something that becomes quite important in the rest of the book). At this point, if we didn't know where Accra was, we'd begin to make assumptions that it might be in Ghana. We now also begin to see why the other passenger asked his initial question. Did all of this really happen or was it invented by the teller? It's very difficult to say. Everything seems real enough. How are we to know? Again, what we do here is make use of our existing knowledge to negotiate and make sense of the story we're reading. The aspects of the story that we do recognize are very important in allowing this process. If London is a real place, a Boeing 777 is a real plane, Ghana is a real country, then it's easier for us to imagine the two characters as possible.

In 'Tent', we don't know very much at all about the location. We know that the protagonist and at least one other companion, Simon, are in a tent, probably at night, since Simon is sleeping and the protagonist is in a sleeping bag, presumably about to fall asleep too. As we read on, we know that the main character has been in a tent many times before and in different parts of the world. Again, depending on our background knowledge, we might realize that all the places the protagonist mentions have mountains nearby. So we can make guesses about the kind of place the two characters are in at the moment, but also where they might be from, their age and perhaps even the protagonist's gender. Even though you may not have slept in a tent, you can somehow visualize the environment as it is described by the teller. As in the previous passages, there's nothing obviously invented about the actors, what they're doing or where they are. There are sufficient elements that make the story feel real.

'Budapest' feels a little different. It's written in the present tense, so it's as if the narrative follows the story simultaneously, like a running commentary. This gives us a sense of 'here and now'. But the names mentioned don't sound very close at all. You probably know that Budapest is the capital of Hungary. But what about the people's names? They sound very unusual and not very Hungarian. Guavas are fruits that grow in the tropics, not in Hungary. And stealing them doesn't seem to be a very normal action. The main character mentions not having eaten in the morning, but the description possibly feels a little exaggerated for someone who hasn't had breakfast. Even the language sounds a little unusual: the expression 'Mother would kill me dead' probably isn't something you would use or hear. Compared to the first three passages, you are more likely to struggle to make sense of who the characters are, where they are and what they're doing. If this is the case, that's because the narrative disrupts your background knowledge in more significant ways, so you have to work harder to accept this as a possible story.

The final passage is the one that is furthest from reality. You might struggle to make any sense of it. There's hardly anything in it that we're familiar with. Having read this first passage, would you want to keep reading the rest of the book?

> ### Activity
>
> Turn to the set text that you have chosen to study for this area of the specification and read the first page. How much background knowledge are you using to make sense of the story's introductory passages? Think about the setting – the time and place – as well as any characters you are introduced to or events you are told about. Are there any details that are puzzling but that you are willing to believe will be explained later?

Possible worlds and the suspension of disbelief

The analysis you have completed of the five short passages has shown two things:

- It is often not easy to decide if a piece of narrative is about a real story or a fictional one.
- The decision seems to depend very much on the extent to which we are willing to accept the story as possible.

This is the theory of **possible worlds**, which explains how we make sense of the 'worlds' – situations, places, people, actions, etc. – that we read about in narrative. This theory says that we negotiate the world that unfolds in the texts that we read according to the knowledge stored in our minds and how this knowledge increases as we keep reading.

Sometimes, when aspects of the story seem to be obviously unreal, as is the case in the passage 'Turtle' above, we latch on, so to speak, to other elements that we do recognize – place names, ordinary situations, laws of nature and so on – and somehow accept the seemingly impossible elements (such as invisible people) too. When we do that, we **suspend disbelief**. This means that we temporarily avoid questioning whether something may be real or not and, instead, choose to go along with the narrative. Of course, we don't *have* to do so, but if we refuse to suspend disbelief, we will probably also stop reading the particular narrative that we find it impossible to accept.

Therefore, we can say that the suspension of disbelief is a condition of narrative. In fact, we do that with all kinds of narrative. Even in the passages 'Princeton', 'Ghana' and 'Tent' above, where nothing stands out as particularly unusual, we won't question the 'reality' of the stories. Much of the pleasure that we derive from reading narrative comes from our ability to identify with the characters, their feelings and so on. If we constantly wondered whether they're real, that pleasure would vanish.

> ### Key terms
>
> **Possible world.** Everything related to a story that readers accept as possible as a result of their suspension of disbelief.
>
> **Suspension of disbelief.** The ability of readers to accept the 'world' of a story as possible, without questioning whether it is real or not.

Having established that 'Princeton' is fictional, how fictional is the character of Ifemelu? This may sound like a strange question – you might object that she's either an invented character or she isn't. That is a perfectly valid point, but if you do a little research, you can find out information that might make you rethink the fiction–reality opposition.

After completing the above activity and reading the feedback on it, you will find that the answer to the question of whether 'Princeton' is fictional becomes more subtle and complex than a simple 'yes' or 'no'.

The extract 'Budapest' comes from NoViolet Bulawayo's *We Need New Names*, a novel that is similar to *Americanah*. As in Adichie's novel, *Americanah,* here too the protagonist is a young African woman who, at one point in her life, leaves her country and moves to America. And, like Adichie, Bulawayo did that herself. The beginning of Bulawayo's novel feels stranger than the opening of *Americanah*, with the unusual names, the odd combination of Budapest and stealing guavas, the language, the very strong feeling of hunger. The narrative is set in a suburban ghetto in Zimbabwe. Budapest is the name of a wealthy neighbourhood, where the protagonist and her friends – a group of children – are planning to go and steal guavas so that they can calm their intense hunger. The world of the text, in 'Budapest', bears hardly any similarity with ours or that of 'Princeton', but is just as real.

So are *Americanah* and *We Need New Names* novels about their authors, like autobiographies? To some extent they are, but while in an autobiography every single aspect of the story is (or is expected to be) real, in a novel there is always a combination of reality and imagination. The balance between them can vary, of course, but the two components are always there. This is true even in narratives where the story seems to be just pure fantasy.

Activity

Read the passage 'Turtle' (pages 64–65) again. What is the balance between reality and imagination? Would you be willing to suspend your disbelief and continue reading the novel?

Much of the description in 'Turtle' is fantastic, in the sense that it is the product of fantasy; but not all of it. If it was, we wouldn't be able to make any sense of it at all. There's a turtle, which is a real animal. There are elephants, which are real animals too. Of course, in reality elephants don't stand on the shells of huge turtles! But, somehow, we can visualize this very large turtle with four elephants on top of it. After all, the shell of turtles is very hard and resistant and can take quite a lot of weight. Weight itself is also real. Elephants are heavy and A'Tuin the Turtle feels their weight on its back.

In fact, the whole idea of the world being supported by elephants standing on a turtle comes from Hindu mythology and is not an invention of the author. So even though, compared to the other passages, there may be more here that you need to suspend your disbelief about, you can still accept the world of the text as possible – thanks to the elements in it that, somehow, you can relate to. The rule about the combination of real and fictional elements still stands.

All the prose-fiction texts set for the specification share the genre of fantasy. They are all different types of fantasy, including **gothic** horror (*Frankenstein* and *Dracula*), the supernatural (*The Lovely Bones*) and **dystopian** science fiction (*The Handmaid's Tale*). So they are all very good examples of what we have just been talking about – works of fiction that are quite far removed from everyday life and realistic events. But they need to make links with the real world in order to give their stories a point. The following activity will start you thinking about how the elements of fantasy and reality have been balanced in the text you are studying.

Key terms

Dystopian. The opposite of 'utopian', which means 'a perfect place'. Dystopian societies are oppressive and full of suffering and misery. *Utopia* was the name of a book written by Sir Thomas More in 1516, where he described his ideal society in the form of a fictional island.

Gothic. The term 'Gothic' refers not just to literature but also to other creative forms, such as painting, architecture, and music. Named after a Germanic tribe called the Goths, a gothic style of fiction includes elements of extreme emotion (such as terror), medieval and dramatic settings, and unnatural events.

Activities

1. Look at how your set text has been marketed. Think about the cover, including the images, use of colour and aspects of textual design. Also look at the blurb on the back of the book, any story details given inside the cover or on preliminary pages, and any other elements that seem to you to have a persuasive function.

   In all these aspects, what is the balance between references to fantasy elements and references to the real world? How are you being 'sold' the idea of fantasy? What are you told about the relevance of a fantasy story to contemporary real life?

2. Read the first chapter of your set text. How does the novel mix realistic details with elements of imagination and fantasy in that first chapter?

   Make a list of some of the elements of each and decide what balance there is between the two. What makes it possible for you to suspend your disbelief and accept the story that is being told?

3. Why do you think the writer has chosen to produce a type of fantasy or unnatural story? What is the value of the fantasy story? (You might need to come back to this idea several times as you study the novel).

4. Think about any connections between the type of fantasy in the novel and the modern versions of that genre we have around us in other novels, films, games and so on. How do we continue to use fantasy elements in modern culture? What are the modern values of fantasy stories?

The teller in fiction

This section focuses on the role of the person who appears to be telling the story: the teller of the tale.

Read through the passages below. All four have something in common: the teller of the story is also the main character in the story.

India

I left India in 1964 with a certificate in commerce and the equivalent, in those days, of ten dollars to my name. For three weeks I sailed on the *SS Roma*, an Italian cargo vessel, in a third-class cabin next to the ship's engine, across the Arabian Sea, the Red Sea, the Mediterranean, and finally to England. I lived in north London, in Finsbury Park, in a house occupied entirely by penniless Bengali bachelors like myself, at least a dozen and sometimes more, all struggling to educate and establish ourselves abroad.

Borstal

As soon as I got to Borstal they made me a long-distance cross-country runner. I suppose they thought I was just the build for it because I was long and skinny for my age (and still am) and in any case I didn't mind it much, to tell you the truth, because running had always been made much of in our family, especially running away from the police. I've always been a good runner, quick and with a big stride as well, the only trouble being that no matter how fast I ran, and I did a very fair lick even though I do say so myself, it didn't stop me getting caught by the cops after that bakery job.

Atlas

In the long fighting, most of us were killed, and my mother, out of her secret nature, promised victory to Zeus. What Titans were left were banished to Britain, where the cold inhospitable rocks are worse than death. I was spared for my great strength.

In a way I was allowed to be my own punishment.

Because I loved the earth. Because the seas of the earth held no fear for me. Because I had learned the positions of the planets and the track of the stars. Because I am strong, my punishment was to support the Kosmos on my shoulders.

Dead

Now that I'm dead I know everything. This is what I wished would happen, but like so many of my wishes it failed to come true. I know only a few factoids that I didn't know before. Death is much too high a price to pay for the satisfaction of curiosity, needless to say.

Since being dead – since achieving this state of bonelessness, liplessness, breastlessness – I've learned some things I would rather not know, as one does when listening at windows or opening other people's letters. You think you'd like to read minds? Think again.

Activity

Having read the passages 'India', 'Borstal', 'Atlas' and 'Dead', can you establish whether each story is fictional?

The passage 'India' feels very real. Many people emigrated from India to Britain in the 1950s and 1960s. Most of them travelled by ship, and not very comfortably. Everything in the passage is absolutely possible and all the place names are real. It's a very credible story and the reader doesn't really need to suspend disbelief to accept it.

'Borstal' sounds quite real, too. The language is a little old-fashioned (such as 'I did a very fair lick') and this might make it feel more distant, perhaps. But, other than that, there isn't anything particularly hard to believe or accept.

'Atlas' is very different. The teller mentions Zeus and the Titans. This immediately sets the story in some mythological world. Depending on your prior knowledge of Greek mythology, you might recognize that the main character is the Titan Atlas, condemned by Zeus to carry the entire world on his shoulders after the Titans lost their battle against the Olympians. In some ways, this is similar to the myth of the turtle and the elephants in the passage 'Turtle' that we looked at earlier. The big difference, however, is that here the teller is Atlas himself. How can this be?

In 'Dead' the teller is even more improbable: someone who is dead! You might find this even harder to accept.

So, 'India' and 'Borstal' seem to be very different from 'Atlas' and 'Dead'. And yet, they all share an important characteristic. Besides being told by the main characters, the stories in all four texts have something else in common: none of the tellers are the authors of the narratives. This is quite obvious in 'Atlas' and 'Dead', but is also true in 'India' and 'Borstal', both of which are extracts from short stories. 'India' comes from a short story by Jhumpa Lahiri, who was born in London in 1967. The story is based on her father, who had arrived from India a few years earlier. 'Borstal' comes from a short story by Alan Sillitoe.

Of course, the tellers of the stories in some of the first batch of passages you looked at are not the same as the authors, either. At this point, it will be useful to compare all nine passages in terms of who the teller is.

Did you know?

The modern word 'atlas' comes, by association, from the name of the Titan Atlas.

The teller is...	The author	Not the author
a witness		*Americanah* (Princeton)
		The Colour of Magic (Turtle)
a participant	*Black Gold of the Sun* (Ghana)	*We Need New Names* (Budapest)
	Touching the Void (Tent)	*The Third and Final Continent* (India)
		The Loneliness of the Long-Distance Runner (Borstal)
		Weight (Atlas)
		The Penelopiad (Dead)

Key terms

First person narrator. A narrator who is an active participant in the story and, therefore, mentions him/herself in the narrative. This figure is more usefully described as a **homodiegetic narrator**.

Heterodiegetic narrator. A narrator who is not an active participant in the story.

Homodiegetic narrator. A narrator who is an active participant in the story.

Third person narrator. A narrator who is not an active participant in the story and, therefore, does not mention him/herself in the narrative. This figure is more usefully described as a **heterodiegetic narrator**.

In terms of how books are categorized in bookshops and libraries, you would find that the books containing the extracts 'Ghana' and 'Tent' are on the non-fiction shelves, while all the remaining six books would be in the fiction section. This shows a very important thing about fiction: what makes certain narratives fictional is not so much the extent to which the events narrated are invented, but the fact that the teller is invented. In fiction, the teller is called the **narrator** and is never the same person as the author. The narrator is an invented character.

The narrator may be a participant in the events of the story or simply a witness, just like the examples we saw above. Sometimes, a narrator who participates in the events is called a **first person narrator**, while one who is only a witness is called a **third person narrator**. Similarly, you might come across explanations where narrative is described as being 'in the first person' or 'in the third person'. All these terms are a bit misleading, because they focus on the use of personal pronouns rather than on the actual roles the narrator plays in the story. All narrators will use the same personal pronouns: third person pronouns 'she', 'he' and 'they' plus, if they (the narrators), are involved in the events, the **first person pronouns** 'I' and 'we'.

Since it is more useful and interesting to focus on the roles of the narrator rather than on the pronouns they use, there are better terms that we can use: **homodiegetic narrator**, for a narrator who is part of the story, and **heterodiegetic narrator**, for a narrator who is *not* part of the story. The following diagrams illustrate this.

Activity

Focus on the set text that you are studying. What type(s) of narrator(s) are involved in telling the story? Are they:

- the authors themselves, talking about their real lives?
- a participant or participants in the story?
- someone who witnesses the events of the story but who is not directly involved in it?
- a mixture of different types of narrator?

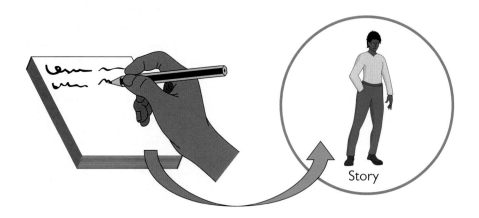

Homodiegetic narrator

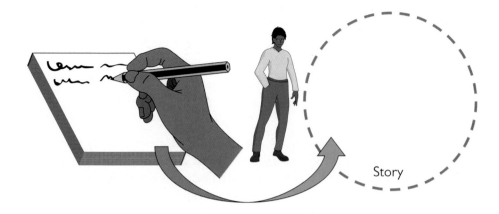

Story

> **!** **REMEMBER**
>
> Thinking about how your story is narrated is an important area of study. It might help if you represent the story visually, by drawing some diagrams showing who tells which part of the story.

Heterodiegetic narrator

Who speaks to whom?

Narrative fiction is a type of verbal communication. There are many ways of representing verbal communication, but one that is particularly useful was developed by Russian linguist Roman Jakobson in 1960. Jakobson's model has six components:

	Context	
Addresser	**Message**	**Addressee**
	Contact	
	Code	

- *Addresser:* the person who speaks/writes
- *Addressee:* the person who listens/reads
- *Context:* everything that is part of the addresser's and addressee's world (things, people, facts, etc.)
- *Code:* the language(s) that the addresser and the addressee use, e.g. English, Russian, etc.
- *Contact:* the physical channel of communication, e.g. phone, Internet, face-to-face, etc.
- *Message:* the words used in the exchange

Let's focus on the addresser and addressee for now. In real-world narrative, the addresser is the teller of a story and the addressee is the listener or the reader. In fictional narrative, this is slightly more complex. We've already seen that the author and the narrator are not the same person. The author is a real man or woman who imagines a story, with its actors, actions and circumstances. The narrator is not a real person, but is part of the author's creation. He or she is a special character who has the task of telling the story. So, using Jakobson's model of verbal communication, both the author and the narrator are addressers. The question then is: Who are their addressees?

The best way to answer this question is to think of the author and the narrator as addressers in two separate processes of verbal communication. This means that they also have separate addressees. The author, the flesh-and-blood person who creates the whole narrative, addresses the reader – someone who is just as real, like you and me. Therefore, one diagram would look like this:

Author	Message	Reader
(addresser)		(addressee)

Who does the narrator address? Let's look at an example. After the passage 'Borstal' shown on page 70, the short story 'The Loneliness of the Long-Distance Runner' continues:

> You might think it a bit rare, having long-distance cross-country runners in Borstal, thinking that the first thing a long-distance cross-country runner would do when they set him loose at them fields and woods would be to run as far away from the place as he could get on a bellyful of Borstal slum-gullion – but you're wrong, and I'll tell you why.

The narrator is a fictional character. Just to reinforce this concept, remember that Alan Sillitoe, the author of this short story, never went to prison and was never a long-distance runner. As in all fiction, the narrator is an invented character and exists entirely within the narrative. Who is the person the narrator addresses and refers to as 'you', then? It can't be the reader: the reader – you, me or whoever else reads the book – is of course a real person and is addressed by the author. But the person addressed by the narrator must exist within the same level, the level of the narrative, and is just as fictional as the narrator. We can call this person the **narratee**.

The diagram below illustrates the relationship between author, reader, narrator and narratee:

Real world   AUTHOR   MESSAGE   READER

Narrative fiction   NARRATOR   MESSAGE   NARRATEE

> **Key term**
>
> **Narratee.** A fictional receiver; the person that the text appears to be aimed at (not the real reader).

> **Activity**
>
> Focus on your set text. Think further about who is telling the story and how readers are addressed.
>
> 1. What is/are the narrator(s) like? How would you describe him or her or them? For example, do they seem trustworthy? Do you find it easy to believe their accounts of events and people, places and times?
>
> 2. Also think about the narratee(s). What assumptions are being made about the person or people who are reading the narrative? Do you find it easy to identify with the assumptions made? If you feel there is miscommunication, can you identify the mismatch between how you are being addressed and how you see things? An example of this could arise from a shift in time, where a novel written a long time ago assumes that you share certain attitudes and values.

Point of view

In the previous section you learned that the narrator is a fictional character – rather than a real person – who has the special role of telling the story.

Compared to a real-world teller, the narrator in fiction can do much more. One of the things that the narrator can do is to shift the **point of view** in the narrative. This is a very important distinction between real-world narrative and fictional narrative. As we saw in the previous chapter, real-world stories are always told from one point of view, a bit like when you take a photograph – the **representation** of your subject will always depend on where you took the photograph from. By contrast, in fiction, the narrator has the capacity to move around, be in different places at the same time and even adopt somebody else's subjective point of view.

Activity

Read the passages 'Snow' and 'Fog below. What difference do you notice in their use of point of view?

Snow

What you will see if you come here where I am standing is the snow. Snow on the leafless trees, snow on the cars, snow on the roads, snow on the yards, snow on the roofs – snow, just snow covering everything like sand. It is as white as clean teeth and is also very, very cold. It is a greedy monster too, the snow, because just look how it has swallowed everything; where is the ground now? Where are the flowers? The grass? The stones? The leaves? The ants? The litter? Where are they?

Fog

Fog everywhere. Fog up the river, where it flows among green aits and meadows; fog down the river, where it rolls defiled among the tiers of shipping, and the waterside pollutions of a great (and dirty) city. Fog on the Essex Marshes, fog on the Kentish heights. Fog creeping into the cabooses of collier-brigs; fog lying out on the yards, and hovering in the rigging of great ships; fog drooping on the gunwales of barges and small boats. Fog in the eyes and throats of ancient Greenwich pensioners, wheezing by the firesides of their wards; fog in the stem and bowl of the afternoon pipe of the wrathful skipper, down in his close cabin; fog cruelly pinching the toes and fingers of his shivering little 'prentice boy on deck.

The passages 'Snow' and 'Fog' are to some extent similar. They both describe scenes where a particular weather condition has transformed the environment – both what it looks like and what it feels like. But now try to visualize what is being described. As if each passage was a clip from a film, try to imagine the position of the camera. In the first passage, the camera will be where the narrator is, where she's standing, outside, somewhere in a town. The reader 'sees' what she sees: snow covering everything. In the second passage, fog covers everything in a similar way, except that our imaginary camera isn't standing still on a tripod in one spot, but moves to different places, very fast, as if it was flying, and the lens zooms in and out.

The narrator in 'Snow' acts very much like a real-world teller of a story – she only follows her own subjective point of view. By contrast, in 'Fog' the narrator chooses to do something that would be impossible for an ordinary teller and offers the reader a wide range of different points of view, all within only a few lines of text.

More than meets the eye

Activity

Apart from describing the look of snow and fog, the passages 'Snow' and 'Fog' also make some references to what these weather conditions feel like. Write down the relevant phrases and, next to them, note the person who experiences those feelings.

There is some feedback on this activity at the back of the book.

First of all, while both texts describe feelings of cold, the narrator in 'Fog' is also able to tell the narratee the feelings of other characters. This is another special capacity of narrators in fiction: not only can they shift the point of view of the narrative, but they can also adopt somebody's own subjective point of view. Again, not all narrators do that. The one in 'Snow' follows her own point of view only.

Secondly, the references to feelings in both texts indicate that point of view isn't just related to sight, but also to sensations, perceptions, feelings. So we can distinguish two types of point of view:

- **spatial point of view**, related to what characters see
- **psychological point of view**, related to what characters feel.

At this level, however, the difference between the two is only superficial. You can think of point of view as anything that has to do with the characters' senses: what they see, hear, touch, taste or smell. This adds an extra layer to our ideas about point of view: it is about physical sensations as well as feelings, emotions and mental states.

Key terms

Psychological point of view. The feelings and perceptions of the narrator or one of the characters in the story.

Spatial point of view. The physical position of the narrator in relation to the events in the story.

Activity

To help you to understand the difference between a narrator who channels everything through his or her own perspective and a narrator who can adopt the point of view of different characters, read through the further extracts below and answer the questions that follow.

The first extract is from the novel *Americanah*, which opens with a description of how the main character (Ifemelu) felt about Princeton. (You read part of this novel in an earlier activity.) The second chapter of that novel then begins with a description of another character's feelings on receiving an email from Ifemelu:

> When Obinze first saw her email, he was sitting in the back of his Range Rover in still Lagos traffic […] He stared at his BlackBerry, his body suddenly rigid. First, he skimmed the email, instinctively wishing it were longer […]
>
> He read it again slowly and felt the urge to smooth something, his trousers, his shaved-bald head.

The second extract is from *We Need New Names* and, again, you read an earlier passage from this same novel. The passage below focuses on the narrator's uncle.

> Uncle Kojo sounds all upset now, and this annoys me very much because it's not like I've done anything wrong. And besides, I've been

> getting all As in everything, even maths and science, the subjects I hate, because school is so easy in America even a donkey would pass, so I don't know what Uncle Kojo wants, what else I'm supposed to do. He looks at me from the rearview mirror and his eyes have this disappointment in them that I know I don't deserve.

Which of these extracts is written just from the narrator's subjective point of view and can't get inside another character's mind? Which extract is able to get inside a mind other than that of the narrator? Try to pick out the language details that helped you to come to your decision.

There is some feedback on this activity at the back of the book.

These two types of narrators are quite typical in fiction. One type of narrator filters the story through his or her own perceptions, so as a reader you get the narrator's version of events and descriptions of other characters.

The other type of narrator is a kind of 'super-teller' who can move around to give you a sense of many different characters' thinking, feelings and perceptions.

Activity

Focus on your set text and see how far you can apply some of the ideas you have learned here about **spatial** and **psychological points of view**.

- Does the narrator of your story appear to be able to get inside the heads of different characters and tell you what he or she sees and feels? Or is the narrator very subjective, telling you only what he or she experiences?

- If the narrator is able to get inside the heads of different characters, how are you given a distinctive sense of each character's thoughts and feelings? For example, is each character's perspective conveyed through a different style of language use?

- Make a list of all the different characters in the novel, and think about how you have a sense of what they are like. How have they been presented to you?

- Find an example of a passage where you can analyse in detail how the point of view within the extract works. Make sure you can give examples of language and explain how they indicate point of view.

The next section will add to your analytical skills further by looking at how narrators behave when it comes to reporting speech and thought.

The presentation of speech

In Chapter 1 you learned about three ways of reporting speech in real-world narrative: **direct speech** (DS), **indirect speech** (IS) and **narrative report of a speech act** (NRSA). To make sure that you're confident with these, complete the following activity.

> ### Activity
>
> For this activity we'll use a simplified version of the dialogue in 'Ghana', from page 64. Your task is to turn the direct speech into indirect speech first, and then into a narrative report of a speech act. Remember that there is more than one way of doing this.
>
> 'Where are you from'? he said.
>
> 'My parents are from Ghana, but I was born in Britain', I replied.
>
> There is some feedback on this activity at the back of the book.

DS, IS and NRSA are the main ways of reporting speech in fiction, too. However, narrators often choose other methods as well.

Free direct speech

> ### Activity
>
> Read the passage 'Airport' below. Some of the words in the passage are a little difficult and you may not have seen them before, but they're not important for the purpose of this activity. Try to identify all instances of reported speech. How many people do you 'hear'?
>
> There is some feedback on this activity at the back of the book.

Airport

There was chaos.

Will someone please explain why we are here? – What are we going to eat? Who has thought of that? – Who is in charge here? Let me speak to him!

A 747 had disgorged its 323 passengers into the middle of a vacant, snow-brushed tarmac expanse, left them to trudge across it through the cold and the floodlit glare to a terminus whose neon name was only illuminated in patches and anyway was in a language most of them could not read; had abandoned them, in short, in the Middle of Nowhere, in a place that was Free of Duty but also, much more importantly, devoid of any obvious egress, like a back corridor between two worlds, two somewheres, where people only alighted when something was seriously kaput with the normal eschatological machinery.

Do you realize I have a vital meeting tomorrow morning? I haven't got time to be here!

Sir: we have already explained it to you several times. This snow-storm breaks all of Tokyo's records. The city is blanketed, completely inaccessible. Do you understand? Absolutely no possibility of landing there. Everywhere in this hemisphere planes are lurching as we speak, U-turning, overnighting where they can. We cannot argue with the weather. These things happen.

Three hundred and twenty-three people clamoured for a hearing for their unique Woes. My husband is waiting for me at the airport. I'm only going to get one honeymoon. I have to be back in New York on Friday: my vacation is Over. Over. This cannot be happening. Heads in hands, bloodshot eyes towards heaven.

The way in which the narrator in 'Airport' reports speech is different. There are no **reporting clauses** and no quotation marks. Speech is simply reproduced freely, with no intervention from the narrator whatsoever. For this reason, this is called **free direct speech** (FDS). In this text, FDS is in its 'purest' form. At other times, speech may be reported in ways that are half-way between free direct speech and ordinary direct speech. Consider the following passage:

> ### Coventry
> Greta was standing at the stove, stirring tinned rice pudding, when Maureen crashed through the kitchen door; coming from darkness into sudden fluorescent light.
>
> 'Coventry has killed Gerald Fox!'
>
> '*Coventry?*'
>
> 'Yes!'
>
> '*Killed?*'
>
> 'Yes!'
>
> '*Gerald Fox?*'
>
> 'YES!'
>
> An explosion of enjoyment filled the kitchen. The two women, trembling and shocked, but also excited and happy, began to talk. Coventry's life was examined for previous displays of aggression. Greta remembered the time that Coventry had spoken to her sharply once.

Here, there are no reporting clauses in the dialogue, as in the passage 'Airport' but, unlike that passage, the presence of quotation marks ensures that we understand that this is a piece of reported speech. It is only from the context that we are able to understand that Maureen is the one revealing the news about Coventry killing Gerald Fox and that Greta is the one asking for confirmation. So this is an example of reported speech that is 'freer' from the narrator's intervention than normal DS but not quite to the extent that FDS is.

Free indirect speech

Free indirect speech (FIS) is a little more challenging to spot and to analyse. It is like indirect speech, but without a reporting clause. It is by far the least common type of reported speech. You can see an example of free indirect speech in the passage below. Grace is a Nigerian woman who reflects on some of the things she was taught at school, when Nigeria was still part of the British Empire. Words such as 'wallpaper', 'dandelions', 'coffee' and 'chicory' didn't mean very much to her, as they were not part of her environment.

> ### Grace
> It was Grace who would begin to rethink her own schooling – how lustily she had sung, on Empire Day, 'God bless our Gracious King. Send him victorious, happy and glorious. Long to reign over us'; how she had puzzled over words like 'wallpaper' and 'dandelions' in her textbooks, unable to picture those things; how she had struggled with arithmetic problems that had to do with mixtures, because what was coffee and what was chicory and why did they have to be mixed?

In this passage, the words of the song are an example of **direct speech**. But the questions 'what was coffee?' and 'why did they have to be mixed?' can be considered examples of free indirect speech, because they seem to report

Key terms

Free direct speech. A form of direct speech in which the narrator does not use any quotation marks or a reporting clause.

Free indirect speech. A form of indirect speech in which the narrator does not use a reporting clause.

speech events in which Grace wondered what these items were. The use of the past tense indicates that it is an *indirect* form of reported speech and, finally, the absence of a reporting clause makes it *free*.

The following table summarizes the different types of reported speech found in narrative fiction.

Direct speech (DS)	Direct speech remains faithful to the original words that were uttered by the characters, with the narrator making it obvious that speech occurred through the use of a reporting clause indicating who is speaking, as well as quotation marks around the words spoken. For example: 'Is it raining?' she asked.
Free direct speech (FDS)	The narrator reports just the words as they were originally uttered by the character, and nothing else. It is called 'free' because there is no reporting clause and sometimes no quotation marks either. For example: Is it raining?
Indirect speech (IS)	Indirect speech is a report of speech that has occurred. It is incorporated within the narrative, but the narrator indicates who spoke, by using a reporting clause. For example: She asked whether it was raining.
Free indirect speech (FIS)	The episode of speech is incorporated within the narrative, but without any indication of who spoke. This is hard to spot, as it can look very much like thought rather than speech. For example: Was it raining?
Narrative report of a speech act (NRSA)	The narrator reports a speech event by summarizing its content. For example: There was a question about whether it was raining.

The five types of reported speech can be placed along a scale, based on the amount of apparent control that the narrator exercises on the way speech events are reported. Of course, the author is in control of the narrator, so how to report things is not the narrator's decision! But the narrator can be made to seem as though he or she is managing the information we are given, to a greater or lesser degree. If characters are speaking but there is no reporting clause, then it doesn't seem as if the narrator is doing very much (FDS in the following diagram). If the narrator offers some speech marks and tells us who is speaking, then they seem to be doing more (DS in the diagram). Indirect speech seems as if it is filtered through the narrator's perspective, because indirect speech is a reported version of direct speech. By the time we get to the final category in the diagram, narrative report of a speech act (NRSA), the speech is so removed from any actual utterance that we seem to be a long way from the original scene, with the narrator stepping in between us and the speech event.

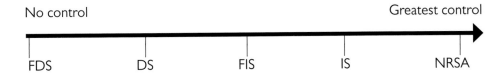

No control   Greatest control

FDS   DS   FIS   IS   NRSA

Let's go back to the passage 'Grace' now (page 79). We said that the two questions about coffee and chicory could be free indirect speech. But the nature of FIS is such that often we can't be sure if it reports words that were uttered or words that were only thought by a character. The absence of a reporting clause such as 'she said' or 'she thought' may make it impossible for us to know for certain. Sometimes we are able to use the context to decide whether it's a character's speech or thought that is being reported. At other times, as in this case, it's not so easy. However, this isn't really a problem, since our ability to follow the narrative isn't affected.

Activity

Focus on your set text and on the presentation of characters' speech.

- Think about the different categories in the grid on page 80 and decide whether the presentation of speech fits a particular category or whether there is a mixture of different types.

- If there is a mixture of different types, think about why the variation occurs. Is the writer trying to do different things with the different approaches to speech?

- Choose a passage where speech occurs and make a **formal** analysis of it, focusing on all the aspects of point of view you have studied so far, but also adding an analysis of how speech is presented.

The presentation of thought

We have seen so far that in fiction the narrator can be a 'super-teller' who can do things that are impossible outside fiction. This is because, thanks to their ability to shift the point of view of the narrative, narrators often know more than real people telling stories would. This means that they are able to know what happens in different places, as well as what different characters feel and think. This kind of narrator is sometimes called an **omniscient narrator**, where the word 'omniscient' means 'all-knowing'.

An omniscient narrator can report not only what characters say, but also what they think. How does that work? Now that you know how speech is reported, the answer to this question is an easy one. In many ways, reported thought is the exact equivalent of reported speech. Think of reported thought as a speech event that occurs only within a character's mind. In comics and cartoons, the difference is represented graphically:

Key term

Omniscient narrator. An 'all-knowing' figure who can report everything, including the thoughts inside all of the characters' heads.

! REMEMBER

Not all narrators are omniscient. Normally, a narrator who is also a participant in the story follows his or her own subjective point of view.

Speech

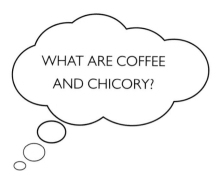

Thought

The forms of reported speech have their equivalent in reported thought:

Direct speech (DS)	Direct thought (DT)
'Is it raining?' she asked.	'Is it raining?' she wondered.
Free direct speech (FDS)	Free direct thought (FDT)
Is it raining?	Is it raining?
Indirect speech (IS)	Indirect thought (IT)
She asked whether it was raining.	She wondered whether it was raining.
Free indirect speech (FIS)	Free indirect thought (FIT)
Was it raining?	Was it raining?
Narrative report of a speech act (NRSA)	Narrative report of a thought act (NRTA)
There was a question about whether it was raining.	There were some thoughts about whether it was raining.

Although these five ways of reporting speech and thought are *formally* equivalent, their frequency of use varies. While direct speech is by far the most common method of reporting speech, a narrative report of a thought act (NRTA) is the most frequent way of reporting thought. At the very end of the passage called 'Coventry' on page 79, for example, there's an example of NRTA when the narrator says that 'Greta remembered the time that Coventry had spoken to her sharply once.' We know that some thought occurred in Greta's mind, we know what the gist of the thought was, but the narrator doesn't say exactly what the words were in Greta's memory.

Direct thought (DT) is much rarer. It tends to be found mainly in literature for younger readers. Consider, for example, the opening of *Alice in Wonderland*:

> ### Alice
> Alice was beginning to get very tired of sitting by her sister on the bank, and of having nothing to do: once or twice she had peeped into the book her sister was reading, but it had no pictures or conversations in it, 'and what is the use of a book', thought Alice 'without pictures or conversation?'
>
> So she was considering in her own mind (as well as she could, for the hot day made her feel very sleepy and stupid), whether the pleasure of making a daisy-chain would be worth the trouble of getting up and picking the daisies, when suddenly a White Rabbit with pink eyes ran close by her.

Activity

Read the passage 'Alice' and identify the forms of thought presentation in it.

There is some feedback on this activity at the back of the book.

When the 'free' modes of thought presentation are used, they tend to produce a '**stream of consciousness**' effect. Indeed, this expression refers to a particular style of writing where the narrator reproduces characters' thoughts freely, and sometimes these may form a very substantial part of the narrative. The passage below is an example of this approach. The character's thoughts are reproduced in their 'freest' possible form, making it seem as if the narrator has simply conveyed them without any intervention.

Key term

Stream of consciousness. A writing technique that attempts to simulate the freewheeling nature of a person's inner thoughts.

Beginning

The beginning

of things – when is it exactly?

Astrid Smart wants to know. (Astrid Smart. Astrid Berenski. Astrid Smart. Astrid Berenski.) 5.04 a.m. on the substandard clock radio. Because why do people always say the day starts now? Really it starts in the middle of the night at a fraction of a second past midnight. But it's not supposed to have begun until the dawn, really the dark is still last night and it isn't morning till the light, though actually it was morning as soon as it was even a fraction of a second past twelve i.e. that experiment where you divide something down and down like the distance between the ground and a ball that's been bounced on it so that it can be proved, Magnus says, that the ball never actually touches the ground. Which is junk because of course it touches the ground, otherwise how would it bounce, it wouldn't have anything to bounce *off*, but it can actually be proved by science that it doesn't.

At this point, we should note a very interesting difference between reported speech and reported thought. In reported speech, when the narrator uses 'free' ways of reporting thought, he or she 'steps back' and lets the characters speak for themselves. As the narrator hardly interferes with the characters' own words, it would seem that this is a rather light-touch approach. This is confirmed by the scale of control shown on page 81 above.

However, in the case of reported thought, the ability to reproduce what is in a character's mind makes the narrator a very intrusive one. That's because speech and thought are quite different. Speech is external to the character, and can be heard, and so it's easy for the narrator to just reproduce it. But thought only takes place in a character's mind. It's invisible and inaudible. So a narrator who reproduces the thoughts of characters is one who has the most power: the power to enter people's minds and reveal exactly what's in them. So we could use a scale for reported thought similar to the one used for reported speech, but this time based on power:

Greatest use of power   Smallest use of power

FDT   DT   FIT   IT   NRTA

Activity

Focus on your set text and explore the way different characters' thoughts are portrayed.

- How are characters' thoughts revealed? For example, are you told about their thoughts from a distance or does it seem as though you are an intimate part of their thinking processes?

- Are there characters for whom there seems to be no access at all to their thoughts?

- To what extent is the story helped by knowing what the characters are thinking, as well as what they are saying?

- Choose a passage where a character reveals his or her thinking process. Are the thoughts relayed directly or through the filter of the narrator?

The presentation of place and time

So far, within the discussion of point of view, the focus has been on some important distinctions between different types of narrator and different ways of presenting speech and thought within narratives.

However, narrators also have a key role in establishing settings and time frames within narratives. These aspects are fundamental to the ways in which a text follows the genre conventions that are expected for certain types of narratives.

The dimensions of place and time are significant in texts of all kinds. In oral narratives, speakers have to give listeners a sense of when events happened, and where. In all of the novel openings that you looked at on pages 64–65, and as you will have seen when you looked at the opening of your set text, a narrative normally gives some information about 'where' and 'when', as well as 'who'. If openings don't do this, it's because they deliberately want to keep you guessing.

 Activity

1. Think about the typical kinds of places – and descriptions of places – that you expect to find in the following genres of fiction:

   - Science fiction
   - Ghost stories
   - Horror stories
   - Romantic fiction
   - Detective fiction
   - Vampire stories
   - Cowboy westerns
   - Fairy stories
   - War stories

2. Can you specify the types of characters that you would expect to find in each of these genres of fiction?

3. When you have finished, go on to think about some aspects of time.

   - Are some of the genres above more likely to be in the past or future?

   - Are some more likely than others to jump around in time?

Place and time are often interrelated. Narrators can do much to further their narrative by using these dimensions creatively; settings and times are not just about openings.

The passage below is from a detective novel, *K is for Killer*, by the American writer Sue Grafton. The novel's narrator is the detective figure Kinsey Millhone. This narrator is a participant in the story, so she offers subjective descriptions of the sights and sounds around her. However, this does not mean that the narrative point of view is limited to one place or one time. Detectives often move around a place and, where they are based in a particular area, they also tend to have some historical knowledge of the community.

Activity

Read the passage carefully and focus on the aspects of place and time contained within it. Look particularly at the verb tenses used in the passage to shift between time periods and to construct different meanings.

- Why are shifts of time important in this text and how are time shifts connected with ideas about place?
- How is this extract typical of the genre of detective fiction?

K is for Killer

I drove east along Cabana, the wide boulevard that parallels the beach. When the moon is full, the darkness has the quality of a film scene shot day for night. The landscape is so highly illuminated that the trees actually cast shadows. Tonight the moon was in its final quarter, rising low in the sky. From the road I couldn't see the ocean, but I could hear the reverberating rumble of the tide rolling in. There was just enough wind to set the palm trees in motion, shaggy heads nodding together in some secret communication. A car passed me, going in the opposite direction, but there were no pedestrians in sight. I'm not often out at such an hour, and it was curiously exhilarating.

By day, Santa Teresa seems like any small southern California town. Churches and businesses hug the ground against the threat of earthquakes. The rooflines are low, and the architectural influence is largely Spanish. There's something solid and reassuring about all the white adobe and the red tile roofs. Lawns are manicured, and the shrubs are crisply trimmed. By night the same features seem stark and dramatic, full of black and white contrasts that lend intensity to the landscape. The sky at night isn't really black at all. It's a soft charcoal gray, nearly chalky with light pollution, the trees like ink stains on a darkened carpet. Even the wind has a different feel to it, as light as a feather quilt against the skin.

The real name for CC's is the Caliente Cafe, a low rent establishment housed in an abandoned service station near the railroad tracks. The original gasoline pumps and the storage tanks below had been removed years before, and the contaminated soil had been paved over with asphalt. Now, on hot days the blacktop tends to soften and a toxic syrup seeps out, a tarry liquid quickly converted into wisps of smoke, suggesting that the tarmac is on the verge of bursting into flames. Winters, the pavement cracks from dry cold, and a sulfurous smell wafts across the parking lot. CC's is not the kind of place to encourage bare feet.

I parked out in front beneath a sizzling red neon sign. Outside, the air smelled like corn tortillas fried in lard; inside, like salsa and recirculated cigarette smoke. I could hear the high-pitched whine of a blender working overtime, whipping ice and tequila into the margarita mix.

Now it's time to put together the different elements that have been covered in this chapter. This final activity will require you to analyse an extract by using all of the different concepts that have been explained so far.

REVIEW YOUR LEARNING

The extract below is from *Oranges Are Not the Only Fruit*, by Jeanette Winterson. The novel is about growing up in the north of England in the 1950s. The narrative is based on Winterson's own experiences.

Answer all the questions below, giving examples of language use from the extract to support your views.

1. What kind of narrator is in evidence in this extract? Is the narrator:

   - a participant in the narrative or outside of it?

   - a subjective narrator, centred on her own perceptions, or an omniscient narrator who can get inside others characters' minds?

2. What aspects of sensory perception are conveyed by the narrator?

3. What kind of narratee is being constructed?

4. How are speech and thought represented?

5. How are aspects of time and place conveyed?

6. What aspects of the narrative are typical of a novel about childhood and growing up?

Oranges

Country dancing was thirty-three rickety kids in black plimsolls and green knickers trying to keep up with Miss who always danced with Sir anyway and never looked at anybody else. They got engaged soon after, but it didn't do us any good because they started going in for ballroom competitions, which meant they spent all our lessons practising their footwork while we shuffled up and down to the recorded instructions on the gramophone. The threats were the worst; being forced to hold hands with somebody you hated. We flapped along twisting each others' fingers off and promising untold horrors as soon as the lesson was over. Tired of being bullied, I became adept at inventing the most fundamental tortures under the guise of sweet sainthood.

'What me Miss? No Miss. Oh *Miss*, I never did.' But I did, I always did. The most frightening for the girls was the offer of total immersion in the cesspit round the back of Rathbone's Wrought Iron. For the boys, anything that involved their willies. And so, three terms later, I squatted down in the shoebags and got depressed. The shoebag room was dark and smelly, it was always smelly, even at the beginning of terms.

References

Jakobson, R. (1960). 'Linguistics and Poetics', in T. Sebeok, (ed.), *Style in Language*. Cambridge, Mass: MIT Press.

Further reading

Bal, M. (2009) *Narratology: Introduction to the Theory of Narrative (3rd edn.).* London: Routledge.

Leech, G. N. and Short, M. (2007) *Style in fiction: a linguistic introduction to English fictional prose (2nd edn.).* New York: Pearson Longman

Rimmon-Kenan, S. (2003) *Narrative Fiction: Contemporary Poetics (2nd edn.).* London: Routledge.

Stories in poetry

In the previous chapter you learned about narratives in fiction, where the focus was on prose texts such as novels and short stories. You looked at many different aspects of fiction, including what fictional narratives share or don't share with real-world stories.

In this chapter, the focus will be on poetry. But that doesn't mean that everything you have done already is irrelevant. Quite the contrary. Poetry is fictional too, so it shares with the other literary genres the same ideas about needing to convince you as a reader to stay with the imaginary world that is being created. Poetry, like the stories in novels, also shares some common ground with everyday narratives. Just as everyday storytellers have to make us feel their stories are worth listening to, writers of both prose and poetry need to make us feel that their messages are worth making an effort to understand.

Poems might not seem to offer such a strong or obvious narrative as either novels or drama, but they are narratives just the same. Each poem has a **narrator** who adopts a particular **point of view** or several points of view. Each poem constructs a sense of time and place. Each poem makes assumptions about the people being addressed by the text. And each poem uses language features that you will be able to refer to in your interpretation of its overall meaning.

You will be able to apply the skills you learn in this chapter to the poetry texts set for study (collected for you in the AQA poetry anthology) as well as to other parts of the specification. For example, in the coursework component 'Making Connections', you are required to compare a literary text with some non-literary material. Understanding how texts of all kinds work is therefore a key skill for this subject area. Details of the relevant exam papers are given below.

Relevant Assessment Objectives

For A level analysis, AO1 and AO2 are tested.

For AS level analysis, AO1, AO2 and AO4 are tested.

- AO1 rewards your ability to take a language approach to the texts that you study, to write coherently and to use terminology appropriately.

- AO2 rewards your ability to explain what texts mean, by showing how meanings are built from the language choices made.

- AO4 rewards your ability to compare and contrast texts, according to the focus that is given in the exam question.

The ability to analyse poetry is tested in exam conditions in Section C of A level Paper 1 (Poetic Voices) and Section B of AS level Paper 1 (also called Poetic Voices). There are some differences between the A level and AS level exams, as follows:

- Section C of the A level exam is open book, while the AS level exam is closed book.

- The AS level exam involves comparison and contrast between two poems printed in the exam paper.

- The A level paper asks you to analyse a poem printed in the exam paper and then choose a further poem appropriate to the question focus.

This chapter will:

- help you understand how to go about analysing poetry

- give you useful frameworks for analysis and opportunities to practise your skills

- show you how to apply what you learn to your set texts.

Introduction

In Chapter 2 you learned about the difference between ordinary, everyday storytelling, which we all do all the time, and narrative fiction. You now have a much better understanding of what labels such as 'fiction' and 'non-fiction' refer to. In this chapter, you'll learn about another term that is used all the time but is hard to define precisely: 'poetry'. Trying to come up with a comprehensive definition of poetry is a bit like trying to define what art is – it seems so vast: Where do you start?

One good starting point is to consider what we already know, and see how we can build on it. First of all, in most bookshops you will probably find a section labelled 'Poetry'. As they do for 'Fiction', those who organize books in shops generally have few doubts about which ones are poetry books. If you pull out a random book from the 'Poetry' section, the chances are that it will be a book with poems in it. Easy!

So what is the issue? Couldn't we just be happy with saying that a poetry book is a book with poems in it? Indeed we could, but then we could also ask another question: What is a poem? One possible answer, of course, might be: a poem is a text contained in a poetry book. But this would be a little circular, since we would define poetry by using the word 'poem' and poem by using the word 'poetry'!

This doesn't take us very far. So in this chapter you will acquire the knowledge and the skills to go further than a bookshop-style definition of poetry (and of a poem).

What is a poem?

Trusting the labels in a bookshop is a good way to begin. Labels are very powerful, because they inform us what something is and therefore condition our responses. If we look at a text that comes from a book labelled 'Poetry', then we treat that text as a poem.

Whether 'Plums' and 'This is Just To Say' in the activity on the left are different texts is an interesting question. The words are exactly the same, but the point is: do we read them in the same way? 'Plums' looks like a note to a housemate written on a piece of scrap paper. 'This is Just To Say' looks very much like a poem. We expect to find the first text on the kitchen table or the fridge door. But the second text could easily come from a poetry book and it's as if it had the 'poem' label on it. Because of that, we are invited to read it as a poem and perhaps to find some profound interpretation in it.

Indeed, 'This is Just To Say' is a poem by William Carlos Williams. This shows that the **context** and the presentation of a text are very important for the way we interpret and respond to it. For example, if you visit the Tate Modern art gallery in London, you will see many works that you would never consider to be art if you saw them outside an art gallery. But displayed in the rooms of a gallery, you will be encouraged to find some meaning in them beyond the surface.

Poems are very similar in this sense. From this perspective, trying to define exactly what poetry is would be pointless, since our circular definition would be quite enough: poetry is anything that is presented to us as poetry! So there's nothing really wrong with this at all.

Activity

1. Read the text 'Plums' below and think of its **context**. Who wrote it? To whom? Why? Where?

> **Plums**
> This is just to say I have eaten the plums that were in the icebox and which you were probably saving for breakfast. Forgive me they were delicious so sweet and so cold

2. Now read 'This is Just To Say' and answer the same questions. Is it any different from 'Plums'?

This is Just To Say
I have eaten
the plums
that were in
the icebox

and which
you were probably
saving
for breakfast

Forgive me
they were delicious
so sweet
and so cold

Something more specific that we can do in our exploration of the concept of poetry is to draw on a language perspective. This means that our job is to see whether there is, perhaps, a special kind of poetic language that might be different from ordinary language, regardless of the label that a text may come with.

Poetic language?

Activity

The two texts below are both advertisements. So obviously, they're not poems. However, does the language in which they're written *feel* in any way poetic to you? Is that true for both texts equally or for one more than the other? There are no obvious right or wrong answers here and it would be useful if you compared your responses with those of your classmates.

There is some feedback on this activity at the end of the chapter.

Activity

Focus on your poetry set text. Are there any poems in your set text collection that involve a narrator addressing someone? If so, and if those examples had not been in a poetry collection, could they have occurred in another **genre**, such as the fridge note in 'Plums' opposite?

HouseBeautiful sofas exclusively at dfs

All sofas in our House Beautiful range are available now, including the Casa Mila, featured here. Inspired by Gaudi's sweeping architecture it's bold and passionate, evoking the spirit of Barcelona. Our House Beautiful designers have scoured Europe to source the finest materials for the sofa, which is then handmade to order by British master craftsmen.

To find the nearest store that stocks the range visit www.dfs.co.uk/house-beautiful

Add a splash of you to your walls.

Express yourself through colour.
Whatever your personality
Crown can bring it out.
So if you're quirky go for it.
If you're sexy, go on, flaunt it.
If you're shy be beautifully subtle.

For hundreds of beautifully crafted colours, trust Crown.

It's not just paint.

It's personal.

It's not very easy to come up with a definite answer to the previous activity. This is normal. It's because you don't have criteria for evaluation and have to rely on your own intuition. Often we tend to think that poetic language is highly descriptive, with lots of adjectives and sophisticated words. The text 'HouseBeautiful' has some of these characteristics: it tries to convey a sense of refinement as it makes references to 'Gaudi's sweeping architecture', described as 'bold' and 'passionate' and 'evoking the spirit of Barcelona'. However, these are more like tricks to make a text sound poetic. In the next sections you'll see how you can make your judgement more objective.

The poetic function

In Chapter 2 you began to learn about Roman Jakobson's model of verbal communication. Jakobson developed this model as part of his search for criteria that could be used to identify poetic language. His idea was that every text fulfils one or more of the following six functions: referential, emotive, conative, phatic, metalingual, poetic. Each one of these six functions is related to one of the six basic elements of communication explained on page 73: context, addresser, addressee, contact, code and message.

What this means is that a text has a particular function if it focuses its attention on the element of communication to which that function corresponds. The table below clarifies this relationship:

A text fulfils this function if ...	... it focuses on this element of communication
referential	context
emotive	addresser
conative	addressee
phatic	contact
metalingual	code
poetic	message

Despite the slightly unusual terminology, this is not very difficult to understand. The function that really interests us is the poetic function, but before we examine that, the table below explains the other five functions in a little more detail.

Referential function	All texts have referential function because all texts will refer to people, things, places and so on. The text 'Plums' on page 88, for example, refers to the plums and the icebox, and that's its referential function.
Emotive function	Some texts may be about the addresser, i.e. the writer or speaker. In that case, they fulfil the emotive function. To some extent, 'Plums' is about the writer – he or she is the one who ate the plums ('I have eaten…'). So there's some emotive function there, too.
Conative function	Some texts are about the addressee. Again, this is the case in 'Plums', because the writer acknowledges that the intended recipient of the note was probably saving the plums for breakfast. The writer than uses an **imperative** ('Forgive me'), again addressing the recipient directly. The text, therefore, has a conative function.

Phatic function	This is a less-frequent function. It is fulfilled when a text refers to the physical channel of communication. For example, if you were on Facebook and made a comment that it's difficult to convey emotion on Facebook, you'd be fulfilling the phatic function, because you'd be talking about the channel of communication (or contact) that you were using (i.e. Facebook itself).
Metalingual function	Like the phatic function, this is not very frequent. A text fulfils the metalingual function if it refers directly to the language in which it is written. If you had a conversation about any aspect of the English language (vocabulary, grammar, etc.), you'd be using the metalingual function.

At this point, the key question is: How exactly do certain texts focus on the *message* to fulfil the *poetic* function? First of all, it is very important that you are not tempted into believing that the message is the same as the content of a text. In fact, a focus on the message is the exact opposite of a focus on the content. The poetic function is fulfilled when the addresser pays special attention to the *form* of the message. This means that he or she chooses words and syntactic structures not only based on their meanings but also because he or she tries to make the message stand out in some way.

Think of this with a trivial example. If you buy a few things at the supermarket, you generally put them in a bag. The bag has a very simple function: to allow you to carry all the items easily. If you buy a present for someone, you won't give it to them in a simple bag, but you might use a gift bag with more attractive colours, decoration, writing, materials, etc. This gift bag has the same function as the supermarket bag – in that it still allows you to carry something – but, in addition, whoever made it has also paid attention to the way it looks. The poetic function is very similar: the writer isn't concerned only with the content of the message, but he or she also wants the message to be, in some way, special.

Foregrounding: language that stands out

The ability of poetic language to make texts stand out is called **foregrounding**. This term comes from the visual arts. When you take a photograph, you might choose to frame it so that something or someone is in the foreground and is more easily noticeable than anything else. By doing this, you direct the viewer's attention to that person or thing. Exactly the same concept applies to poetic language: it puts certain things (words, sentences, paragraphs or even whole texts) in the foreground and makes them more noticeable. A foregrounded part of the text waves and shouts at the reader: 'Hey, look at me! I'm special!' Poetic language does this in two main ways: **deviation** and **parallelism**.

Deviation

Deviation is one of the two forms of foregrounding. To deviate means to take a sudden turn from a planned route. In English, this tends to have a negative **connotation**, since it often refers to behaviour that doesn't conform to an expected norm. In our case, the basic meaning is the same – but without the negative connotation. Think of it like a road diversion that takes drivers along an alternative route. Similarly, language deviates when it does something unexpected.

Key terms

Deviation. A form of foregrounding. It is achieved when a piece of language moves away from the normal use of grammar, vocabulary, graphology or meaning.

Foregrounding. The capacity of a piece of discourse to make something (words, sentences, or even an entire text) stand out and be noticeable to the reader.

Parallelism. A form of foregrounding. It is achieved when two (or more) pieces of language exhibit similar patterns, without being identical.

M1 NORTH CLOSED
Alternative route
follow ▲

The best way to understand the concept of deviation is by looking at the text 'ordnung – unordnung' by Timm Ullrichs below. In this text there is a very regular pattern – the word *ordnung* – repeated a number of times and arranged along two parallel columns. This pattern is, however, broken at a specific point, where the fifth and the sixth letters of the word *ordnung* have shifted to the front of it, creating the string 'unordn g'.

ordnung – unordnung

ordnung	ordnung
ordnung	ordnung
ordnung	ordnung
ordnung	ordnung
ordnung	ordnung
ordnung	unordn g
ordnung	ordnung
ordnung	ordnung
ordnung	ordnung
ordnung	ordnung
ordnung	ordnung

The second half of the sixth line is a clear example of deviation: something that stands out because it breaks a pattern. Significantly, *ordnung* is a German word that means 'order'. The string of letters 'unordn g' represents the word *unordnung*, which means 'disorder'.

It is also worth noting that, in this text, deviation takes place on another level too. That's because the two-column layout is quite unusual and breaks away from conventional text layout. The line where the regular pattern is broken is an example of **internal deviation**, whereas the entire text represents an example of **external deviation**. So this means that internal deviation violates a norm *within* the text, whereas external deviation occurs when a whole text violates a more general norm that exists *outside* the text.

Key terms

External deviation. The way in which a language feature stands out for being used differently from how it is used in texts of different kinds.

Graphology. All the visual aspects of textual design, including colour, typeface, layout, images and logos.

Internal deviation. The way in which a language feature stands out for being used differently from elsewhere in the text.

Activity

Look again at the two advertisements on page 89. Do you notice anything in the language that is in any way unexpected?

There is some feedback on this activity at the back of the book.

Deviation in language can be of different types. You've already begun to see this in the previous activity. This depends on which aspect of language departs from a norm: sounds, lexis, grammar, **graphology** or meaning.

Phonological deviation

The introductory chapter covered a number of different aspects of **sound symbolism** and sound patterning, when discussing the language level of phonology and **prosody**. In that chapter, you completed a preliminary exercise on one of Seamus Heaney's poems (see page 15). The aspects of sound that were covered included **onomatopoeia**, **alliteration** and **assonance**. There was also discussion about how writers can manipulate spellings and use a variety of punctuation marks to suggest prosody and achieve **phonological approximation**.

In our everyday discourse, if we accidentally say something that rhymes or that is highly alliterative, we tend to view it as funny or embarrassing. We might even make a remark such as 'I'm a poet and didn't know it'. The idea of sound patterning, then, is seen as something that belongs to crafted language use rather than to regular, spontaneous interactions. However, when we want to memorize something, it can be useful: rhymes and other patterns of sound can help us to remember because they stand out from the norm.

Activity

What types of sound patterning can you find in your set text collection? Think about such areas as:

- rhyme
- pararhyme (sometime called 'half rhyme': the consonants are repeated but the vowels vary, e.g. grain/groan)
- assonance (repetition of vowel sounds: e.g. grain/grate)
- alliteration (technically an example of consonance, which refers to the repetition of consonants: e.g. 'Peter Piper picked a peck of pickled pepper')
- onomatopoeia.

Think about the **connotations** of different sounds and the way in which writers sometimes play sounds off against written **symbols**.

Draw some conclusions about how your set text poet uses sounds in order to suggest certain meanings.

Lexical deviation

Lexis is another word for vocabulary, so lexical deviation is connected with words. This type of deviation takes place when a writer/speaker uses words in an unexpected way. The instance of deviation in 'HouseBeautiful' is a good example, as the words 'House' and 'Beautiful' are combined into one in a creative, 'deviant' way. Exactly the same thing happens in the text 'Cake' below.

> **Cake**
> i wanted one life
> you wanted another
> we couldn't have our cake
> so we ate eachother.

Like 'HouseBeautiful', 'Cake' uses lexical deviation by joining together two words, in this case 'each' and 'other'. As a consequence, both 'HouseBeautiful' and 'eachother' are foregrounded and noticeable to the reader. In an advertisement, this is useful because it helps to grab the reader's attention.

Of course, one important difference between the two texts is that 'Cake' is a poem. As mentioned at the beginning of this chapter, text that presents itself as a poem invites readers to do some interpretive work. This is precisely the purpose of foregrounding in poetry. In making itself noticeable, a foregrounded piece of poetic language doesn't just wave and shout at readers to grab their attention, it also asks them to stop and think about its meaning.

It's important that you understand that interpretation doesn't mean searching for some hidden meaning that is waiting to be discovered. For the same item – a single word, a sentence or a whole text – there can be more than one possible interpretation. When you discuss your interpretation, what matters is that you're able to explain it, not that you 'guess' the 'right' one.

Activity

How do you interpret the use of the word 'eachother' in 'Cake'? Compare your interpretation with those of your classmates.

There is some feedback on this activity at the back of the book.

Of course, lexical deviation is not just about words joined together in an unusual way. Words could be split or even invented completely. Before computers – and especially the Internet – were in common use, it was difficult to know whether a word that looked unfamiliar was a new invention, or just one that you'd never seen before. Of course, dictionaries have always acted as reference guides, but they leave out a lot of words that may be being used in everyday language but are not yet sufficiently established to be included in the dictionary.

Now it is much easier to measure how unusual a word actually is. When you type into a Word document, you will notice that words are underlined in red if they are not recognized by Word's dictionary. Like all other dictionaries, this isn't very reliable, but it begins to give an indication that such words are, at least, quite rare. If you want to find out with much more confidence whether a word exists, you can look it up in a corpus. You were introduced to the idea of language corpora in the introductory chapter, where there was a link to the British National Corpus (page 24).

There are different types of corpora. If you go to www.corpus.byu.edu, you will be able to access some very large and varied collections of language. A good one to try is called Global Web-Based English (GloWbE), because it contains nearly two billion words from 20 countries where English is used as a first or second language. You can then enter any word in its search box to see how many occurrences of that word are found. If no occurrences are found, you can be confident that the word is a very good example of lexical deviation. (You could still claim this if there were only a few occurrences.)

! REMEMBER

You can use a corpus for many different searches on the use of words. The simplest kind of search allows you to check how frequently a word is used.

Conducting a search on a term can also help you to pinpoint possible language change, and to see the term's semantic field. For example, in his poem 'A Valediction: Forbidding Mourning', John Donne uses the word 'sublunary', which means, literally, 'under the moon', or 'earthly'. Searching the BNC shows that it is rare, with only three occurrences. GloWbE has more examples but only from certain countries; and you can see that the semantic field is very much about planetary movements when you look at its context of use in the **concordance lines**.

Another interesting strategy for using words in an unexpected way is in creative combination. For example, in 'Porphyria's Lover', Robert Browning uses the phrase 'shut bud', to mean a closed bud. There are no occurrences of this in corpora, so you can be confident in labeling this phrase as lexical deviation, too. Seamus Heaney uses the phrase 'squat pen' in his poem, 'Digging'. The only corpus examples of this phrase are actually his, from this poem.

Activity
Focus on your poetry set text collection and identify any unusual combinations of words. What do you think the poet is trying to communicate by choosing this combination?

Try a corpus search to see whether this combination exists anywhere else.

Grammatical deviation

Sometimes poets break grammar rules and, again, when this happens, it is noticeable.

Activity
'Yes' is the first **stanza** of a poem by Edward Estlin Cummings. Identify any instance(s) of grammatical deviation in it.

Yes
yes is a pleasant country:
if's wintry
(my lovely)
let's open the year

E. E. Cummings is famous for his very creative use of language. Many of his poems use different types of deviation and so does this one. In this stanza (a stanza is like a paragraph in a poem), there is something very unusual going on in the language. The words 'yes' and 'if' are used as if they were nouns, even though 'yes' is normally an adverb and 'if' a conjunction. So this deviates from normal grammar and is **foregrounded**. Again, as is often the case in poetry, foregrounding isn't for its own sake but is used to invite the reader to think about the meaning of certain words and phrases.

As always, interpretation is personal and subjective. Here, one possibility is that by describing 'yes' as a pleasant country and 'if' as a wintry place, the poet is saying that he really prefers it when the person he's speaking to (presumably his partner) agrees with him (says 'yes') but he doesn't like it so much when there's doubt.

Did you know?
Many ordinary words in English have been invented by poets. William Shakespeare created many words that are now very common, such as 'amazement', 'arouse', 'compromise', 'dawn', 'exposure', 'hint', 'impartial', 'lonely', 'undress', 'worthless'.

REMEMBER
Identifying language features is important (AO1) but it is only part of the story. You have to be able to say why the feature is there. How does it contribute to meaning? (AO2).

Key term
Stanza. A set of lines that are grouped together in a poem and set apart from other lines.

Did you know?
The origin of the word 'stanza' is Italian, meaning 'a standing place'. This fits the idea of the stanza as a visual unit in a poem, rather like a paragraph in prose.

Now let's look at something slightly different. The text below contains two stanzas from a poem by John Agard, entitled 'Listen, Mr Oxford Don'.

> I ent have no gun
> I ent have no knife
> but mugging de Queen's English
> is the story of my life
>
> I dont need no axe
> to split / up yu syntax
> I dont need no hammer
> to mash up yu grammar

There seems to be quite a lot going on here. We can make a list:

- The word 'ent' – this is an unusual spelling of 'ain't', which is a non-standard negation.

- Double negative – the word 'ent' is used together with 'no', which makes a double negative; this doesn't normally occur in Standard English. Double negatives also occur in the second stanza in the combination of 'don't' and 'no'.

- The word 'de' – is an unusual spelling of 'the'.

- The word 'yu' – is an unusual spelling of 'you'.

In this case, however, deviation has a different function. It's not so much the product of linguistic creativity, but the **representation** of a particular **regional variety** (or dialect) of English. John Agard is originally from Guyana, a small country in the Caribbean that used to be a British colony. People there speak a variety of English that is different from Standard British English but is similar to other varieties in nearby countries in the Caribbean, such as Trinidad and Tobago. John Agard moved to Britain in the 1970s, when he was in his twenties, and many of his poems are about his mixed **identity**. In 'Listen, Mr Oxford Don' he associates the use of language with the struggle of Caribbean immigrants in Britain to convey their identity as non-violent and non-dangerous people.

What's really interesting here is that the narrator in the poem says that to break grammar rules ('mash up yu grammar') is the only way he will use a weapon to affirm his identity. So grammatical deviation is used for a very distinctive purpose. Also, the rules that he breaks are those of Standard British English, but his way of using English is fairly common among Caribbean speakers of English. This means that what appears to be deviant to some readers may be perfectly normal to others.

Key term

Regional variety. A form of a language with its own distinctive features of vocabulary and grammar, used by speakers in a particular geographical region.

Did you know?

English is spoken by approximately one billion people (maybe more) in the world and, as a consequence, there are many different 'Englishes'. Even within Britain there is tremendous variation in the types of English used in different parts of the country.

Extension activity

Find and collect five poems by poets from different parts of Britain showing features of regional variation. Then show them to your classmates and ask them to guess where each is from. Be prepared: they will do the same for you!

Graphological deviation

The word '**graphology**' refers to what a text looks like. This includes layout, colour, and the size and shape of fonts. We've already seen an example in 'A Splash of You' (page 89), where one line of the text looked very different from the rest. In 'ordnung – unordnung' on page 92 **graphological** deviation is based on layout. In 'Smoking', below, you can see how the creative use of font size contributes to conveying the meaning of this anti-smoking campaign.

'The Altar' is a poem by George Herbert. It is an example of 'concrete poetry', a type of poetry where the physical layout of the text is part of its meaning.

The Altar

A broken ALTAR, Lord, thy servant rears,
Made of a heart and cemented with tears;
Whose parts are as thy hand did frame;
No workman's tool hath touch'd the same.
A HEART alone
Is such a stone,
As nothing but
Thy pow'r doth cut.
Wherefore each part
Of my hard heart
Meets in this frame
To praise thy name.
That if I chance to hold my peace,
These stones to praise thee may not cease.
Oh, let thy blessed SACRIFICE be mine,
And sanctify this ALTAR to be thine.

The concrete poem above has some very clear cut-off points at the ends of lines, showing quite a simple connection between aspects of meaning and aspects of design and layout. But some poets deliberately play visual design and meaning off against each other. Unlike prose, where lines continue until sentences end, the ends of poetic lines are not necessarily where a thought or idea is completed, or where punctuation occurs. This means that the physical shape of the text can be played off against its grammatical structure or another aspect of language. This tends to be the case where a poet wants to achieve more of a conversational feel, rather than follow a traditional 'poetic' format.

Key terms

End-stopped line. A line in a poem which stops at the end of a phrase or a sentence. The opposite of enjambment.

Enjambment. This occurs when a line in a poem stops before the end of a sentence, which continues to the next line. The opposite of an end-stopped line.

Sonnet. There are different types of sonnet, but a common type is one formed of three quatrains (stanzas with four lines) and one couplet (a stanza with two lines), with a very regular rhyme pattern.

Did you know?

'Enjambment' comes from the French *enjamber* meaning 'to stride across'.

Activity

Focus on your poetry set text and pay attention to the layouts of the poems in the collection. How would you describe the way the lines are set out?

- Are there any conventional poetic formats, such as a **sonnet**?
- Are there poems where lines finish visually and are also complete in sense (called **end-stopped lines**)?
- Are there poems that carry meaning across lines in a more irregular way (called **enjambment**)?

Whatever visual aspects you find, try to explain how they contribute to the poem's overall meaning.

Semantic deviation

Of all the types of deviation, semantic deviation is the most common. The word 'semantics' is related to meaning, so semantic deviation has to do with anything that we perceive isn't quite right with the meanings of words or phrases in a text. The text 'A Splash of You' (page 89), for example, uses this kind of deviation. What does 'a splash of you' mean exactly? How can there be a 'splash' of someone? The text is an advertisement for a paint product, so the unusual phrase combines the idea of paint – a liquid that can splash – with the idea of the ability of potential customers ('you') to personalize their homes by choosing the colour they like (presumably from a wide range).

This is an example of semantic deviation because, based on the normal meaning of the word, a 'splash' can only be of something liquid, not of a person. Advertising slogans use this technique quite often. Here are some famous examples:

- Eat football. Sleep football. Drink Coca Cola.
- Let your fingers do the walking.
- Don't just book it. Thomas Cook it.
- The future's bright. The future's Orange.
- Be more dog.

Activity

Explain why the five slogans above are semantically deviant and explain your interpretation for those deviations. Discuss and compare your answers with those of your fellow students.

When you have finished, add to the list with some more examples of your own.

The various types of deviation seen in this section don't need to occur only one at a time. In fact, texts often exploit different types of deviation together. A very good example is '40 Love', a poem by Roger McGough.

40 -------------------------- **Love**	
middle	aged
couple	playing
ten	nis
when	the
game	ends
and	they
go	home
the	net
will	still
be	be-
tween	them

Activity

Read '40 Love' and:

- identify all the instances of deviation in it
- attempt an interpretation of the poem
- compare and discuss your answers with your classmates.

There is some feedback on this activity at the end of the book.

One special type of semantic deviation is often found in poetry: **metaphor**. This was discussed in the introductory chapter, where an initial activity asked you to look at your poetry set text and identify some metaphors. The next section explores this aspect of semantic deviation in more detail.

Metaphor

What does it mean, exactly, to say that the 'net' in '40 Love' is a metaphor? The first thing to point out is that if a word or expression is used metaphorically, it means that it shouldn't be taken literally. In '40 Love', the net that is still 'between them' isn't a real net that you'd find on a tennis court, but stands for something else. In this case, the net represents lack of communication or separation. So, to use a very basic definition, metaphor is the use of one concept in order to talk about another concept.

How does all of this work? We use a metaphor when, in talking about something, we treat it as if it were something else. The thing we talk about is called the '**target**', whereas the something else is called the '**source**'. (If you have previously studied metaphor using a literary approach, you will know the equivalent terms 'tenor' for the target and 'vehicle' for the source). In '40 Love', the target is the kind of separation that sometimes exists between middle-aged partners, but it is treated as if it was a net, which is therefore used as the source in this particular metaphor.

Key terms

Source. An alternative term for a base text or original text. Note that in discussing metaphor, this term has a different meaning: it refers to the idea or thing that the target is being compared with.

Target. This has two different meanings. In a metaphor, it refers to the concept being talked about by comparing it with the source. For example, if we say 'love is a drug', the target (the thing you are trying to understand) is love; the source (the thing it's being compared with) is a drug. But in discussing audiences for writing, 'target' means the person or group being aimed at.

The basic structure of all metaphors is:

TARGET IS SOURCE

In our example, this translates into:

SEPARATION	IS	A NET
Target		Source

In more general terms, we could say that the poem is about middle-aged love, which is compared to a tennis match. So, the resulting metaphor is:

MIDDLE-AGED LOVE	IS	A TENNIS MATCH
Target		Source

Poetic language tends to make heavy use of metaphor because poetry – and, arguably, literature in general – tries to give us a new perspective on ideas and experiences. Sometimes metaphors are very obvious, sometimes more subtle. In 'Yes' (page 95) the first two lines are both explicit metaphors:

YES	IS	A PLEASANT COUNTRY
Target		Source

IF	IS	A WINTRY PLACE
Target		Source

The fourth line is also metaphorical, since one can't literally 'open' the year. So the year is described as if it was something than can be opened, like a box:

THE YEAR	IS	A BOX
Target		Source

What's really interesting about metaphors is that, although they're used a lot in poetry, they're common in everyday language too. You were introduced to this idea in the introductory chapter. Generally, metaphors are used to talk about something that is a bit difficult to grasp – perhaps because it's far away, abstract, complex, very big or very small. What we tend to do is talk about these things as if they were closer to us, more concrete, simpler.

For example, the human body is often used as a source for different kinds of targets. The base of a mountain is its 'foot'. The person who manages an organization is its 'head'. Indeed, an organization is often called a body. A clock, has a 'face' and 'hands' (and in shop displays the hands are nearly always shown positioned at ten to two, which creates a smiling expression!). The human body is the closest thing to us and that's why it's used so much in metaphors. All these metaphors have the human body as the source:

A MOUNTAIN	IS	A BODY (HAS A FOOT)
AN ORGANIZATION	IS	A BODY (HAS A HEAD)
A CLOCK	IS	A BODY (HAS A FACE AND HANDS)
Target		Source

Activity

1. Consider the following three expressions:

- The pot-holed path to happiness
- 10 steps to true love
- Turning 65 is not the end of the road!

What do you think may be a possible metaphor that describes all three of them?

2. What is the basis for the following three metaphors?

- I'm feeling a bit rusty.
- I couldn't crank myself into action, I'm so tired.
- I can't process it all.

There is some feedback on this activity at the end of the book.

Extension activity

The text 'Metalheads' is the first paragraph of a news article. Find some metaphorical words or expressions in it and try to explain why they are metaphorical. Additionally, you could also try to come up with a 'target is source' formula for them.

Metalheads

Female metalheads feel marginalized by mainstream radio, but as Radio 1 gives its Rock Show a primetime slot, more and more girl rockers are flocking to the moshpit.

Activity

If you completed the activity in the introductory chapter where you examined your poetry set text for the use of metaphor (page 22), go back to the metaphors you listed.

If you did not complete that activity, first compile a list of all the metaphors you can find in the collection. Make sure you keep notes about which metaphors occur in which poem.

- Analyse the metaphors by identifying the part of the metaphor that is the target and the part that is the source.
- What do the metaphors contribute to the overall meaning of the poem where they occur?
- Are there recurring metaphors across different poems by the same poet?
- Are certain metaphors connected with particular ideas?

Metaphor isn't exclusive to poetry, but pervades all language. Can we say the same thing for poetic language in general? To some extent, we can. Many of the texts seen so far in this chapter are not poems, but still exhibit features of deviation. This is beginning to show one very important fact: although poems are texts that are 'self-labelled' as poems and are different from other kinds of texts in the way they invite readers to interpret them, the material of which they are made – poetic language – is found in many other types of texts.

The next section explores the second type of foregrounding: **parallelism**.

Parallelism

The word 'parallel' is generally used to describe two lines that run side by side, close to each other, without touching, like in a dual-carriageway road. Sometimes, writers employ a technique that achieves a similar result. The poem '40 Love' (page 99) does this by giving every line a big gap in the middle, so that the overall layout of the text appears to be arranged along two parallel columns. The **graphological** deviation in '40 Love' – its unusual layout – is an example of parallelism.

In McGough's poem, the effect is one where readers have to move their eyes from left to right and back again, as when watching a tennis match. However, parallelism is often of a different kind. Rather than being a matter of visual layout, parallelism is more structural. You'll understand what this means by working with a few texts.

If you go back to 'A Splash of You' on page 89, you'll find an example of parallelism. Let's focus on these three lines:

> So if you're quirky go for it.
> If you're sexy, go on, flaunt it.
> If you're shy be beautifully subtle.

Notice that there's a repeated pattern in the structure, where something stays the same, while something else changes. This can be represented with a simple formula:

IF YOU'RE X DO Y

Here the X and the Y stand for the things that change. The X represents the words 'quirky', 'sexy' and 'shy', whereas the Y represents the phrases 'go for it', 'go on, flaunt it' and 'be beautifully subtle'.

All parallelism in language works in the same way – there will be two or more chunks of text (of any size) where some elements are repeated and form a recognizable pattern and some other elements vary. When we represent parallelism with a formula like the one above, all we need to do is include all the parts that are the same and use letters (normally, X, Y and Z) to represent the parts that vary.

The best way to get to grips with this is through some practice.

Activity

Below are examples of parallelism taken from some of the texts in this chapter. Write a formula for each one of them.

The future's bright.	The future's Orange.
i wanted one life	you wanted another
yes is a pleasant country	if's wintry
I ent have no gun	I ent have no knife
I dont need no axe to split / up yu syntax	I dont need no hammer / to mash up yu grammar

There is some feedback on this activity at the back of the book.

Writing these formulae isn't just doing something that looks a bit like maths with poetry. They're useful because they help us to see relationships between the various words involved in parallelism. Let's consider one more example. Below are two lines from 'How sweet I roam'd' by William Blake:

> He caught me in his silken net,
> And shut me in his golden cage.

As usual, we have some words that are the same (in the second line 'he' is assumed to be there) and some that are different:

He	caught	me in his	silken	net
	shut		golden	cage

The formula to describe this instance of parallelism is:

HE X ME IN HIS Y Z

So parallelism **foregrounds** a piece of text thanks to an evident pattern and this induces the reader to see a relationship between *all* the elements involved, including those that vary. In this case, the reader is invited to see a relationship between the pairs of words represented by each variable – 'caught' and 'shut', 'silken' and 'golden', 'net' and 'cage'. Here, the relationships between these pairs of words are quite obvious. In other cases, the poet may exploit parallelism in order to impose a relationship between words that aren't usually related.

Activity

'Spain 1937 'is a poem by W. H. Auden. It is set during the Spanish Civil War. Below and on page 104 is an extract from the poem. Explore the way in which parallelism works in the poem.

Spain 1937
To-morrow, perhaps the future: the research on fatigue
And the movement of packers; the gradual exploring of all the
Octaves of radiation;
To-morrow the enlarging of consciousness by diet and breathing.

> To-morrow the rediscovery of romantic love;
> The photographing of ravens; all the fun under
> Liberty's masterful shadow;
> To-morrow the hour of the pageant-master and the musician.
>
> To-morrow for the young the poets exploding like bombs,
> The walks by the lake, the weeks of perfect communion;
> To-morrow the bicycle races
> Through the suburbs on summer evenings: but to-day the struggle.

Adding up your knowledge

The technical aspects you have been learning in this chapter do not replace the basic knowledge of language levels that were covered in the introductory chapter of this book or the work that you did in Chapters 1 and 2 on **narrative**. You should see the technical aspects in this chapter as adding to the knowledge you have already acquired.

For example, the topic area of **connotation**, or the associations certain words carry, is a very powerful aspect of meaning and you will need to refer to it regardless of how deviant the techniques of a particular poem are. Equally, all the poetry chosen for the set text list is characterized by strong narrative voices and/or strong perspectives on ideas and experiences, so all the work you have done so far on **narrators**, on speech and thought **representation**, on audience, purpose, **mode** and **genre**, is relevant here. How many of your poetry texts tell stories? How many appear to be addressing another person directly? How many express strong emotion? What kinds of emotion? The poetry sections on both A level and AS level exam papers are called 'Poetic Voices' for a good reason. All the poets have things to say about life, about memories, about times and places, about events, and about relationships with others and with the natural world.

You should regard the focus on language as part of a toolkit which you can use to help you analyse and interpret what your set text poems have to say. But, of course, your starting point in understanding your set poetry is to read and respond to the poems as pieces of communication – not as laboratory dishes containing examples of sound symbolism and metaphor. Your language knowledge is there to help you to analyse how a writer has put together a piece of communication and explain how you have interpreted it.

Adding a poem of your choice to a set poem

The A level assessment of poetry will give you a focus as a basis for choosing a further poem. The choice you make needs to follow that focus; therefore you need to do plenty of work on how the different poems in your collection relate to each other in terms of their **themes** and ideas, and how these are approached in different poems. One way to do this, after you have read and responded to the poems as whole texts, is to list all the topics and approaches of each poem, recognizing that any one poem can cover several ideas. You will then be able to see all the possible connections between the poems, so that in the exam you will quickly be able to locate an appropriate poem. The exam is open book, but that doesn't mean you have time to browse.

Comparing and contrasting poems

The AS level assessment is closed book and provides you with the text of two poems from your set text collection to analyse. Comparing and contrasting means exactly that: it doesn't mean analysing one poem, then analysing another. It means reviewing the two poems using the focus that is provided by the question, considering some common ground between the two poems but also what is distinctively different about each one. Again, if you work on your set text poetry as a collection from the start, and plot what the different poems have to say, you will know how to approach the task.

REVIEW YOUR LEARNING

- What are the two main aspects of foregrounding?
- Name some different ways in which poetic language can be deviant.
- What is a metaphor?
- Does poetic language exist outside of poetry? If so, where?
- Name some of Jakobson's language functions.

Further reading

Montgomery, M., Durant, A. and Fabb, N. (2006) *Ways of Reading: Advanced Reading Skills for Students of English Literature (3rd edn.)*. London: Routledge.

McRae, J. (1998) *The Language of Poetry*. London: Routledge.

This chapter will:

- help you develop your writing and editing skills
- show you the connections between analysing texts and writing texts
- give you some frameworks for applying your skills to exam tasks.

Key terms

Commentary. In this specification, a set of analytical comments about a re-creative task.

Creative writing. All writing is of course creative to some extent, but this term is frequently used to describe writing that is an individual's original creation. Traditionally, the term referred to literary creations but more recently it has widened to include any type of text.

! REMEMBER

At AS level, **re-creative** and **commentary** work offers a good foundation for the more complex A level versions.

At the heart of English Language and Literature study is an engagement with the different ways in which writers and speakers use language. Your study of different texts, both literary and non-literary, will prepare you for the production of your own re-creative writing. By reading a range of texts you will become a more-critical reader and become more sensitive to the choices that writers and speakers make to create meaning. A clear understanding of the choices that others make will help to inform you about the language techniques that will be most effective in your own writing.

The specification requires you to re-create texts. There is a difference between **creative writing** and **re-creative writing**. While all writing is of course creative to some extent, creative writing as a subject area can involve starting from scratch with your own idea, while re-creative writing – as a tool for understanding texts, as here – is about the creative adaptation of material that already exists.

There are re-creative writing tasks on both the AS level and the A level specifications, and they progress in difficulty from AS to A level. This chapter focuses on the AS task, which is based on re-creating material from the AQA Anthology: *Paris*, in Section B of Paper 2. If you are an A level student and not intending to take AS exams, don't simply miss out this section and move on. The AS work has been designed as a helpful earlier stage in preparation for the more challenging A level task. Details of the re-creative writing task for AS are given below. Chapter 5 has details of the A level task.

Both AS and A level tasks also involve writing a **commentary**, where you explain how you have made your choices of language and the effects you were aiming for. Again, AS level involves a simpler version of this activity, so if you are an A level student, use this opportunity to develop your skills.

Relevant Assessment Objectives

For the AS level re-creative writing task, AO5 is tested.

- AO5 rewards you for your creativity and originality – the ability to produce a new piece of writing from the material given.

For the AS level commentary, AO2, AO3 and AO5 are tested.

- AO2 rewards your ability to show how the language choices you have made contribute to meanings.
- AO3 rewards your understanding of **context** in such areas as audience, purpose, **genre** and **mode**.
- AO5 rewards your ability to communicate what you have done clearly.

People, places, times and stories

It is a mistake to think that describing people and places is simply about facts and figures. In reality, writers and speakers often try to capture the essence of people and places by weaving a **narrative** around their experiences. This means that all the work you have done so far on storytelling in the earlier chapters can help you to understand how representations of people, places and times work.

And the more you can be analytical about the different perspectives constructed in texts, the better you can employ those strategies in your own writing.

When producing your re-creative writing at AS, you will be provided with material taken from the AQA Anthology: *Paris* as the basis for your writing. This means that you are required to draw on the source material, extracting useful and **salient** detail which you will be able to adapt to create your original writing. You will be required to transform the material from one form into another, so a clear understanding of specific conventions is essential to enable you to shape and manipulate genre features.

Audience and purpose will be clearly specified, so it is important that you craft your writing appropriately. Your language choices need to be suitable for the target audience, which may be very different from the one intended for the original text (called the **base text**). When you have chosen the style for your writing, it is important that you sustain this throughout. Your main purposes also need to be clear – any audience needs to understand why you have written this text and understand what your intentions were.

Your commentary will require you to identify four features of language that you have used, and to explain why you have used them and what you were hoping to achieve.

The *Paris* Anthology

Paris is a culturally rich city, a truly cosmopolitan place at the forefront of the world's style, fashion, art, café culture and cuisine. It has proved a place of endless fascination to the millions of people who visit it every year and to those who have made it their home.

This cultural diversity is reflected in the Anthology, with its wide range of non-literary texts reflecting different people's experiences of Paris: people who are visiting the city for the first time, those who have returned to Paris many times – drawn by the vibrancy and *joie de vivre* that embodies the city – and those who are interested in the art and culture for which Paris is famous.

The texts have been gathered together from many different sources, from web pages to personal narratives, from song lyrics to journalism. Each of these texts tells a different story about Paris. Studying these texts will develop your understanding of the different ways in which people construct their own narratives in different genres.

This chapter will offer you a range of texts for analysis and as starting points for re-creative writing. Although some of your Anthology texts may be referred to in activities and in discussion, none of the extracts printed in this chapter are part of the Anthology. That is deliberate – there is no point in filling the pages of this book with extracts that you already have access to. However, some of the extracts in this chapter are about Paris, so you will see that this same theme has been continued. This will help you to see that there are endless textual variations that could form part of any collection about a specific place.

The aim of the extracts in this chapter is to help you develop your skills in encountering and producing texts of different kinds. All of the extracts reflect the types of material that feature in the Anthology, so you will be getting extra hands-on experience of working with equivalent texts. This will extend your class-based experience and offer you some wider reading as well as new material for re-creative writing exercises.

> **Key term**
>
> **Salient.** Most important, prominent, or noteworthy.

> **Did you know?**
>
> The term 'anthology' is derived from Greek and means a collection of flowers. It originally described a collection of poems, so in its Greek origins, the word 'anthology' is really a metaphor.

Activity

As explained previously, the extract below is not part of the Anthology set for study, but the approaches suggested here can be applied directly to any of the texts that are part of the collection. The extract is from the introduction to *The Little Paris Kitchen* by Rachel Khoo, a cookery book providing classic French recipes. How has the writer used language to present each of the following?

● People: those that she encounters
● Places: her experience of Paris, and the ways in which she views Paris as being different from London
● Times: the temporal framework of her text
● Stories: how she narrates her experiences of living in Paris

As you work on this analysis, use some of the techniques and frameworks from the previous chapters to help you.

The Little Paris Kitchen

Five years ago, I made the decision to pursue my sweet dream of studying patisserie at Le Cordon Bleu. So I packed my belongings and waved goodbye to London. A short train journey across the Channel and it was '*Bonjour, Paris*'.

And so my edible Parisian adventure began. The bakeries would entice me with their perfume of freshly baked baguettes and croissants. The cheese-monger would lure me with his perfectly ripe, oozing Brie displayed in the window, conveniently located next to a little wine shop. Its owner, who I nicknamed 'the wine fascist', would interrogate me with a thousand questions in order to find the perfect wine match for my dinners.

The outdoor produce markets overflowed with the season's bounty, brightly coloured fruits and vegetables, and the market traders would shout '*Mademoiselle, goûtez le melon. C'est delicieux!*' ('Miss, taste the melon. It's delicious!') It was a world away from the markets in London and the traders' cockney cries of 'Pound of bananas, a pound!' I soaked up the French ambience in the little cafés and bistros, with the locals sipping their glasses of wine, and watched the world go by.

But discovering '*la vie parisienne*' wasn't just about eating it up. I had some hard work to do.

> **! REMEMBER**
>
> Referring to language levels in any analysis shows that you are familiar with the terminology of the subject area.

Understanding context to inform your re-creative writing

To produce successful re-creative writing, you need to demonstrate a detailed understanding of at least the following dimensions:

● mode
● audience
● purpose
● time/era
● genre.

Mode

It is traditional to consider speech and writing as different **modes**, following particular conventions to achieve their various purposes. However, it can be simplistic to divide modes in this way, because there are many overlaps between them. For example, many writers will incorporate aspects of represented speech into writing, and modern forms of communication such as blogs and forums are termed **hybrids**, because they draw both on spoken and written features. Many of our mode choices are influenced by the **constraints** (or the nature) of a particular type of communication. Constraints include both **affordances** – what a text or communication tool is able to do – and **limitations**, or what is more difficult to do. For example, something like a blog or other interactive site is good at being accessible, immediate and inclusive. However, that very openness and inclusivity means that sites can accrue huge amounts of material that it is difficult to wade through; also if there is no limitation on any individual post, writers can often contribute lengthy texts.

Audience

We make very careful choices about our language to engage our audiences, to attract their attention to our stories and to maintain an interest in what we communicate to them. And audiences will have particular expectations of us: they expect to be introduced to a topic in a clear manner and then led through a text or interaction in an interesting way. Audiences can be broadly categorized according to such factors as age, gender and personal interests, but understanding audience is more complex than that; when you produce your re-creative writing, it is therefore important not to generalize and over-simplify language by **stereotyping** your audience.

The relationship that writers have with their audience will also influence the style of language used: **informality** may be appropriate if there is a close connection, while a more **formal** style might be suitable if the audience is more distanced. If people share a field of experience, then using a particular **register** is appropriate and shows that the writer is part of a **community of practice**. However, registers can also be excluding of those who do not have the same status of group membership.

Purpose

The purpose of a text is closely linked to the target audience. Notions of text production and text reception must be connected: does a writer's or speaker's aim in communication match what a reader requires from a text? Purpose is often multi-layered, with writers and speakers often having multiple purposes. For example, persuasion involves giving information, too. The mode or relationship a text producer has with the audience will also affect how language might be used to achieve purposes. A distanced relationship might require a more-explicit level of information, while a closer one could mean that not everything has to be spelled out because there is more shared meaning and context. A closer relationship could also encourage a speaker to use more emotive and impassioned language if attempting to persuade.

Time issues

The Anthology covers a range of texts from different times, from the 18th century to the present day. The different narratives reveal Paris in very different

Key terms

Affordances. Things that are made possible. For example, a website can be read by many people simultaneously.

Community of practice. A group of people who share understandings, perspectives and forms of language use as a result of meeting regularly over time.

Constraints. Overall shaping factors, including both affordances and limitations.

Hybrids. Blends of two or more elements. For example, new forms of communication are often seen as having some of the characteristics of both spoken and written language.

Limitations. Things that are prevented or restricted. For example, an SMS has no way to convey the subtleties of non-verbal communication (hence the need for emoticons).

Stereotyping. Assuming that whole groups of people conform to the same, limited, range of characteristics.

! REMEMBER

Studying the Anthology does not involve evaluating the texts and saying whether one is better than another. The aim is to help you understand textual variation.

Link

Look back to the work that you did on narrative point of view in Chapter 2 of this book, to help you think about audience.

ways, illustrating how the city has evolved over time. And of course, writers and speakers use language that reflects their era and the social conventions of the time.

Genre

There is considerable diversity of **genres** within the Anthology, and also diversity within genres. For example, travel journalism takes many forms: web pages, travelogues, guide books and so on. Having a clear understanding of all these factors will enable you to analyse the texts in your Anthology carefully and will also help you to understand the requirements specified for your re-creative task.

Classifying texts

One way to approach your Anthology is to classify the different texts according to their mode, genre and so on, so that you can begin to see patterns and links between them. Here are some examples of different categories that you could use as a starting point, with some possible examples in each:

Mode	Genre	Audience	Purpose	Time
• Spoken • Written • Multimodal • Mediated by technology	• Personal narrative • Memoir • Travel guide • Journalism • Letter • Diary/blog • Podcast • Advertisement • Web page • Comic • Conversation • Report of historical events • Song lyrics • Video clip	• Adults in various age groups • Parents/families • Children • Specialist interest, e.g. those interested in art, architecture, history • Wide audience – attempting to attract as many people as possible • Specific audiences, e.g. a known individual	• To entertain • To inform • To persuade • To advise • To guide • Interactional • Reflective	• Historical • Present day • Written in the present about events or incidents in the past

It is important to note that there is considerable diversity within these categories. Let's take spoken language as an example:

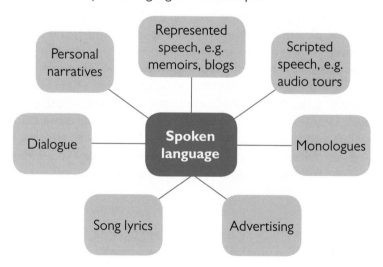

Activity

Use your Anthology to explore the various modes and genres in more detail, thinking about subtle differences within them.

Extension activity

In Chapter 1, you identified texts in your Anthology that represented spoken language in different ways. Return to your findings from that activity (page 60) and choose two texts that are very different in how they convey the idea of spoken language. This can include texts that don't represent any speech directly, but still give you a sense of a narrator's 'voice': for example, social media posts often convey a strong sense of personal expressiveness. Do a piece of re-creative writing by swapping the genres of the texts and writing one in the style of the other. For example, you could change a blogpost into some song lyrics, a monologue into some comics panels with speech bubbles, or a memoir into a blog. Playing with texts in this way is a good way to discover how they work.

Research idea

Record someone talking about their memories of a place and compare this with how that same place is represented in another genre – for example, in a novel. See Chapters 8 and 9 for ideas about how this could tie in with your coursework task. ●

Working with journalism

Carrying out the activity above should have helped you to realize that even an apparently straightforward label such as 'speech' hides a great deal of complex variation. The same can be seen with many of the other labels. For example, the 'journalism' we see around us in everyday life can come in many forms, ranging from very opinionated 'rants', such as those of Charlie Brooker, to the understated comic styles of journalists such as Caitlin Moran or Mark Steele, and from highly political and persuasive editorials to much more factual-seeming accounts of places and activities.

However, it is important to realize that even where a piece of writing seems very factual, the author has had to make choices about language use to suit the particular type of journalism that he or she is producing.

Activity

Read through the following text, which was published in *The Guardian*. Note that this is not included in your Anthology, but working on a text like this will help you to analyse any of the media texts that are included in the collection. This article's primary purpose is to inform, and the intended audience would be people who enjoy travelling and cycling and who wish to combine these two interests. It could be argued that this could also appeal to those who are environmentally conscious and who wish to consider alternative ways of seeing European cities.

What features of the text provide evidence for its audience, purpose and genre?

There is some feedback on this activity at the back of the book.

Freewheeling Paris

Parisians may have gone Vélib mad, but cycling in the city can be scary. Resident *Agnès Poirier* finds a quiet route via the best bistros and markets.

The novelty factor may have worn off but the romance between Parisians and le Vélib continues. Back from their long summer holidays, 215,000 of my fellow Parisians have renewed their annual subscription to the citywide bicycle scheme. These, together with other occasional cyclists, such as tourists, make up the 100,000 daily rentals. Needless to say, the scheme is a 'succès formidable'.

Young entrepreneurs have turned the Vélib into businesses, organising paid-for Vélib tours for American tourists in the Latin quarter. You can spot the riding hordes with their red jackets on, led by a lean Parisian student in a yellow vest. For those who prefer to go at their own pace, we thought the time right to devise a *Guardian* Vélib tour.

My favourite route starts with a cycling flânerie through the streets of St-Ouen that bear revolutionaries' names (the area has had communist mayors for a century). In St-Ouen, the urban landscape changes drastically from that of bourgeois Paris: low-rise 19th-century red brick factories and typical tiny 1930s workers' houses.

At the weekend, I often stop at *La Chope des Puces* (point 1 on the map) for live jazz (122 rue des Rosiers, +1 40 11 02 49; jazz every Saturday and Sunday, 2pm-7pm) and the bistro *Paul Bert* (point 2) for a pâté sandwich (20 rue Paul Bert, +1 40 11 90 28). The waiter there is always grumpy; it's part of the folklore.

From St-Ouen, I usually cycle through Porte de Clignancourt, with its French West Indies locals living in 1930s council estates, and ride up, up, up rue Hermel where the view over the Sacré Coeur gives me just enough strength to keep going. My favourite 18th-arrondissement street is rue Lamarck, a winding road of blond stone Haussmannian buildings encasing the Montmartre hill like a snake.

In Montmartre, the best bit comes when you suddenly realise that from there on, it's all downhill. Among my favourite stops in the descent is the leafy square sheltering the artists' cafe, *Le Botak* (point 4) (1 rue Paul Albert, +1 46 06 98 30).

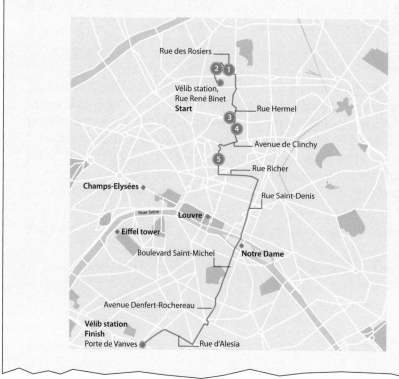

Activity

Now look at those texts in the Anthology that you would classify as journalism, and consider which language features are used by the different writers to suit the different types of journalism they are producing.

Travel writing

As with journalism, travel writing can take on many different forms, from personal travel memoirs to more conventional travel guides such as *Rough Guides* or *Lonely Planet*. Travel guides themselves vary greatly, depending on whether texts are print based or web based.

Activity

Look at the following two extracts. Text A is taken from the website WhyGo.com and Text B is taken from the *AA Spiral Guide to Paris*. Both focus on the Père Lachaise Cemetry in Paris. These texts are not part of your Anthology but offer a perfect opportunity for you to contrast an online source with a paper-based one. You will be able to use the insights you have gained and apply them to your Anthology.

- How is each text structured and how does its structure shape the way you read it?
- What language features are used to convey information about the cemetery?
- What language features are used to engage and interest the reader?

There is some feedback on this activity at the back of the book.

A

Web Browser   ⊟ ☐ ✕

◀ ▶   https://jessica.blog.com

Père Lachaise Cemetery in Paris: Where the In Crowd is Buried

By Jessica, 31 July 2008

I'll be the first to admit that on my first visit to Paris, after the big-ticket items like the Eiffel Tower and the Louvre Museum one of the things I most wanted to see was Père Lachaise cemetery – in fact, my French cousins were so amused by my fascination with the cemetery (they really didn't see the point) that they found an old book about it and gave it to me. I still don't read French, so I have no idea

what gems are contained within that book, but I still have it – along with a lasting love for Père Lachaise.

Now, I'll also admit that when I first visited Père Lachaise (yes, I've been there multiple times) it was primarily to visit the grave of former Doors lead singer Jim Morrison. I'm not now, nor have I ever been, a massive fan of The Doors – but Morrison's tomb is at least as famous as the man ever was, so I had to see it for myself. Little did I know how many other famous tombs I'd see there.

Père Lachaise is not only the largest cemetery in Paris, it's one of the world's best known cemeteries. Certainly this is partly due to Morrison's grave, but the

cemetery is almost literally packed with so many famous names that even someone who had no idea who Jim Morrison was would find someone to be impressed by. What's amusing about that is the fact that when the cemetery was originally built in 1804, it was deemed too far from the city, so few people chose to be laid to rest there. It wasn't until nearly 1820 that cemetery administrators had the bright idea of moving some famous remains to Père Lachaise – and it wasn't long until ordinary folks wanted to be buried in the same cemetery as the notables. Even in death, they wanted to be in with the in crowd.

• *Some of the most famous graves in Paris are in Pere Lachaise, but there are other cemeteries where you can find celebrities, too!*

B

The Grave Side of Gai Paris

Step inside the three great cemeteries of Paris, where the seemingly endless celebrity guest list of illustrious dead are conveniently assembled, and you will begin to understand why they say 'You haven't lived until you've died in Paris'.

The largest cemetery, Père Lachaise boasts 43 hectares (the size of the Vatican State) of higgledy-piggledy headstones and sepulchres, lined up like bathing huts along the tranquil, tree-shaded avenues. Since 1804, when it was first opened on the edge of the city to put an end to the over-crowding of inner-city graveyards, and the great French playwright Molière and lovers Abélard and Héloïse were reburied here, it rapidly became the place to be interred – the ultimate status symbol for the rich and famous. Once inside the walls of Père Lachaise, scarcely a sound disturbs the other-worldly calm, except for the cawing of the black crows that swirl ominously overhead.

By no means all of the great who are buried here are French. Many, including Marie Curie and Maria Callas, Gertrude Stein and Alice B. Toklas, were foreigners who came to live and work in France. Others – Oscar Wilde, Rossini, Isadora Duncan – simply had the misfortune to die here. The most visited grave is also the most controversial – that of Jim Morrison, lead singer of The Doors, who died in Paris of a drug overdose while on holiday in 1971. His simple tomb, always surrounded by adoring fans (and protected by a security guard), is covered with cigarette stubs, magazines, dead flowers and beads – trinkets intended as homage here, but which elsewhere would be considered merely rubbish.

25   *the Paris guide*

Activity

Choose a paper-based extract from the Anthology and transform it (or part of it) into a digital version. Think about how you will structure your text and the language features you will use to engage your readers. What headings, images and links will you include?

Personal writing

There are many different examples of personal writing in the Anthology, and these can be used to gain insights into the different ways in which people have experienced the city.

Activity

Look at the text below, taken from *Paris Letters* by Janice Macleod, an American who moved to Paris for 'two years of freedom in Europe'. Janice writes illustrated letters home, commenting on her experiences in Paris. As with previous activities, this text is not part of your Anthology, but offers you valuable practice in thinking about how writers choose different formats to convey their personal experiences.

- How does the writer create a sense of place in this letter?
- Janice has written this letter to a friend. How have her audience and purposes influenced the language choices she has made?

There is some feedback on this activity at the back of the book.

Dear Georgia

For my first two months in Paris, I was like Goldilocks, traipsing all over the city in search of the best café – a place I could call my own. One café would have a cozy atmosphere but terrible coffee. Another would have great coffee but terrible food. Then I came upon the café that was just right. It had it all – great coffee, cozy atmosphere and delicious traditional French cuisine. Plus its location on the pedestrian-friendly rue Mouffetard makes it the perfect perch for people watching.

Being here makes me feel like I'm in a timeless Paris – the version you see on all those postcards. People still sit and write letters, read the paper, and catch up on the latest gossip. I often linger here with my journal – sipping, dreaming and listening to French words flutter by on the breeze. I plan on putting in plenty of time here, and at the end of my days I'll likely haunt it ever after. We all must find our place in this world. Here in Paris, I believe I've found mine.

À bientôt!

Janice

Research idea

Some writers use letters in order to construct a literary text. Compare the use of letters in a non-literary text or collection with their use in a novel. See Chapters 8 and 9 for ideas about how this could tie in with your coursework task. ●

Extension activity

Referring more widely to your Anthology, examine some of the different ways in which writers have presented their own personal experiences of Paris. You might want to focus on memoirs, diary entries, blogs or letters. Select two different **genres** and compare the ways in which writers and speakers present a sense of place and time.

Producing a re-creative text

The diverse texts in your Anthology illustrate some of the different types of text that you could be asked to produce in your own writing. Below are some variations of genre, audience and purpose, to get you thinking about possible parameters.

Activity

Study your Anthology and choose some material that could be your source for each example. This list is not definitive nor is it a prediction of what may be required in any future assessment. You need to add to the list with your own ideas about the variations that are possible. Then, if you can, try some of these out as simulations:

- Web pages: find material that would enable you to write a web page promoting an aspect of Paris to visitors, for example, food, fashion, transport, art.
- Articles: find some material that would enable you to write a column for a newspaper from a historical angle.
- Tourist factsheet: find some material that would enable you to promote Paris for a specialized audience.
- Magazine advice column: find a text that would enable you to write informatively about Parisian customs, aimed at a foreign audience.
- Diary or blog entries: find some material that would enable you to convert personal memoirs from speech or continuous prose into a diary or blog format, or convert graphics or other visual media into continuous prose.
- 24 hours in Paris: find some material that would enable you to write a double-page spread for a newspaper's travel section on how to make the most of Paris in a day.

For each of these tasks, you should think carefully about genre, audience and purpose in the production of your writing.

Approaching the re-creative task

Activity

Work through Stages A to E below.

A When you are undertaking this task in the exam, read through the question carefully, so that you are clear about the text type you are being asked to produce, as well as its audience and purpose. The example below is from AQA's own specimen material.

Sample task:

Source text

Refer to Text A from *The Most Beautiful Walk in the World: A Pedestrian in Paris* by John Baxter.

Recast this as the section of the Café Danton's website where the café's location in Paris is described. You might consider:

- what will appeal to visitors about the location
- how the local area might best be described.

(200 words)

Genre: section of website; produced by the café for promotional purposes

Audience: visitors to the local area; people who have searched for this web page

Purpose: to inform and persuade

Content focus: the local area

B   Use your source material carefully. You will be directed specifically to a text from your Anthology and an extract will be provided for you. Re-read this carefully and highlight key sections that you might be able to adapt for your own writing.

Below is the extract that features in AQA's specimen material. Remember that your task is to produce re-creative writing: John Baxter focuses his writing on the people he encounters every day, while *your* task is to focus on the location and to consider how you can develop the details provided here into more descriptive writing that is suitable for the website.

> Every day, heading down rue de l'Odéon toward Café Danton on the corner of boulevard Saint-Germain or toward the market on rue Buci, I pass them.
>   The walkers.
>   Not all are walking, however. They'd *like* to be – but their stroll around Paris isn't working out as they hoped.
>   Uncertain, they loiter at the foot of our street, at the corner of boulevard Saint-Germain, one of the busiest on this side of the Seine. Couples, usually, they're dressed in the seasonal variation of what is almost a dress uniform – beige raincoat or jacket, cotton or corduroy trousers, and sensible shoes. Huddling over a folded map or guidebook, they look up and around every few seconds, hopeful that the street signs and architecture will have transformed themselves into something more like Brooklyn or Brentwood or Birmingham.

The highlighted sections may be useful in helping you to start shaping the content of the source text. Remember, you will use the source material as the basis for your own writing. Your task is to *adapt* the source material, not to copy from it.

C   Make notes about genre, audience and purpose.

Genre:

- What makes a website different from a more conventional, paper-based advertisement?
- What structural and discourse features are important for a website?

Audience:

- What language and style will be appropriate for an audience who have searched for this page online?
- What language and style is appropriate for tourists?

Purpose:

- Your task is to describe the local area so that it is appealing for tourists. How will you shape your language so that it persuades the audience that this is an interesting area of Paris to visit?
- How much information will you include about the local area, the architecture, events/activities and so on?

D   Write your response, thinking carefully about how you will shape your content.

- How will you engage your readers in the title and introduction?
- What language style will you adopt? What kind of narrator will you be? Will you address your audience directly? Will you use mainly **formal** standard English or will you vary your formality? Will you include humour?

- How will you shape the content so that it includes enough information but is not simply a list of facts?
- How will you build in persuasive elements so that you are convincing your audience of your perspective?
- How will you guide the reader through the text?
- How will you conclude your writing so that you have a strong finish?

E Check through your work and reflect on the success of your writing. As well as checking for accuracy, this stage is important as it will help you to shape your **commentary**, allowing you to select the most **salient** language choices you made in the production of your re-creative task.

Evaluating your writing

All writers think about their language choices, but not everyone writes about what they have chosen and why. However, this is something that you must learn to do if you are to be successful in producing a commentary on your work. You must be able to stand back and review your writing, which means analysing it and not just making sure that it reads fluently and is accurate. You need to look at your own writing in the same way as you look at any other piece of writing you analyse. In fact, a good way to start learning how to reflect is to exchange your writing with fellow students and ask them to tell you how they interpreted it; you can do the same for their work. In both your AS and A level exams, you are required to reflect on the specific language features you have used; this reflective commentary carries a significant number of marks in each case.

For the AS level commentary, you are required to *identify* and *comment on* four key features that you have used in your writing. You will be familiar with applying language levels to your set texts and to the *Paris* Anthology. For this task, you will apply those language levels to your own writing.

When you have completed your writing task, read through your work and begin to extract points that you think are the most salient in your writing. These might be:

- specific examples of sound symbolism, to create memorable patterning
- aspects of textual design that make your text distinctive and/or indicate its genre
- particular semantic fields that are appropriate for your intended audience
- particular adjectives that create layers of descriptive detail
- pronoun choices to set up narrative perspectives and different points of view
- deictic features that help to establish time and place
- interactive features that engage the target audience
- discourse features to structure or shape your content.

You can comment on any of the different language levels, but you should aim to discuss *different* language aspects in order to show the *range* of language choices you made when producing your work.

Producing your commentary

Activity

Now write your commentary.

You will have only about 200 words for your commentary, so it is important to be concise in your approach and not repeat yourself. Avoid simply describing the text you have produced and identifying four key language features. Anyone marking your work will have read it; you need to say *why* you have done what you've done, not just describe what is there.

Using a table like this can help you to organize your commentary:

Language levels	How meanings are constructed (AO2) (How do your language choices create particular meanings?)	Significant contextual factors (AO3) (How do your language choices relate to mode, audience, purpose, genre, etc?)
Example 1:		
Example 2:		
Example 3:		
Example 4:		

Remember that you will also be assessed on your ability to write clearly and accurately (AO5).

Adopting this approach can also be a useful starting point for writing your commentary at A level, where you are expected to reflect more fully on the different language features that you have used in your writing. Extracting key language examples from your own writing and thinking about how they create meanings will help you to understand how meanings are created in texts of all kinds, whether texts set for study or your own re-creative pieces.

REVIEW YOUR LEARNING

- How are the tasks of analysing texts and re-writing texts connected?
- What ideas have you used from the earlier chapters to help you with your analysis and re-writing work in this chapter?
- What is the difference between creative writing and re-creative writing?
- How can you best use the Anthology to prepare for your re-creative writing task in the AS level exam?
- What is a commentary and how is it assessed for AS?

Further reading

O'Toole, S. (2003), *Transforming Texts*. London: Routledge. This book refers back to older versions of English A levels, when the Assessment Objectives were different. However, all of the activities in this book are still extremely relevant for current courses.

Part 2: Exploring Conflict

This chapter will:

- help you develop your writing skills further
- show you the value of **re-creative writing** as a way to **critique** texts
- give you some frameworks for applying your skills to exam tasks.

Key term

Critique. A critical analysis that pays attention to all aspects of a text or topic, seeing different perspectives.

In Chapter 4 you examined different text types in the AQA Anthology: *Paris* and considered ways in which you can transform texts from one **mode** or **genre** into a different one, to suit different audiences and purposes. In this chapter you will develop your analytical skills to examine extended set texts, focusing on either a non-fiction or a fiction text for the exam. In the exam (Paper 2 of the A level; see below) you will analyse your set text – not by writing a traditional essay, but by producing a re-creative response to it.

As with the AS re-writing task, you will write a **commentary** to accompany your writing. In Chapter 4, there were some starting points for thinking about commentary writing, but the A level commentary needs to be more detailed, analytical and reflective. This chapter focuses on the A level re-creative writing task. Chapter 6 explores the A level commentary. Because the two activities are so closely aligned, it would make sense to read and work on this chapter in parallel with Chapter 6.

The overall A level exam featuring the re-creative task is called Exploring Conflict. The re-creative task is in Section A of this paper (Paper 2), which is called Writing About Society. Section B of the paper is called Dramatic Encounters and, as the title suggests, focuses on drama texts. Drama texts are covered in Chapter 7 of this book.

For Section A of Paper 2, the main focus for your re-creative skills will be on the study of one of four set texts.

Non-fiction texts:

- *Into the Wild* by John Krakauer
- *The Suspicions of Mr Whicher, or the Murder at Road Hill House* by Kate Summerscale

Fiction texts:

- *The Great Gatsby* by F. Scott Fitzgerald
- *The Kite Runner* by Khaled Hosseini

Relevant Assessment Objectives

For the re-writing task, AO5 is tested. AO5 rewards you for your creativity and originality. You need to follow the instructions given in the exam task and, staying with what's possible and feasible within the world of the text, create a new perspective that was not previously there or was not given prominence in the original story (called the **base text**).

Published writers and new perspectives

The focus of this chapter is on *adopting new perspectives*. This means that you will be studying your set text closely so that you can identify key patterns of language use in order to understand narrative and characterization, and then use this to inform your own writing.

This activity is one that many published writers have completed in order to extend the repertoires of their favourite novelists. For example, in 2012 Anthony Horowitz successfully resurrected Sir Arthur Conan Doyle's Sherlock

Holmes in his novel *The House of Silk*, and there have been many attempts at continuing the various stories of James Bond, long after the death of Ian Fleming, most recently with the publication of *Solo – A James Bond Novel* by William Boyd. The work of crime writers Agatha Christie and Dorothy L. Sayers has also been continued in new stories developed by the modern authors Sophie Hannah and Jill Paton Walsh, respectively.

In order for these re-imaginings to be successful, a writer needs to have a detailed and thorough understanding of the language choices made by the original writer, as illustrated in this review of *The House of Silk*:

> Enthusiastically replicating the spirit, style, suspense and atmosphere of Conan Doyle's stories, this skilfully crafted homage is an irresistible read.
>
> (Peter Kemp, *Sunday Times*)

For any transformed writing to be successful in this way we, as readers, need to believe the presentation, not only of the central characters and the events they may be involved in, but also of the world they inhabit. All of the contemporary writers noted above create convincing and believable evocations of the time and landscape of their texts – echoing those presented in the original stories.

It is not just the continuation of a story that lends itself to such creative transformations. Many texts are written from the perspective of a particular character, as you saw in Chapter 2 of this book. Often these perspectives are presented in a particular way, because of the social or historical circumstances under which they were originally produced. But what happens if we alter these perspectives? In her poetry collection *The World's Wife,* Carol Ann Duffy gives voice to the silent women of the past, the women who were present at important events throughout history, but whose perspective was not deemed as important as that of the men involved. Thus, Duffy offers a voice to Ann Hathaway and Frau Freud, the wives of men who changed the way we see the world. These speakers offer a contrasting, intelligent and ironic view of their husbands' lives and important works.

Social class issues have also offered fertile ground for re-creations. For example, in her novel *Longbourn*, Jo Baker offers a refreshing insight into the world of Jane Austen's *Pride and Prejudice* through the eyes of the servants: ' "If Elizabeth Bennet had the washing of her own petticoats," Sarah thought, "she would be more careful not to tramp through muddy fields." ' Novels published in the 19th century rarely focused on the lives of the servant classes, but we can now appreciate how much these marginalized or alternative voices can tell us about the so-called 'reality' of a text's depictions.

> **Did you know?**
> The art world has also seen some interesting re-creations from a gender perspective. For example, Sally Swain's *Great Housewives of Art* comments on the work of famous artists as if from their wives' perspectives. To see some examples, search Google images for 'Great Housewives of Art'.

From these examples, we can see that a clear understanding of narrative, events, characters and place is crucial to understanding a **source** text fully. It is only then that we can begin to consider ways in which to develop or shape elements which have perhaps been under-explored or under-represented in the original text.

To work towards your exam task, you need to acquire a clear understanding of the set text so that you can:

- develop aspects of the text that you are studying to present absent or underplayed perspectives
- consider how groups or individuals who either do not have a voice, or who might be marginalized in your set text, can be given a voice or perspective.

You will be able to explore these elements by:

- showing a clear understanding of narrative events so that you can shape or develop missing events

- examining the dominant points of view and considering alternatives to these

- examining speech or thought processes to consider what these reveal about particular characters and their interactions with each other.

When we think about adopting new perspectives, some key areas we might think about are:

- *Altering* perspectives – Offering insight from different characters' perspectives can provide alternative interpretations or responses to particular events and stories. All of the set texts have clearly defined characters, but some are developed more than others. By altering perspectives, we can gain a different insight into how characters interact with each other. Different characters can also offer us a different experience of the world of the text. For example, a woman's account of life in Afghanistan might offer us a very different insight into the world of *The Kite Runner*.

- *Developing* perspectives – Texts will often have layers of storytelling running through them. Sub-plots or additional points of narrative may be included to add to our understanding of central characters. Sometimes, a text's narrative voice can offer only a restricted view of key events. Thus, it can be useful to consider under-explored story lines so that we gain a fuller understanding of events and different characters' reactions to them. For example, much of what we learn about Mr Whicher is from accounts of previous cases throughout his career.

- *Adding* perspectives – Many writers will offer us essential information, but hold back some key aspects so that a reader is engaged in the text. We are expected to make logical assumptions and inferences based on the information that has been provided. Adding perspectives can allow us to explore some of these missing elements – helping us to piece together some of the plot and narrative, so that we can understand events more clearly. For example, the brevity of Chris's journal in *Into the Wild* means that there is much we don't know about his final days.

- *Externalizing* perspectives – The set texts are told from very particular perspectives with clearly defined narrators, who are often deeply involved in the plot and events that take place. It can be useful to step outside of the narrative voice to consider how an outsider might view particular characters or events.

The theme of conflict

As explained earlier, the re-creative work outlined in this chapter is linked to the overall theme of Exploring Conflict. Ideas about conflict are explored further in Chapter 7. However, it is important to note that conflict is multi-dimensional. Many different types of conflict operate within the set texts, with a powerful interplay of different themes and issues. And conflict can seem most powerful when it is understated, simmering below the surface, just waiting to explode. This chapter offers you the opportunity to examine some of these hidden tensions, considering how different characters might respond to them, and how the exploration of further information and detail might help to explain or resolve issues.

The conflicts presented in the set texts all illustrate some key issues about different societies and their values, whether these are based on a clash of social classes, different cultures and traditions, or particular concerns related to the time in which the texts are set. For example, some of the restrictions imposed on Mr Whicher during his enquiries are very much linked to the era in which he carried out his investigations; forensic evidence would probably lead to very different practices in a modern setting.

Producing different modes and genres

As you saw in Chapter 4 with its focus on AS level Paper 2, one aspect of re-telling stories can be to change the **mode** or **genre** of a text, so that it appears in a different form. This is an effective activity which can help you to understand a text and a writer's language choices. The process of transforming a text from one genre to another will also be useful when you consider your set texts for Paper 2 of the A level.

If you are studying the non-fiction texts, make a list of the different text types that are included. There will be many different types, such as diary entries, news articles, reports and interviews.

For example, each chapter of *Into the Wild* begins with a quotation from other texts. What other text types are used in this text? Think about why the author has chosen to use a variety of genres. What do the different genres add to the overall narrative? What different perspectives does this allow the reader to gain for key events?

The fiction texts may include fewer examples of different text types, but this means that you can be more creative in thinking about how different modes and genres might be used to explore different viewpoints or interpretations of events.

Activity

Read through the following short story by Ernest Hemingway. Although it is very short, Hemingway creates an evocative scene, capturing the intense emotions of the people who are forced to flee their homes. The environment is described only briefly, but reference to the rain and mud, and the struggle of both the people and the animals through the rain, creates a powerful atmosphere.

This story could be transformed into a variety of modes and genres. Try one of these:

- Transform this story into a news article for a British newspaper, reporting on the evacuation of women and children from a war-torn environment to a place of safety. You might want to focus on the circumstances faced by the evacuees. Shape your writing so that you can target your reader's conscience about unfortunate events that occur in other parts of the world. You should write about 200 words.
- Transform this story into a script for a 3-minute TV news report delivered by a foreign correspondent.
- Transform this story into a diary entry, told from the perspective of the woman giving birth. Focus on how the woman might feel having to go through a traumatic experience while being forced to leave her home behind. You should write about 200 words.

Did you know?

There are many claims about who has written the shortest short story. Here are two examples:

1. A horror story, by Fredric Brown: 'The last man in Earth sat alone in a room. There was a knock on the door.'
2. A **dystopian** romance, by Margaret Atwood: 'Longed for him. Got him. Shit.'

Minarets stuck up in the rain out of Adrianople across the mud flats. The carts were jammed for thirty miles along the Karagatch road. Water buffalo and cattle were hauling carts through the mud. There was no end and no beginning. Just carts loaded with everything they owned. The old men and women, soaked through, walked along keeping the cattle moving. The Maritza was running yellow almost up to the bridge. Carts were jammed solid on the bridge with camels bobbing along through them. Greek cavalry herded along the procession. The women and children were in the carts, crouched with mattresses, mirrors, sewing machines, bundles. There was a woman having a baby with a young girl holding a blanket over her and crying. Scared sick looking at it. It rained all through the evacuation.

Exploring narrative voice in fiction

REMEMBER

A **narrator** who is a character will often have quite a restricted view of events; this can convey strong impressions, as the character relays his or her experiences, but other perspectives are absent.

As we have seen in previous chapters (particularly Chapter 2), narrative point of view and voice are very important when examining a text, whether the text is fiction or non-fiction.

The two novels that are optional set texts both have a narrative where the story is told from the perspective of one of the characters; no further insight is provided. Thus, Amir in *The Kite Runner* is able to recount events from his own **point of view**, but does not have knowledge of how other characters think and feel. Similarly, while Nick Carraway has some knowledge and understanding of the different characters in *The Great Gatsby*, the narrative is limited to his own perspective only.

Activity

If you are studying *The Kite Runner* or *The Great Gatsby*, answer these key questions:

- Who is the narrator of the story?
- What role does the narrator play in the events of the story?
- How much does the narrator know about the events of the story?
- Why has the author chosen this character to present the narrative?

This then brings us to the bigger question:

What happens when we alter the perspective and see the story from a different character's point of view?

So, what if Hassan told us his story in *The Kite Runner*? And what might we have learned if Gatsby told us his own story?

Transforming a narrative from one perspective to another will allow you to move beyond **spatial point of view** (commenting on what a character sees) to **psychological point of view**, thinking about how different characters feel about the events and incidents of the novel.

Activity

Look at the short extract below, taken from *What is the What* by Dave Eggers. In this passage, the narrator Achak's flat has been burgled. He is lying on the floor, bound with phone cable by the burglars. A young boy is in the flat, guarding Achak to make sure he doesn't call the police. This boy is referred to as 'TV Boy' in the text.

- How is Achak's role as a victim presented here?
- Achak tries to establish a connection in his own mind between the young boy and himself. How does he do this?
- Now that you have paid close attention to the language features that Eggers uses to present this situation, re-write this scene – but from the perspective of 'TV Boy'. Imagine how he feels, left in this apartment guarding an injured man he does not know. You should use a **homodiegetic narrator (first person narrator)** to capture the young boy's feelings about the situation he is in.

I lie on the carpet, wondering whether I should make another attempt to move. I do not even know who this boy is; he could be in the same sort of trouble I am. I try to find my arms and realize they are behind me, tied with what I assume is the phone cord.

***

I see only the profile of this boy's head, and he is not so different than I was at his age. I do not want to diminish whatever is happening or has happened in his life. Surely his years have not been idyllic; he is currently an accomplice to an armed robbery and is staying up much of the night guarding its victim. I will not speculate about what he is or is not being taught at school and at home. Unlike many of my fellow Africans, I don't take offense at the fact that many young people here in the United States know little about the lives of contemporary Africans. For every young person who is ill informed about such things, though, there are many who know a great deal and have respect for what we face on the continent. And of course, what did I know about the world before high school in Kakuma? I knew nothing. I did not know of the existence of Kenya until I set foot in it.

Look at you, TV Boy, settling into that kitchen chair like it was some kind of bed.

Exploring narrative voice in non-fiction

For the non-fiction texts you are studying, narrative voice operates in a different way, but these texts still enable you to explore and develop voice creatively.

Both *Into the Wild* and *The Suspicions of Mr Whicher* have an authorial voice which distinguishes these texts from the two novels set for this part of the specification. The authorial voice intrudes into the text at different times to offer a personal comment on the events and characters involved in the stories. This presents us with a very different view of the texts: the writers inform readers about their aims in writing the texts and about which aspects of the stories inspired them to write in the first place.

Activity

If you are studying the non-fiction texts, answer these key questions:

- Who tells us about the main events of the story?
- What is the relationship of the teller to the main character in each text?
- How involved is the teller in the events of the story? Does the teller become more involved as the story continues?
- How much does the teller know about the main events of the story? Is the teller objective? Does this affect the reliability of the narrative?
- Are other perspectives introduced? If so, how do other characters present their views? (Think about the use of interviews, news reports, diaries and so on in these texts.)

This then can lead us to explore the different narratives in more detail:

Which characters' perspectives are important in understanding the events of the story, but not fully developed in the text?

So, for example, what more could Jan Burres tell us about her impressions of Chris as he embarked on his journey in *Into the Wild*?

What details could Carine McCandless tell us of her childhood growing up with Chris?

Speech and thought

Characters are not only realized through descriptions of them, but also through the spoken voice they are given and the ways in which they interact with other characters (see Chapter 2 in this book).

In prose texts, the **representation** of dialogue is not expected to be a faithful representation; instead, there is careful crafting of speech. Readers expect highly conventionalized dialogue, with suitable **reporting clauses** so that we are able to glean information, not only from what is said but also from aspects that remain unstated.

 Activity

Read the following extract from *Stoner* by John Williams. In this extract, Stoner becomes aware that his wife Edith has full knowledge of the affair he is having. Grace is their daughter.

- What does the exchange that takes place between Stoner and his wife reveal about the nature of their relationship with each other?
- How is punctuation used to convey aspects of the conversation?
- What other language features are used to present the conflict in this situation?

There is some feedback on this activity at the back of the book.

She spoke of it casually one morning while he lingered over his breakfast coffee, chatting with Grace. Edith spoke a little sharply, told Grace to stop dawdling over her breakfast, and that she had an hour of piano practice before she could waste any time. William watched the thin, erect figure of his daughter walk out of the dining room and waited absently until he heard the first resonant tones coming from the old piano.

'Well,' Edith said with some of the sharpness still in her voice, 'you're a little late this morning, aren't you?'

William turned to her questioningly; the absent expression remained on his face.

Edith said, 'Won't your little co-ed be angry if you keep her waiting?'

He felt a numbness come to his lips. 'What?' he asked. 'What's that?'

'Oh, Willy,' Edith said and laughed indulgently. 'Did you think I didn't know about your – little flirtation? Why, I've known all about it all along. What's her name? I heard it, but I've forgotten what it is.'

In its shock and confusion his mind grasped but one word; and when he spoke his voice sounded to him petulantly annoyed. 'You don't understand,' he said. 'There's no – flirtation, as you call it. It's –'

'Oh, Willy,' she said and laughed again. 'You look so flustered. Oh, I know all about these things. A man your age and all. It's natural, I suppose. At least they say it is.'

For a moment he was silent. Then reluctantly he said, 'Edith, if you want to talk about this –'

'No!' she said; there was an edge of fear in her voice. 'There's nothing to talk about. Nothing at all.'

And they did not then or thereafter talk about it.

Activity

Referring to the set text you are studying, closely examine an example of conversation between characters. This might be:

- Chris's conversation with Franz while they are travelling to San Diego in Chapter 6 of *Into the Wild*
- the cross-examination of Emma Moody in Chapter 11 of *The Suspicions of Mr Whicher*
- Nick's first meeting with Daisy at her house in East Egg in Chapter 2 of *The Great Gatsby*
- Baba and Rahim Khan discussing Amir in Chapter 3 of *The Kite Runner*.

Of course there are many examples that you could focus on, but when you examine the speech and thought in your set text, you should focus on:

- types of spoken language that are used: direct speech, free direct speech, indirect speech, free indirect speech, narrative report of a speech act (see Chapter 2 of this book)
- language features that are typical of each speaker – what language features might reveal about social status, gender, age, dialect and so on
- language features indicating hesitation, indecision, directness, challenge, provocation and so on
- particular reporting clauses that might suggest details about the relationship between characters or the sensitivity of a particular topic
- particular thought processes that might appear alongside the spoken communication – think about what characters might choose to leave unstated and why these points are not discussed

- prosody or non-verbal communication that might reveal a character's inner thoughts or anxieties (see the introductory chapter).

Having examined the spoken language in your set text, imagine that you are adding to the narrative by including additional dialogue between some of the characters.

Referring closely to your set text, choose a character who is not the main focus of the events of the narrative. For example, you might wish to focus on:

- Carine in *Into the Wild*
- Reverend Wagner in *The Suspicions of Mr Whicher*
- Jordan Baker in *The Great Gatsby*
- Soraya in *The Kite Runner*.

Pay close attention to the language the writer uses to present your chosen character, referring to the points above. A detailed understanding of the character will help you to develop your chosen character, producing convincing dialogue.

Imagine that your chosen character is having a conversation with another character from your set text, where they discuss some of the key events of the narrative. Pay close attention to the setting or environment: this should be a situation that a reader can imagine occurring.

Write about 200 words, imagining what each character's reactions might be to key events. Remember, you do not need to focus solely on the dialogue. You should also think about careful shaping of your writing to include a clear narrative voice, suitable reporting clauses and language choices that might reveal important information about the dynamics of the relationship between the characters.

Developing character

Does character or story drive the narrative forward? When reading a text are you eager to find out what has happened? Or are you more interested in how a character has developed and progressed throughout the narrative?

Characters are used to enliven a narrative; a successfully drawn character can help us to engage with the events that he or she is involved with. An effective character should be multi-dimensional, with flaws, imperfections, secrets, hopes, ideals and inner thoughts, allowing us to gain a deep understanding of him or her.

You may be focusing on real or fictional characters, depending on your set text. However, writers will often present them in a similar way. Real or not, we need to feel that characters have some substance in order for us to engage with them and follow them. Many strategies are used to create the idea of a character, including:

- physical description
- names, which can have strong **connotations** (e.g. the connotations of the names Daisy and Myrtle in *The Great Gatsby*)
- an exploration of the inner thoughts and feelings of a character

- their relationship with other characters
- their relationship with the environment
- characters' actions and how they impact on others or on the main plot.

Activity

Look at the following short extract, which is again from *Stoner*, by John Williams. What is revealed about the character by the physical description given?

There is some feedback on this activity at the back of the book.

> By his second year he was a familiar figure on the campus. In every season he wore the same black broadcloth suit, white shirt, and string tie; his wrists protruded from the sleeves of the jacket, and the trousers rode awkwardly about his legs, as if it were a uniform that had once belonged to someone else.

When examining characters in your set text, it is useful to focus closely on the lexical choices used to refer to them. The word cloud below focuses on Nick Carraway's first introduction to Myrtle Wilson in *The Great Gatsby*:

Activity

Select a character from the text you are studying and find a passage that describes that character. You could create a similar word cloud to that above by using wordle.com. It would be useful to select a minor character, one that the writer has perhaps only sketched rather than fully presented.

Which words are significant? Is there a pattern which **foregrounds** particular attributes or qualities of the character?

From your text or word cloud, select 10 words and use these to shape a description of your chosen character, developing the description to consider personal qualities and attributes, rather than just physical description. Or make the physical description represent aspects of character, as in the *Stoner* passage.

If we look at the example word cloud above, we can see that there is a mix of both positive and negative description: 'smouldering', 'lips', 'vitality' and 'light' create a fairly sensuous image of Myrtle. But this is presented alongside the terms 'stout', 'thickish' and 'coarse', which all present a very different view of her; and she seems to be overshadowed by the presence of her 'husband'.

A useful way of thinking about the characters in your set text is to make a list of all main characters and their relationships with each other. It would be helpful to present this as a diagram. For example:

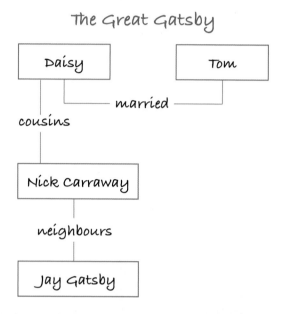

Activity

Construct a similar diagram for the text you are studying and add all the main characters, paying close attention to the relationships which the different characters have with each other.

Make another list, this time of the minor characters, thinking about when they appear in the text and why they are important to the overall narrative.

For *Into the Wild*, it would be useful to record these characters on a map to illustrate where Chris McCandless met particular people during his travels.

Similarly, it can be useful to compile a historical timeline, prior to the murder at Road Hill House, charting the different cases that Mr Whicher has worked on and the different people he encounters throughout his career.

Continue to add to these lists while you are reading your set text.

The impact of setting and location

Each of the set texts is located within a very particular environment, whether it is Alaska or West Egg, Afghanistan or Wiltshire. And in each of the set texts, the place and setting is a key part of understanding the events of the narrative. A landscape can deeply intensify the conflict in which a character finds himself or herself.

Read through your set text carefully, paying close attention to the way the writer presents important locations. For example:

- How does Krakauer present Alaska? You could compare Chris's descriptions with that of his parents when they come to see where their son died.
- How does Summerscale present Wiltshire, and Road in particular? You might want to think about how Mr Whicher perceives the environment as a newcomer to the area.
- How does Fitzgerald present the opulence that surrounds Gatsby's home? You might want to focus on one of the many parties that he hosts.
- How does Hosseini create a contrast between the Afghanistan of Amir's childhood and his adulthood following his time in America?

Each of the texts for study for this paper has varied landscapes that help us to understand the different characters who inhabit them and the different events that take place there. Different characters will respond differently to the various landscapes; setting and location can lead to a sense of release and escape for one character, and yet the same setting might be quite oppressive for another character. Try transplanting a character from one book's setting to another and you will soon see how closely characters and settings are aligned.

Activity

Read through the following extract, which has been taken from *Twelve Years a Slave* by Solomon Northup. In this passage, Solomon describes the nature of his imprisonment, having been forcibly taken as a slave.

What language features does Northup use to describe his physical environment?

There is some feedback on this activity at the back of the book.

The light admitted through the open door enabled me to observe the room in which I was confined. It was about twelve feet square – the walls of solid masonry. The floor was of heavy plank. There was one small window, crossed with great iron bars, with an outside shutter, securely fastened.

An iron-bound door led into an adjoining cell, or vault, wholly destitute of windows, or any means of admitting light. The furniture of the room in which I was, consisted of the wooden bench on which I sat, an old-fashioned, dirty box stove, and besides these, in either cell, there was neither bed, not blanket, nor any other thing whatever. The door, through which Burch and Radburn entered, led through a small passage, up a flight of steps into a yard, surrounded by a brick wall ten or twelve feet high, immediately in rear of a building of the same width as itself. The yard extended rearward from the house about thirty feet. In one part of the wall there was a strong iron door, opening into a narrow, covered passage, leading along one side of the house into the street. The doom of the colored man, upon whom the door leading out of that narrow passage closed, was sealed. The top of the wall supported one end of a roof, which ascended inwards, forming a kind of open shed. Underneath the roof there was a crazy loft all round, where slaves, if so disposed, might sleep at night, or in inclement weather seek shelter from the storm. It was like a farmer's barnyard in most respects, save it was so constructed that the outside world could never see the human cattle that were herded there.

> **Activity**
>
> Referring closely to your set text, write 200 words where you describe the physical landscape of a distinctive place. For example, you might wish to describe West Egg as seen by Jay Gatsby.

The importance of time

Setting is clearly important in a text, but so too is how particular events are presented to readers. As you saw in Chapter 1, there is a difference between a **story** and a simple **recount** of events. While recounts just describe one event after another in a series through time, stories can jump around, and often do, in order to keep readers engaged by working to piece parts of the story together for themselves.

Look at the events in your set text. Are they told in a simple chronological way, with a logical progression throughout the text? Or does the narrative have a more complex chronology, moving backwards and forwards to address different events and stories at different times?

Where there is a complex chronology, you need to think about why you have been told the story in this way.

> **Activity**
>
> Read the following passage, the opening to *Catch a Fire*, a biography of Bob Marley by Timothy White.
>
> - How does the writer present the sequence of events in this extract?
> - How does the writer use time and place to analyse the politics of the social context?
>
> There is some feedback on this activity at the back of the book.

It was just before midnight, and the cheers from the distinguished audience were mingling with the shouts of the ragged crowd climbing over the walls surrounding the Rufaro Stadium in Salisbury, the capital city of Zimbabwe. The wind suddenly shifted, and billows of tear gas being used by police outside the arena to control the throng had blown across the grounds to inflame the eyes of the man performing on the small stage in the center of the arena. Momentarily disorientated, he darted about, eventually stumbling through an opening in the stinging fog. Soldiers brandishing M-16 rifles led him off to the side and down into a trailer, where he dabbed his eyes with a water-soaked cloth.

The concert, which had been in progress for about twenty minutes, was part of the official Independence Day ceremonies on April 18, 1980, for the new nation-state of Zimbabwe. The paying customers and dignitaries (among them Marxist Prime Minister Robert Mugabe and England's Prince Charles), who had assembled to celebrate the casting off of white colonial tyranny, were now witnessing a demonstration of another form of repression: thousands of adulatory peasants and the rank and file members of the revolutionary army had amassed outside the arena hoping to see the performance of international reggae sovereign Bob Marley, hero of black freedom fighters everywhere and the most charismatic emissary of modern

Pan-Africanism. Hearing the reggae rhythms pulsing within, wave upon wave of idolators attempted to storm the gates. Police responded with tear-gas grenades and rifle volleys over their heads, but the people would not be held back, and they surged over the walls.

Marley pushed back the thick, ropy strands of his 'dreadlocks' (long matted strands of hair) away from his swollen eyes, peering into the darkness beyond the blinding lights onstage. There were shouts, screams and the muffled thuds of police batons against bodies as what looked from a distance like a swirling tide of people was beaten back from the crest of the stadium's parapets. Rallying to rejoice over their deliverance from white oppression, much of the black population of the city was now fighting for the simple right to hear reggae.

'Madness,' Marley muttered. He felt the firm grip of a soldier's hand on his left arm, and was escorted to safety.

Extension activity

Choose a text that has interesting uses of time, and analyse how the time-shifts work.

Activity

Plot all the main events and incidents that occur in your set text on a timeline. This will help you to see the chronology of the text clearly.

- Identify different events and stories within the text that you feel could be developed more fully.
- Choose one event or incident that you have identified and write a fuller account of it. Choose your perspective: you could remain with the existing perspective or select a new one.

Each of the set texts has very a good film adaptation which can offer you a different interpretation of events. Some of the texts might have more than one adaptation.

Activity

Watch the film version of your set text. Remember, it is important to read through your set text *before* you watch the film version.

- Are events relayed in the same order as in the original text?
- Is the film chronological? Or are flashbacks used to move between present and past events?
- Film versions of texts cannot present every scene from the original text, so directors will make choices about which details and events are included in the film and which aspects are omitted.
  - Make a list of omitted scenes. Why do you think the director chose to leave these out of the final film version?
  - Do you think any of the omitted scenes added crucial detail to your understanding of the set text?

- ○ Are any scenes added to the film that do not appear in the original text? What might these add to your reading and interpretation of the original text, events and characters?
- Just as readers will often interpret texts in a particular way, so too do directors. Does the film adaptation of your set text tie in with your interpretation of the text? Are characters and events presented in the way that you expected them to be presented?

Approaching the transformation task

When responding to this question in the exam, carefully read through the question so that you are clear about the text type that you are required to produce as well as the audience and purpose. The example below is from AQA's own specimen material. This question is about *Into the Wild*.

> Read the opening of Chapter One from 'Jim Gallien had driven four miles out of Fairbanks' to 'he couldn't wait to head out there and get started'.
>
> Here the writer describes the meeting between Gallien, a working man travelling to Anchorage, and Alex, who is hitchhiking.
>
> Recast this description into an account that Gallien might give to his wife later that evening.
>
> You should write about 300 words.
>
> In your transformation you should consider:
> - Gallien's perspective of the meeting, his views on Alex and attitudes towards travellers
> - Gallien's relationship with his wife in the way he conveys his recent experience.

A careful reading of what you have been provided with above should help you to see the following:

1 You have been clearly directed to a specific part of your set text. Re-read this section carefully and begin to extract details that you might find useful in this task.

2 You have been provided with details about the writing that you are required to produce: an account that the character Gallien might give to his wife later that evening.

3 This means that you need to understand that the text you will be writing will be in the form of a conversation. Therefore, you will need to think about how you will structure the conversation, whether you will use **direct** or **indirect speech** and which narrative elements you will include to help shape the conversation.

4 You have been given guidance about the content of your writing:

a Gallien's perspective about the encounter with Alex

b His attitude towards Alex

c His attitude towards travellers.

5 You have also been directed to think about the relationship between Gallien and his wife, and how this might affect how he tells his story to her.

6 You will be producing only about 300 words. Therefore, you need to be selective about the amount of detail that you will include, as well as developing the nature of Gallien's feelings and attitudes towards Alex and other travellers.

Creating a successful transformation

When producing your transformation task, it is important that you do the following:

1 Show clear understanding of the set text you have been studying. This means that you must have detailed knowledge about the different events that take place and the characters who are affected by the various events. For the above task you may wish to:

- consider Chris/Alex's method of travelling across America by hitchhiking and how different people might feel about this
- reflect on Chris/Alex's character and whether he is a 'typical' hitchhiker.

2 Produce writing that is within the parameters of the set text. All events and situations must be appropriate to the text and to the different characters. Your transformation will be convincing only if readers believe that the events and developments you have created are possible. The events for this task are included in the text, so you are required to develop the perspective that was told to Krakauer in more detail.

3 Use language that is reflective of the style of the set text, the narrative voice and key characters, so that your writing appears to be part of the wider text. Your writing should demonstrate understanding of Gallien's use of language in order to effectively replicate it in a conversation with his wife.

4 Pay close attention to the writer's use of language to present ideas and attitudes about key issues, themes, characters and events, and use similar language to develop these ideas. Here, you have the opportunity to explore some key ideas that Krakauer explores in his text:

- Chris/Alex's desire to survive in the wilderness
- the appeal of nature to young men
- notions of survival in difficult terrain.

5 Make careful and judicious use of dialogue to illustrate conflict, characterization and key themes. Dialogue should always be used carefully. The text you are producing here is an imagined **representation** of a conversation, not a transcript, so think about the conventions of representing speech in prose texts. Think about the relationship between the speakers and how this will affect the language that is used.

6 Think about incorporating key motifs or images to illustrate your understanding of the whole text. Think about the possessions that Chris/Alex carries with him as he embarks on his adventure and whether these are sufficient for survival.

REVIEW YOUR LEARNING

Try to answer the following questions:

- How does re-creative writing help you to take a critical view of your set text?

- How can changing a perspective offer an insight into the way a story is told?

- Why is knowledge of the characters, events, times and places in your set text essential for undertaking a re-creative writing task?

- How is the A level re-creative task assessed?

Further reading

Pope, R. (1995), *Textual Intervention*. London: Routledge

The A level **commentary** forms the second task that you are required to complete in Section A of Paper 2. A crucial difference between the AS and the A level commentaries is that, at AS level, you are asked to identify four different features of language that you have used in your re-writing of the **base text**. At A level, you are not given a set number but, as with the AS version, you are expected to select the most **salient** features to discuss. This means picking out some key aspects and some *different* aspects of language. You don't have room to talk about everything you've done. You are advised to write 400 words, which is about a page of A4, so each of the examples you pick needs to offer something different.

You might find it surprising that the A level commentary is highly rewarded in terms of marks. Why is this?

As noted at the start of Chapter 4, re-creative writing is not just another label for creative writing. It has a completely different purpose: it's an alternative to writing a traditional essay about the way a literary text works, especially focusing on the language use of the writer.

Producing a piece of re-creative writing shows that you understand key aspects of the base text. In the process of planning and producing your writing, you should develop insights into how the base text works, but the job is not complete until you explain those insights in the form of your commentary. Think of your commentary, then, as a form of **critique**, with language at its heart. Obviously, the commentary relies on your re-creative writing. But even if your re-creative writing isn't exactly how you wanted it to be, you can still earn a considerable number of marks by explaining what you were trying to do, showing that you understand the base text and that your intentions were along the right lines.

> **This chapter will:**
>
> - help you understand how the A level commentary compares with the AS commentary
> - show you how to go about writing an effective A level commentary
> - give you an understanding of how the A level commentary will be assessed.

> **! REMEMBER**
>
> In your commentary, don't be tempted to evaluate yourself by including remarks such as 'I think I was very successful' or 'If I'd had more time, I could have done things better'.

Relevant Assessment Objectives

The following Assessment Objectives are tested in the A level commentary:

- **AO2** rewards you for showing how the language choices you have made in your re-creative writing contribute to meanings.

- **AO4** rewards you for making connections – in this case, between the base text and your own writing. While AO2 focuses more on your own work, AO4 requires reference to the base text.

- **AO5** rewards you for communicating what you have done clearly.

The focus of these different Assessment Objectives is reflected in the way the sample AQA questions are set out and phrased. Below is an example to show you the way the question is expressed in AQA's sample material for *Into the Wild*; this same format is repeated for each of the text options. The first bullet point refers to AO2, the second to AO4 and the third to AO5.

Write a commentary explaining the decisions you have made in transforming the base text for this new account and the effects of reshaping Krakauer's original description.

You should write about 400 words.

In your commentary you should:

- consider how you have used language to shape your intended meaning
- demonstrate the connections between the base text and your transformed text
- structure your writing clearly to express your ideas.

What kinds of features are salient ones?

The aspects you choose as the most salient will depend entirely on what you have done in your re-creative task. Some examples of re-creative approaches and their likely features are described below. These approaches were set out and discussed in Chapter 5.

Altering perspectives

In Chapter 5 (and earlier in Chapters 1 and 2) it was suggested that altering perspectives can offer a new reading of the text. This can be achieved in a number of ways. You could, for example, change the narrative point of view radically so that a narrator who was part of the story (a **homodiegetic narrator**) becomes removed from the story and views it from an external perspective (**heterodiegetic narrator**). In this case, in the exam you would obviously be pointed to a specific part of the text and your salient features would be those where you have altered the language use in order to signal the change in perspective of the narrator. You would compare what you have produced with the way the base text worked in its original format.

A more straightforward shift of perpective would be from a character who is a homodiegetic narrator in the base text, to another character fulfilling the same role.

In Chapter 5, it was noted that some characters are more developed than others and that bringing out the views of characters who are marginal figures in the original story can be a way to represent the voices of those who we often don't hear from in society. The example given in Chapter 5 was the idea of a female character's account of events in *The Kite Runner*. Adopting this kind of change requires a rethink of the events pointed to in the text, so that you imagine how that character would experience things. It would require a creative elaboration of that character's voice and you would, in effect, be adding something completely new to the text. But it would need to fit in with the events as they occurred – you couldn't suddenly invent a whole new part of the plot.

With this approach, you would need to make your language consistent with how that character would speak and think. So your salient features would be those aspects, plus how you have described the event from a new point of view. This approach can be regarded as altering perspectives because, as with the first example of changing narrative positions, it disrupts notions of 'reality' – of whose account we see as 'the truth'. You would compare your re-created version with the base text, showing how they differ and explaining why.

Research idea

For a masterclass in shifting perspectives, read *Gone Girl*, by Gillian Flynn, which has now been made into a film directed by David Fincher. Consider the ways in which the shifts in perspective have been achieved. ●

Activity

Go back to the writing activities in Chapter 5, where your re-creative work focused on shifting the perspective from one character to another (for example, idea number 3 for the Hemingway text in the activity on page 125; the activity on the Dave Eggers extract on page 127; or the description of landscape from a different perspective in the activity on page 134).

Write a reflective commentary on your re-creative work. Try responding to the AQA exam format, below, which is taken from the specimen materials. Obviously, each task in a real exam will have a slightly different initial instruction, because it will relate to the specific task and extract. However, the bullet points will remain the same and these give you a possible shape for your response.

Write a commentary explaining the decisions you have made in transforming the base text for this new account and the effects of reshaping [name of writer]'s original description.

You should write about 400 words.

In your commentary you should:

- consider how you have used language to shape your intended meaning
- demonstrate the connections between the base text and your transformed text
- structure your writing clearly to express your ideas.

Developing perspectives

In Chapter 5, the idea of under-explored parts of the story was discussed. As with marginalized voices and characters, there may be parts of the plot that are not fully described. Obviously, the descriptions of events are from a specific point of view, so events are not separate from the characters who observe them. But some events are more elaborated than others. The approach of expanding part of a story, then, would again be adding detail, but your invention would need to stay within the likely parameters of the event: for example, you couldn't suddenly have a war breaking out when that would call into question the whole of the base text and the way it was plotted.

Salient aspects of your re-creative work would be those that were consistent with how the original event was described, and in making connections with the base text you would therefore be showing how you tried to make your work consistent with it. This is the kind of work that has been undertaken by writers who finish novels that remained incomplete at the time of another writer's death.

Did you know?

Jill Paton Walsh completed a half-finished Dorothy L. Sayers novel (*Thrones, Dominations*) by continuing Sayers' style. It is very difficult as a reader to see where one writer finished and the other began.

Activity

Go back to the writing activities in Chapter 5 where your re-creative work focused on writing some dialogue between characters in your set text (pages 129–130, which focuses on the task in the sample materials). The idea in both tasks was to capture the characters' reactions to a named event or events. In every real assessment, you will be pointed to a specific place in the book from which to start your writing.

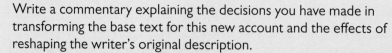

Write a commentary explaining the decisions you have made in transforming the base text for this new account and the effects of reshaping the writer's original description.

You should write about 400 words.

In your commentary you should:

● consider how you have used language to shape your intended meaning

● demonstrate the connections between the base text and your transformed text

● structure your writing clearly to express your ideas.

Repeat the activity above, but this time focus on the writing you did in Chapter 5 to develop an event (page 135).

Adding perspectives

This aspect is about gaps and omissions – things that, if a novel were a drama, could be said to happen 'off stage'. No writer explains every detail: readers are expected to work from inferences and fill in the gaps in their own way. Again, your additions would need to be feasible. Chapter 5 refers to the brevity of Chris's journal in *Into the Wild* as an example of something that could be added to. Salient features would, again, be those aspects that would work within the story frame without contradicting the overall narrative.

Externalizing perspectives

The idea of altering perspectives, above, refers to a change of narrative position. The idea would be that the re-creative writing would be in the same **genre** as the base text. But an external perspective could also be achieved by changing the genre of the text from a fiction or non-fiction extract to something else entirely. In doing this, you automatically change the narrative point of view, along with other dimensions of **context**, as you will see below.

Change of genre

How would events in the base text be described in a different genre, such as a news article, TV or radio news bulletin, magazine article, blog, private letter, phone call, police report or conversation between two characters? Each of these types of text has its own genre conventions, and potentially new audiences and purposes. Your salient features would need to include examples of how you followed those conventions.

The narrator in each of these examples could be external – for example, a journalist reporting on events – or it could be that one of the characters is communicating in a way not seen in the base text. Therefore another aspect of salience, in addition to genre features, is narrative point of view. You would compare your re-created text with the base text with these differences in mind.

Change of mode

A change of genre can involve a change of **mode**, requiring you to pay attention to some of the distinctive aspects of different spoken and written modes in your re-creative writing. If you are representing speech, you need to think about how spoken language works in reality and how it is represented on the page. This has been discussed in the earlier chapters of this book and more will be said in Chapter 7, part of which focuses on differences between real speech and drama scripts.

Changing text from represented speech to another written mode – such as a written report – will also involve changing aspects such as reporting clauses, verb tenses and so on (see Chapters 1 and 2). Digital texts such as emails, blogs and websites have further distinctive features that are hybrids of spoken and written features. Your salient features will therefore be aspects of mode difference as well as the ways in which the base text and your re-creative writing cover similar ground – if similar ground is what the task requires.

> ### Activity
>
> Go back to the writing activity you completed in Chapter 5 involving changes of mode and/or genre (all three tasks on the Hemingway extract, pages 125–126). Focusing on tasks 1 or 2, do the following:
>
> Write a commentary explaining the decisions you have made in transforming the base text for this new account and the effects of reshaping the writer's original description.
>
> You should write about 400 words.
>
> In your commentary you should:
>
> - consider how you have used language to shape your intended meaning
> - demonstrate the connections between the base text and your transformed text
> - structure your writing clearly to express your ideas.

Task 3 on the Hemingway text has already been discussed above (page 141). However, all the tasks on Hemingway also involve changes of genre and task 2 involves a distinctive change of mode. If you have already written a commentary on task 3 of the Hemingway activity, did you discuss the change of genre as well as the change to narrative perspective? If not, why not?

What are *different* salient features?

You should have noticed from the explanations above that aspects you might be required to change in any re-creative task can be strongly interconnected. A new type of narrator might be needed, communicating ideas about something under-played in the base text, but expressing himself or herself in a new genre and a different mode. You will therefore have plenty to write about in selecting your features.

The idea of discussing *different* salient features is important because it shows that you are aware of all these changes and their likely effects. So choosing examples from different areas of change – narrative viewpoint, development of event details, genre, audience, purpose, mode – would be much better than taking one area and writing about several examples of it.

REVIEW YOUR LEARNING

Try to answer the following questions:

- What is the purpose of the commentary?
- What does the phrase 'different salient features' mean?
- What aspects of the commentary are assessed via the different Assessment Objectives of AO2, AO4 and AO5?

Staging perspectives

Drama involves a special kind of storytelling, and in this chapter you will be exploring what makes drama distinctive, both from a language point of view and as a literary genre in its own right. The whole of the A level Paper 2 exam is concerned with the theme of conflict, as explained in Chapter 5, and this idea is very much at the centre of the drama text options. In all the texts, conflict is the raw material of the storyline, and the drama texts specifically centre on domestic conflict within families and within relationships.

However, the plays aren't just about families in conflict: each dramatic story gives us messages about the larger society in which the play is set and about human behaviour in general. You need to be able to analyse your chosen play on a number of levels if you are to produce a successful exam answer.

You have seen in Chapters 5 and 6 that rewriting exercises can help you to develop a critical view, and this approach forms the assessment for your chosen fiction or non-fiction text for the theme of conflict in Section A of Paper 2. With the drama texts in Section B, however, the assessment is a more traditional essay, with a given focus and point of reference within the play. Further details are provided below.

Relevant Assessment Objectives

The drama texts are part of the A level specification only. They are not assessed in the AS specification.

For A level analysis, the Assessment Objectives tested are AO1, AO2 and AO3.

- AO1 rewards your ability to take a language approach to the texts that you study, to write coherently and to use terminology appropriately.

- AO2 rewards your ability to explain what texts mean, by showing how meanings are built from the language choices that writers and speakers make.

- AO3 rewards your understanding of context – the effects produced by variations of such aspects as audience, purpose, genre and mode.

Paper 2 of the A level is open book, meaning that you will have your text with you in the exam, so you will be pointed to a particular scene within the play as the starting point for your essay. The part of the play that you are pointed to will illustrate the focus of the question, giving you an example of what the question is referring to. It is your job to analyse this part of the play; to connect that part with other parts, according to the focus of the question; and to go beyond the play text itself in order to explore the larger themes that are being presented dramatically.

Questions about drama involve exploring both *how* and *why* something is the case. Exploring how the drama text works is the *how* (AOs 1 and 2); exploring the ways in which the play conveys messages about the larger society we live in is the *why* (AO3), because it focuses on why the writer chose to write the drama in this way in the first place.

This chapter will:

- help you understand how to go about analysing drama

- give you useful frameworks for analysis and opportunities to practise your skills

- show you how to apply what you learn to your set texts.

Link

As with the other text types that you study on the specification, drama can be explored further in your coursework component, *Making Connections*. You can read more about this in Chapters 8 and 9.

What is drama?

In Chapters 1 and 2, you explored the question of what a story is and what we mean by fiction. When we think of drama, those two earlier ideas may already be part of our thinking: drama can be seen as another form of storytelling and as a fictional **representation** of real life. But we also have certain expectations of drama that we don't have of prose fiction: drama is a visual medium where we are shown things happening, not just told about them.

When someone tells you a real-life story, they may well act out aspects of it, using gestures and impersonations of speakers in order to 'dramatize' the story for you. In prose fiction, we create these aspects ourselves, in our minds. But in drama performances, it is there before us, being enacted. In a way, then, your study of drama needs to start with the recognition that reading a playscript is no more like experiencing drama than reading a transcript is like experiencing real speech. Both of these written versions are representations, and both need something to be added in order to bring them to life.

But although they are both representations, they are very different: a play is a script, for the most part written before it is acted, so the writing was written to be spoken; a transcript is the result of an earlier performance – it is a representation of what speakers did in the past. If you recorded a performance of a play and wrote out what the actors said, it would become a transcript.

If drama is merely a set of actions, then, does that mean that any activity is a drama? Clearly not: we have a sense even when we use the word 'drama' in an everyday context that what we are referring to is larger than life or more exciting than a run-of-the-mill set of actions. Having your breakfast isn't a drama – at least, not unless the toaster explodes and sets fire to the kitchen curtains.

> **Did you know?**
>
> The term 'drama' comes from a Greek word referring to taking action, to doing things.

> **Activity**
>
> In Chapter 2, you saw some uses of the term 'fiction' in a **corpus** of English, the British National Corpus. Below, from the same source, are some examples of how the term 'drama' has been used.
>
> 1. What meanings are suggested by the ways in which these examples use the terms 'drama' and 'dramatic'?
> 2. What can we infer from these meanings about our expectations of drama as a literary form?
>   - 'It is that real-life *drama* that Singleton decided to explore and recreate on film.' (film review)
>   - 'He had watched the *drama* unfold from a support vessel.' (newspaper article)
>   - 'The *drama* begins about 210 million years ago, when the North American plate finished some 600 km inland, roughly where California now meets Nevada and Arizona.' (geology text)
>   - 'No *Drama*' (sub-heading in an advice book about giving a party)
>   - 'Ken particularly used to enjoy the murder trials — not for any morbid curiosity, but for the *drama* unfolding.' (biography of the actor and comedian Kenneth Williams)
>   - 'We won't make a *drama* out of a crisis.' (Commercial Union insurance advertisement)

- 'Insignificant flowers produce *dramatic* orange-berried seed heads in late autumn, for use fresh or dried.' (gardening book)
- 'This section is one of the most *dramatic*, weaving in and out of sheltered coves and exposed headlands.' (travel book)
- 'We should further note the *dramatic* increase, postwar, in numbers of old people living alone.' (article on elderly care)
- 'Senior officers say the now familiar fixed cameras have already had a *dramatic* effect in reducing speed.' (police report)

Drama and 'reality'

As you will have realized from the above activity, our expectations of drama are that we will be presented with more than a set of everyday, normal events. Just as we saw in Chapters 1 and 2 that both factual and prose-fiction narratives are more than just neutral **recounts**, a drama is a carefully constructed narrative involving particular characters, settings and actions.

Even so-called 'reality TV' is a highly shaped art form. Programmes such as *The Only Way is Essex* use 'real' people but put them in constructed situations; lines are not scripted, but scenes are planned. Such programmes come very close to drama series such as soap operas, except that, of course, soaps use professional actors. It is arguable whether people trying to act themselves are any better or worse than actors trying to seem like 'real' people. One thing is for sure: the scenes in both types of dramatic representation aim for as much heightened feeling and emotion as possible. One way to achieve this is to set up conflict between the characters.

> ### Activities
>
> 1. Read the following transcript, which is an extract from *The Only Way is Essex*. Note that this is a transcript of what the characters said – it is not a script.
>   - How do the 'real' people create a sense of drama in this extract?
>   - Is it convincing as a dramatic scene?
> 2. When you have read the transcript, go to YouTube and watch the clip at https://www.youtube.com/watch?v=JEUo5TcviRI
>   - How does watching the scene and listening to it differ from reading the transcript?

> **Did you know?**
>
> Soap operas got their name from the fact that early programmes were sponsored by soap-powder companies and had soap-powder advertising at transmission breaks. Nowadays, the preferred term for soap operas such as *EastEnders* and *Coronation Street* is 'drama series'.

> **Transcription key**
>
> (.) normal pause
>
> (1.0)   numbers in brackets indicate length of pauses in seconds
>
> || speech between two vertical lines indicates words spoken simultaneously
>
> [ ] square brackets normally indicate non-verbal elements such as facial expressions or vocal effects such as laughter. In this transcript, they also indicate inaudible speech.

Lucy: I wanted to meet you today because erm I've never been completely honest about that night night | (.) and | I think you know that a little bit | [sighs 2.0] |
Mario: | okay | | so what happened that night then |

Lucy: okay from start to finish (.) so you [inaudible] in | the morning (.) | me and the girls
Mario: | umm umm |

Lucy: in the club (.) and the manager came up to me about half an hour into it (.) and said just to let you know (.) Mark's booked a last-minute table (1.0) and he got there (.) and I had a gut instinct that I should leave (.) but I thought (.) it's my friend's birthday and I'll stay (.) and anyway [sigh] I carried on with the night (.) got more and more drunk (2.0) and the last really bit I remember of the night is leaving and going back to (.) Jess and Mark had like a joint party (2.0) and I honestly (.) I really (.) the rest is a fuzz (.) I'm not gonna (.) I can't sit and | say no |
Mario: | where did you wake up |

Lucy: at Mark's
Mario: okay (.) well | then it's | needless to say it's | over | |
Lucy: | but I was | | but Mario | can | you just (.) can you just hear me out |
Mario: | | no (.) no (.) no (.) right you've had |
your say (.) you've lied for the last two months (.) not just to me (.) but to my sisters (.) to my mum's face (.) my whole family

In completing this activity, you have been exploring two areas that you will need to think about carefully in order to analyse your drama set text: how conflict forms an important part of dramatic narratives and the nature of dramatic dialogue, both on the page and in action.

Drama and conflict

In Chapter 1, you learned about the shape of many real-world stories: Labov's idea of **natural narratives** was that real speakers make a story worth telling by introducing a **complication** as part of its structure. We can see whether the same thing is true for the genre of literary drama.

When asked to think about conflict, most of us would probably call to mind the idea of argument. But is argument dramatic enough? If not, how can it be heightened to create a dramatic narrative?

Key term

Natural narratives. A term used in Labov's study of storytelling to label the everyday stories that people tell each other.

Activities

1. Here is a list of some everyday conflicts experienced by a student. What complications could be introduced for each of these situations in order to create a dramatic narrative?

   - Argument with parents over clothes worn to college
   - Argument with a driver while cycling to college
   - Argument with a tutor over deadlines for submitting work
   - Argument with a friend on Facebook
   - Argument with brother about using the computer at home
   - Argument with mother about mobile phone charges

2. Choose one or more of the situations and introduce a complexity to it that would make it into a story worth telling. Once you have thought of a potential plotline, write some lines that could form part of the drama.

If you prefer to focus on your own experiences, devise a list of examples of conflict that you have witnessed or been involved with.

Research idea

How far can Labov's ideas about the shape of narrative in everyday storytelling compare with the way playwrights construct their plays? Ask some people to recall a dramatic experience from their lives, record what they say, and analyse how their narratives compare with the plotline and characterization of a play of your choice (but not a set text). See Chapters 8 and 9 for information about how this could form the basis for your coursework folder. ●

If you have managed to create a sense of drama from any of the ideas above, or from any of your own experiences, you will have embedded the argument in a larger sense of deep-rooted differences between characters, possibly involving the history of their relationships or their fundamental outlook on life. A basic difference between argument in real life and argument in drama is that in real life we argue in order to assert our own position – not in order to tell a story. In drama, the characters argue in order to further the action of the play and to move the narrative along in a dynamic way.

The conflicts that form the basis for the dramatic narrative that unfolds in your set texts may well appear as localized arguments at specific points in the play; and these may be episodes that you are referred to as your starting point for questions. You then need to see how those localized arguments, oppositions and tensions are part of the larger narrative of the whole play and be able to describe why the characters are in conflict with each other and/or the world around them.

Activities

Choose one of the main characters from your set text.

1. List the occurrences throughout the play of episodes of conflict or opposition to others.

   a. Does this character have internal conflicts?

   b. Is this character in conflict with some of the ideas in the society in which the play is set?

2. Set your ideas out visually, by creating a diagram showing the various types of conflict that the character is engaged in.

How do they do it?

You will remember that in exploring questions about your drama set text, you need to show how and why conflicts occur. So far, you have been thinking about who might be involved in conflict, but not how or why they act as they do.

Key terms

Idiolect. An idiolect is the language that is unique to each individual (the language equivalent of fingerprints).

Logos, pathos, ethos. Different appeals that can be made in order to persuade others, according to the classical Greek field of rhetoric, which originally focussed on speech-making. Logos is an appeal to logic, or rationality. Pathos is an appeal to the emotions. Ethos is an appeal to authority, for example by referring to the speaker's credibility.

Did you know?

Experts in analysing speakers' and writers' idiolectal patterns are called forensic linguists and are often employed in court cases where the authorship or authenticity of texts is in dispute. We all have a set of linguistic fingerprints that are uniquely our own.

Looking at how characters interact means analysing the language chosen by the playwright for those characters. How does the writer convince us that the characters are plausible?

To answer this question, you need to think about how playscripts compare with our real-life behaviour in a number of areas.

- In real life, we all have our own individual way of speaking, our **idiolect.** How does the writer give each character a distinctive 'voice'? Are there lexical features, aspects of phonology and **prosody**, or non-verbal behaviour that are used to characterize different speakers?

- What interactive features of **discourse** are used to simulate real speech and, in particular, dissent and conflict?

- What are some of the strategies that we use in our real relationships to establish and defend our views and positions? The ancient Greek philosopher Aristotle suggested, in his *Art of Rhetoric*, three strategies that we often use in order to persuade others: **logos**, or reasoning, where we put forward apparently logical reasons for believing certain things; **pathos**, where we appeal to others on an emotional level; and **ethos**, where we trade on our own credibility – our good name, trustworthiness and loyalty.

Conflict is therefore not just about simple oppositions. It works alongside, and relies on, our connections with others. The family-based nature of the set-text dramas show you explicitly how conflict and connection are two sides of the same coin.

Looking at spontaneous speech or loosely planned improvised drama can help you to explore the aspects above, before you work on your set text in any detail.

Activities

1. On the next page is a further extract from *The Only Way is Essex*.

  a. Are the two characters distinctive in the way they use language?

  b. What features of real speech do they enact in order to simulate spontaneous dialogue?

  c. What strategies are being used by the speakers for asserting and defending their positions?

Refer back to the coverage of spoken language in the introductory chapter, particularly in the sections on phonology and **pragmatics**.

2. Now watch the clip at this link: https://www.youtube.com/watch?v=bZltCVxfroA

  a. Are there further aspects that are observable and were not evident in the transcript?

  b. How does watching the scene and listening to it differ from reading the transcript?

There is some feedback on this activity at the back of the book.

Joey: look (.) I was gonna say (.) I thought that you and me was pals (.) and you've been going behind my back talking (.) talking about me (.) you said to me (.) you said to some of those girls that you thought that I was a boy

Ricky: I didn't even know that I said it innit

Joey: come on you think that funny Ricky (.) if you think that I'm a boy yeah and you think that you're a man (.) why would you not say that to my │face│ (.)

Ricky: │ no │(.) no (.) course not (.) oh come on (.) come on man (.) listen (1.0) look I haven't even denied it (.) look (.) I don't remember saying it (.) I don't remember doing it (.) I don't even remember being at that place (.) I was that out of ma nut (.) and as soon as I found out that I did (.) I tried to …

A playscript is not simply something designed for the page. While it clearly needs to make sense on the page, it also needs to function as a set of prompts for actors to use in their performances. For this reason, playwrights often signal the characteristics of speech that they want actors to aim for, as well as suggesting the types of non-verbal behaviour that would suit the characters and the events being portrayed.

As well as the physical appearance of the actors themselves, playwrights of course have control over the larger physical space that the actors occupy. It is therefore important to consider aspects of stagecraft, such as how the actors are positioned and how they move; the physical backdrops presented; and the time frame that unfolds as the story proceeds.

Activities

1. Read the extract below from Tennessee Williams' play *Cat on a Hot Tin Roof*. It is taken from the opening scene of the play set in the bedroom of Maggie (Margaret) and Brick. Maggie is describing how Mae (her sister-in-law) has been 'parading' her children in front of 'Big Daddy', Brick's father, to win favour with him and get the inheritance that Maggie feels Brick deserves. Maggie and Brick do not have children, and this is a source of tension for Maggie.

2. Compare this extract with that from *The Only Way is Essex*, above. What are some of the similarities and differences?

3. Then, focusing just on the playscript, see if you can answer the following questions:

   a. How does Tennessee Williams suggest aspects of spoken interaction in the way he has written the characters' lines?

   b. What aspects of **non-verbal communication** does he include, and how do they contribute to meaning?

   c. The interaction involves conflict between the characters. How is this conveyed? What part is played by the features you have identified above?

There is some feedback on this activity at the back of the book.

MARGARET: Susie didn't think so. Had hysterics. Screamed like a banshee. They had to stop th' parade an' remove her from her throne an' go on with – [*She catches sight of him in the mirror, gasps slightly, wheels about to face him. Count ten.*] Why are you looking at me like that?

BRICK [*whistling softly, now*]: Like what, Maggie?

MARGARET [*intensely, fearfully*]: The way y' were lookin' at me just now, befo' I caught your eye in the mirror and you started t' whistle! I don't know how t' describe it but it froze my blood! – I've caught you lookin' at me like that so often lately. What are you thinkin' of when you look at me like that?

BRICK: I wasn't conscious of lookin' at you, Maggie.

MARGARET: Well, I was conscious of it! What were you thinkin'?

BRICK: I don't remember thinking of anything, Maggie.

MARGARET: Don't you think I know that –? Don't you –? – Think I know that –?

BRICK [*coolly*]: Know *what*, Maggie?

MARGARET [*struggling for expression*]: That I've gone through this – *hideous!* – transformation, become – *hard! Frantic!* [*Then she adds, almost tenderly*:] – *cruel!!*

Activities

Now focus on your drama set text.

Look at the list or diagram you made previously, where you explored a specific character and the various conflicts they experience (see page 149).

1. Choose an episode where this character is in conflict with another, and answer the following questions.

   a. How does the playwright use aspects of speech to create meanings? You could think about:

   - phonology, such as suggested pronunciations

   - prosody, such as intonation, volume, speed, timing

   - paralinguistic effects, such as whispering, sighing, laughter and other speech-like noises

   - lexis and semantics: vocabulary differences between the characters, the connotations of terms, taboo language, archaic expressions, dialect words, formality, idioms and metaphors

   - pragmatics: characters' shared understandings and assumptions, inferences, adjacency pairs such as question and answer sequences, instructions and compliance or resistance, greetings and farewells, naming and other features that suggest claims to power

   - grammar, including aspects of speech grammar such as non-standard language, incomplete utterances, cohesive features such as deixis and reference

   - discourse, including aspects of mode such as overlaps and interruptions, reinforcements, monitoring features, hesitations, mistakes, false starts and changes of direction; and aspects of function and genre (storytelling, humour and playfulness, talking to oneself, talking to the audience).

   b. How does the playwright use the physical aspects of communication to create meanings? You could think about:

   - aspects of non-verbal communication suggested for the characters, such as facial expressions, bodily gestures, physical movements, aspects of dress and appearance

- aspects of dramatic placement, such as position on the stage and movement around it
- aspects of setting, including backdrops for different scenes, changes in time frame, lighting, sound and other special effects.

c. How does the playwright set up the characters' strategies for positioning themselves and their interlocutor? You could think about:

- claims based on ideas about 'evidence' and appeals to reason and logic (logos)
- claims based on credibility from aspects such as power, status, good character (ethos)
- claims based on emotional appeal such as being part of a family, previous relationship, favours owed, knowledge of the others' weaknesses (pathos)
- other claims or defences that don't fit into the above.

2. Drawing on all you have found, now think about how the conflict between the characters is portrayed in your chosen episode. What part is played by the features you have identified?

If you are able to watch your drama text being performed as well as study it on the page, you will be able to think about the differences between the play on the page and the play in performance. You will be able to consider how the playwright's plans and suggestions are enacted.

Conflict and speaker roles

In order to create a sense of dynamic conflict, playwrights have to think about how to make speakers' roles consistent. Conflicting ideas need to be set out and tension built up gradually. Readers of plays and audiences listening to performances need to feel that speakers hold their line of argument and, if they give way, that this process happens for a reason – people don't just whimsically change their minds.

To see some examples of characters in conflict and how arguments are built, look at this list of famous film arguments taken from the website Total Film: http://www.totalfilm.com/features/50-nastiest-movie-arguments

The top five of all time are listed as:

1. *Twelve Angry Men* (1957)

2. *Do The Right Thing* (1989)

3. *Raging Bull* (1980)

4. *Who's Afraid Of Virginia Woolf?* (1966)

5. *Revolutionary Road* (2008)

The title of the winning film *Twelve Angry Men* leaves no doubt in the audience's mind that this film will centre on conflict. The plot is a very simple one: the film follows 12 jurors on a murder trial as they reach their verdict. Initially, all bar one indicate that they want to find the accused, a young uneducated Puerto Rican boy, guilty. One juror stands alone, convinced of the boy's innocence, and one

! REMEMBER

Don't ignore body language – it can be very expressive. The non-verbal communication in this toilet sign says it all, without any need for words!

by one he changes the minds of his fellow jurors, questioning evidence and citing the prejudice and failures in the legal process that have led up to this point.

Activity

The extract below is from an early part of the film, just after the jurors have taken their preliminary vote. All voted guilty apart from juror eight. Look at the language in the extract and think about how the conflict is built up, focusing particularly on the language of juror eight.

There is some feedback on this activity at the back of the book.

3RD JUROR

I mean, let's be reasonable. You sat in court and heard the same things we did. The man's a dangerous killer. You could see it.

8TH JUROR

The man! He's sixteen years old.

3RD JUROR

Well, that's old enough. He knifed his own father. Four inches into the chest.

6TH JUROR

(to the 8th Juror)

It's pretty obvious. I mean, I was convinced from the first day.

3RD JUROR

Well, who wasn't?

(to the 8th Juror)

I really think this is one of those open and shut things. They proved it a dozen different ways. Would you like me to list them for you?

8TH JUROR

No.

10TH JUROR

Then what do you want?

8TH JUROR

Nothing. I just want to talk.

7TH JUROR

Well, what's there to talk about? Eleven men here agree. Nobody had to think twice about it, except you.

10TH JUROR

I want to ask you something. Do you believe his story?

8TH JUROR

I don't know whether I believe it or not. Maybe I don't.

7TH JUROR

So what'd you vote 'not guilty' for?

8TH JUROR

There were eleven votes for 'guilty'. It's not easy for me to raise my hand and send a boy off to die without talking about it first.

7TH JUROR

Who says it's easy for me?

8TH JUROR

No one.

7TH JUROR

What, just because I voted fast? I think the guy's guilty. You couldn't change my mind if you talked for a hundred years.

8TH JUROR

I'm not trying to change your mind. It's just that we're talking about somebody's life here. I mean, we can't decide in five minutes. Suppose we're wrong?

Activity

Visit the webpage http://www.totalfilm.com/features/50-nastiest-movie-arguments and look again at the list of films. Choose a film that you think has been overlooked in the list, and which you know well, and write a short explanation of why it should be included. You can even give it a number if you wish.

If this is done as a group activity, you could defend your opinions to your classmates and compare your views with those of your fellow students.

The play as a story

So far, you have been focusing quite narrowly on the idea of a particular character and a specific episode where characters are interacting and are in conflict with each other. But any character and any episode are, of course, part of the wider story of the whole play. Any play as a whole is a series of scenes where people, events, times and places are interwoven. The different and varied themes of any play are also part of its larger context, in which playwrights hope to offer perspectives on life and society at the same time as providing entertainment.

As we saw in Chapter 1 and also earlier in this chapter, any story needs to be considered worth telling. In the case of fiction, publishers usually write blurbs for their book jackets and/or inside covers to act as a kind of trailer for the story, hoping that customers will be intrigued enough to buy the book. Trailers can act in the same way for films. But how do plays display their wares?

One answer to this question, of course, is that drama scripts in published form use the same strategies as prose fiction, with carefully designed covers and blurbs. Dramatic performances have different strategies, using both traditional media such as newspaper advertising and flyers, and online media such as the homepages of individual theatres. Whatever the channel chosen for promoting plays – either in book form or in performance – readers do not have endless time or patience to read large amounts of material, so they need to be given interesting images and punchy outlines of the play's story in order to get their attention.

The Oxford Shakespeare
Othello

OXFORD WORLD'S CLASSICS

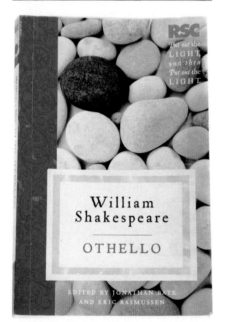

Two contrasting book covers for different editions of *Othello*

Activity

Publishers will have their own distinctive style for the covers of their books, and their own way of encapsulating the theme of a play within the cover design. It is useful to look at the ways in which a single text is marketed, because you can observe different strategies at work to communicate what is seen as the main focus of the story.

How do the two publications pictured represent what *Othello* is about?

The first text uses an **iconic** approach, featuring an image of an individual. The second text uses a **symbolic** approach, where there is no real connection between the image and the **referent**.

- What are the advantages and disadvantages of these two approaches?
- The drama set texts are all about conflict and relationships. To what extent do the *Othello* covers suggest those ideas?
- Do the approaches suggest a slightly different interpretation, in each case?

Activity

Below are four promotional texts advertising performances of upcoming plays at Manchester's Royal Exchange Theatre.

1. How does each text suggest the nature of the play? Is there a difference between the texts promoting well-known plays and those promoting new plays?
2. How does each text attempt to create a sense of dramatic excitement? Do any of the plays' titles add to this effect?
3. Would any of these texts entice you to go and see the play?

CAT ON A HOT TIN ROOF
TENNESSEE WILLIAMS

**THE STIFLING HEAT OF THE PLANTATION.
A RELATIONSHIP ON THE BRINK. A NIGHT OF BOURBON-SOAKED CONFRONTATIONS AND A FAMILY DYNASTY IN CRISIS.**

Tennessee Williams' Pulitzer prize-winning CAT ON A HOT TIN ROOF remains one of the stage's most seductive evocations of the Deep South. Brimming with emotional intensity, this powerful family drama sees Maggie the Cat and her husband Brick return to his home on the night of patriarch and cotton tycoon Big Daddy's 65th birthday. Keeping from him the news that he is dying, the evening spirals into disaster as the family scramble to secure their part of his inheritance.

Key term

Iconic. In semiotics, the term iconic refers to an image that is a picture of its referent, as in a photograph, for example.

HAMLET

HAMLET'S FATHER IS DEAD AND DENMARK HAS CROWNED A NEW KING. CONSUMED BY GRIEF, HAMLET STRUGGLES TO EXACT REVENGE WITH DEVASTATING CONSEQUENCES.

HAMLET is Shakespeare's most iconic work. Exploding with big ideas it is the ultimate play about loyalty, love, betrayal, murder and madness.

GROUNDED

BY GEORGE BRANT

SHE'S A HOT-ROD F16 FIGHTER PILOT. SHE'S PREGNANT. HER CAREER IN THE SKY IS OVER.

Now, she sits in an air-conditioned trailer in Las Vegas flying remote-controlled drones over the Middle East. She struggles through surreal 12-hour shifts far from the battlefield, hunting terrorists by day and being a wife and mother by night.

Grounded is a gripping, compulsive play that flies from the heights of lyricism to the shallows of workaday existence. This extraordinary story targets our assumptions about war, family, and what it is to be a woman.

CROCODILES

BY LEE MATTINSON

IN A SLEEPY SEASIDE TOWN, CORNELIA GLASS IS BUSY SPINNING YARN.

Witches are burning in the town centre. Crocodiles lurk in the shallows. Boys who go to the big city are skinned alive by tramps.

Cornelia's older son, Rudolph, must give up Punch and Judy to work in the local factory. Matilda his wife is secretly penning her first romantic novel. And baby granddaughter Lucy can see into the future. But when Vincent Glass comes home from his glitzy TV job in the city, the stories that once knitted the family together are in danger of smashing them to smithereens.

Lee Mattinson's dark new play CROCODILES is a ferocious Northern fable, a world where strange things are normal, and normal things are very strange.

Extension activity

Focus on your set text and research the interpretations suggested by the covers used on different editions of the play. Go to Amazon, or another online bookstore – or to a real bookshop – and look at the various covers available. You could think not just about different publishing companies, but also about different audiences. For example, are there older editions that show the social values of the time? Are there editions aimed specifically at students or younger audiences? In other words, how do the publishing companies themselves set the stage for the plays?

Activity

When you have finished looking at the texts above, turn your attention to your set text. Write some new promotional copy for the play you are studying. Try to give an indication of the story without explaining it all, and aim to make your play sound as exciting as possible in order to attract an audience. Write no more than 100 words.

Drama and genre

All the set texts – and all the texts being promoted above – have strong storylines that include elements of suffering. A classical tradition in drama dating back to ancient Greece is that of **tragedy**, which in classical form involved the depiction of human suffering with the idea that the audience could learn from witnessing human actions and their consequences.

As we have seen with the terms 'fiction' (in Chapter 2) and 'drama' (in this chapter), there are often connections between everyday uses of a term and its classical, more traditional reference. A search of the British National Corpus for the term 'tragedy' found the following:

- 'It is the second *tragedy* to hit the family in nine months.' (*Daily Mirror* article)
- 'But *tragedy* struck again in 1970 when Jochen Rindt, Chapman's third world champion, was killed at Monza.' (non-fiction book about motor racing)
- 'Corry was affected by personal *tragedy* following the bombing.' (Belfast news article)
- 'She was quite perfect and that those eyes could not see was a great *tragedy*, one that Maggie felt deeply at that moment.' (romantic novel)
- 'The *tragedy* is that Offiah did some very good promotional work in Gateshead a couple of days before the game — and then blew all the goodwill.' (*Daily Mirror* sports article)
- 'I don't think you'll and I suppose I make no apologies for including it, because I think we are all very well aware of the terrible *tragedy* that is happening in in Yugoslavia It's not not an anthem that I would have recognized, erm, I was fortunate to go to Yugoslavia on, I think, two occasions, in happier times, and it saddens me tremendously, to see, on the television, to hear on the radio, to read in the newspapers, just what has happened to what was emerging as, not only a very beautiful, but a very successful country' (from a radio broadcast)
- 'Smiling nurse in car smash *tragedy*' (headline from *Liverpool Echo*)

As you can see, regardless of whether the text is spoken or written, whether it is from a newspaper article, a novel or a radio programme, the term 'tragedy' implies a serious event with powerful consequences for those involved. In the examples above, you'll also note that contrasts are drawn between the tragedy mentioned as the main focus of the comment and another event or quality. In the first three examples, the tragedy is the second misfortune to occur. In all the other examples, tragedy is highlighted by being contrasted with something positive: the beauty of a person's eyes; the good behaviour of a rugby player; a successful country; a smiling victim. It is as if the idea of tragedy is made more powerful when the fortunes of a person or a place have fallen from a great height.

Classical Greek tragedy centred on the idea of a central figure (seen as a **tragic hero**) being implicated in his or her own tragic fate, through making a mistake or misjudgement. Sometimes this was seen to be the result of wilful pride (termed **hamartia** in Greek drama) or another character flaw. This created an emotionally charged context for the audience, because they could see the extent of a character's fall from grace. The approach to tragedy in more modern times can involve ideas about the circumstances that surround the characters in a play as much as the nature of the characters themselves.

Activity

1. Think about our modern ideas about figures in the public eye and how we react to their misfortunes. For example, think about our attitudes to celebrities. Do we still have the classical idea of a tragic story being more powerful when the person involved has been very successful? Is someone's downfall seen as more dramatic if he or she appears to have been partly responsible for it?

2. Think about the TV programmes and films you've seen where a tragedy is part of the story. Are there many examples where the tragedy is the result of a tragic hero's mistake or character flaw? Or are modern tragedies more likely to be the result of circumstances (such as natural disasters, poverty, diseases)?

3. Do we still have many stories that involve **heroes** and **villains**? What about **superheroes** and **anti-heroes**?

4. Now think about your set text.

   a. Are there characters in your play whose fate is partly or wholly the result of their own actions?

   b. To what extent are circumstances beyond the characters' control responsible for what happens in the play?

   c. Are there characters in the play who qualify as 'heroes' or 'villains'? Or are things not so clear cut? In order to think about this question, read Ben Bova's 'tips for writers' below, where he sets out his views about villains. Do you agree with him?

In the real world there are no villains. No one actually sets out to do evil. Yes, there are madmen and murderers and rapists and crooked politicians and greedy land developers and all sorts of villainous behaviors. But each of those people believes that he is doing what is necessary, and maybe even good […]

There are no villains cackling and rubbing their hands in glee as they contemplate their evil deeds. There are only people with problems, struggling to solve them […]

You could write *Hamlet*, for example, from the viewpoint of Claudius, the king who murdered Hamlet's father (his own brother) and married his widow. You might even make a truly powerful story about a man who loved his brother's wife too much, and dared to do what he did to win her.

But he wouldn't be a villain.

Dramatic structure

Genre in plays is not simply about definitions of types of drama or about different types of character. It is also about the way plays are structured. You saw in Chapters 1–3 that there are structures that typify both real-world

Key terms

Anti-hero. A figure who is not expected to show courage or any other qualities normally ascribed to a hero, but who does so eventually.

Hamartia. Deriving from Greek, this word is used to suggest a tragic weakness or flaw that leads to a protagonist's downfall. Although often identified as a single weakness, it can be more complex than this.

Superhero. A hero with superhuman powers.

Villain. A stereotypical bad character in stories that have very black and white, simple concepts of 'good' and 'evil'.

Did you know?

The term '**villain**' comes from Latin via French and originally meant a 'farmhand' (someone attached to a Roman estate, which was called a 'villa'). The connection between social class and perceptions of bad behaviour therefore goes back a long way. Do we still portray this idea in modern stories?

texts and literary texts. So, just as prose fiction has paragraphs and poetry has **stanzas**, drama typically has 'acts' and 'scenes'. The idea of typicality is important, because not every play has the same number of acts and scenes, and literary authors are constantly trying new formats. For example, one of the set texts, Kinnear's *The Herd*, has no conventional divisions of this kind.

Different scholars and critics over the years have proposed different kinds of 'ideal' structure for drama. In ancient Greece, the ideal in Aristotle's *Poetics* was a three-part structure, with a beginning, middle and end. In ancient Rome, the writer Horace in his *Ars Poetica*, advocated five acts. In modern times, there is tremendous variation and, just as poetry and prose comes in many different shapes and sizes, plays do not have to conform to any set structure in order to count as drama.

One writer who suggested not just the number of stages appropriate for drama but also what those stages should consist of was the 19th-century German playwright and novelist Gustav Freytag. His *Die Technik des Dramas* focused on the classical drama of ancient Greece and on Shakespearean drama, but critics have used it to analyse the structure of modern plays too. Freytag proposed a five-part structure with a turning point in the middle, as follows:

1. ***Exposition***: we are introduced to the basic elements of the play, including setting, characters and aspects of the major conflict that will drive the narrative.

2. ***Rising action***: once the main characters have been established, events are developed and conflicts become more complicated.

3. ***Climax***: this is the turning point of the narrative – characters may be in danger or the possibility of resolving the conflict seems unlikely.

4. ***Falling action***: characters respond to the climax and begin to address issues connected with the conflict.

5. ***Resolution***: loose ends are tied up, outcomes (happy or sad) are revealed and conflicts are concluded (although they may not be resolved).

Other practitioners and critics – for example, Yves Lavandier – have suggested that many modern plays follow the older tradition of Aristotle's three-part structure. Lavandier's timeline is as follows:

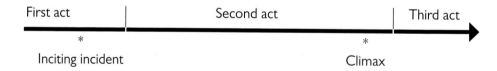

Inciting incident   Climax

> ### Activity
> Look at the structure of your set text. Does it follow any of the patterns above, either in terms of numbered acts and scenes, or in terms of what happens in different parts of the play? If not, write your own timeline for your play, with notes on what happens at each stage you identify.

Now that you have thought a little about the structure of your set text, focus on how the play begins. The overriding theme for all of the plays as described in the specification is conflict – and conflict of different kinds will always provide the basis for exam questions.

But is there some idea of conflict right from the start? Advice for would-be literary authors is often to plunge the reader or audience into the middle of the action, as this is much more likely to capture their interest than a long, slow build-up from a standing start. Ben Bova, quoted below, calls this idea 'the narrative hook' and, although he talks here principally about prose fiction, the same ideas can be applied to drama:

> It is vitally important to capture the reader's interest on the first page of your story. On the first line, preferably. This is called 'the narrative hook'.
>
> It's like fishing. You want to hook that reader so thoroughly that she can't let go of your story until it's ended.
>
> The best way to do this is by starting your story in the midst of brisk, exciting action. Start in the middle! Don't waste time telling the reader how your protagonist got into the pickle he's in. Show the protagonist struggling to get free. You can always fill in the background details later.
>
> Particularly in a novel, it's tempting to 'set the scene,' explain the protagonist's background, describe how she got to where she is. Cut all that out. Or at least save it for later. Start in the midst of action. Hook the reader right away or you won't hook him at all.
>
> In a short story there simply isn't time for static explanations. All the background details have to be worked in through action or dialogue. Show what they are doing, don't tell what they did.

Activity

Focus on the way your set text begins.

1. How closely does the beginning seem to put you, as the audience, into the middle of some ongoing action? Is it constructed to make you feel as though the action was already under way before you 'arrived' as viewers/readers?

2. How much of the play's later conflicts are foreshadowed in the opening scene?

Drama and themes

The set plays all share the common theme of conflict. But there are, of course, many types of conflict. The plays also share domestic settings, but that doesn't mean that the plays are only about issues within households.

Earlier in this chapter, you focused on a specific character and you listed the conflicts that character had with others throughout the play. You also looked at a specific episode where that character was in conflict and you studied the moves the characters made to position themselves and others. Now it's time to expand those ideas and think more broadly about all the characters and issues that are raised by the play as a whole.

For any story to be relevant beyond its own specific point of reference, it has to connect with some themes that we all recognize as significant in our lives. If you look back at the promotional material you studied (pages 156–157), you will see that several themes within the larger idea of conflict are advertised, including the following:

- death
- wealth and inheritance
- alcohol problems
- marital problems
- grief

- revenge
- loyalty and betrayal
- love and loss
- murder
- madness

- war
- conflicting gender roles
- violence
- specific cultural tensions and issues.

These themes are addressed via the actions of the characters; they arise from how the story unfolds and from the personal stake that each character has in the story. To think about the themes in your set text, therefore, you need to think about how your particular story unfolds and how each of the characters behaves throughout the play. You also need to think about how any conflicts are resolved – or not.

Activity

1. Look back at the promotional material you wrote earlier for your set text. What themes did you advertise?

2. Look again at your set text. Are there further themes that you could add now that you are expanding your ideas? Are there any ideas from the list above that also emerge from your set text?

3. Now think about all of the characters in the play. How do the themes you have identified link with the actions and nature of the characters? For example, do any of the characters benefit or learn from the conflicts that arise in the play? Are the issues that are presented in the play ever resolved, and in whose interests?

One way to map out your ideas is to do this visually. For example, take a list of themes and attach relevant characters to it, or make a list of characters and attach themes to it.

Drama and interpretation

Clearly, you will be able to find a wealth of interpretive material online telling you what your play 'means'. But be wary about sources that appear to give you easy answers. Interpretation is a very fluid concept and you will always be credited for seeing things in an open-minded way, recognizing that there is more than one way in which a text can be understood.

You can, of course, access sources of information about any playwright. You might, for example, learn more about the writer by reading some more of his or her plays. This could help you to see whether repeated themes emerge in those other works and how conflicts are treated there. You could also learn much about the context of the writer's life and the social values that were prevalent at the time of writing. Be aware, though, that it is problematic to pin down the themes of the play to a fixed point in time. We have already said that for plays to achieve a continuing audience, their themes need to go beyond a very specific setting and be relevant to people in different times and places. Ideas about family inheritance, about loyalty and betrayal, about love and war, and all the other themes that your work in this chapter may have listed, are not limited to one particular time or place. At the same time, plays written at a certain point in time and from a certain cultural viewpoint will have a set of values that may be very different from contemporary perspectives, and it is important to recognize that.

You are working from a playscript and of course it will be beneficial to see how that script is realized by going to see a live theatre performance or by watching a filmed version. Always remember that, although your interpretation of the play will undoubtedly be enhanced and enriched by your experience of performances, you have to come back to the original script in the discussions you write for your exam answers. However, recognizing the different ways in which actors, directors and producers re-interpret dramatic stories can give you some insights into the power of the original story to address issues of relevance, regardless of time and place. For example, the film *'O'* is a modern reworking of *Othello*, locating the themes of race and power within an American high school, where 'O' is a basketball player named Odin. *Blue Jasmine* takes *A Streetcar Named Desire* as its inspiration and transports its central figure – a Manhattan socialite fallen on hard times – to the San Francisco of 2013.

The performance of *Hamlet* advertised in the flyer you studied on page 157 is a re-working of the play with female actors in four of the male roles, including that of Hamlet himself, who is played by Maxine Peake (an actor who has featured in many TV roles, including *Silk* and *The Village*). The flyer maintains that this shift is right for the time and place of the performance:

> Every Hamlet is defined by the actor. In this stripped back, fresh and fast-paced version, Maxine Peake creates a Hamlet for now, a Hamlet for Manchester.

All these versions are fascinating re-interpretations, showing that some plays have themes that transcend individual places, times and even people. From the point of view of your exams, enjoy these versions and take insights from them, but remember that in your assessments you need to work from the original written scripts and not from particular performances.

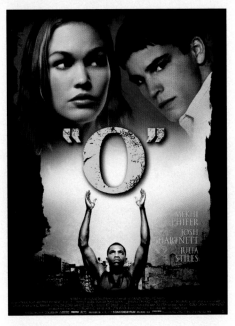

The film *'O'* is a modern reworking of *Othello*

The film *Blue Jasmine* takes *A Streetcar Named Desire* as its inspiration

REVIEW YOUR LEARNING

Try to answer the following questions:

- What makes a story a drama rather than just a set of events?
- What aspects of spoken interaction can you look for in analysing a drama extract?
- How is your set play structured?
- What are some of the conflicts that occur in your set play? Between which characters?
- What are the major themes in the play? To what extent is the story one of tragedy?

References

Ben Bova's tips for writers can be found at: http://benbova.com/tips2.html [Accessed 6.12.14.]

Freytag, G. (2004) [1863]. *Technique of the Drama*. University Press of the Pacific.

Lavandier, Y. (2005). *Writing Drama: a comprehensive guide for playwrights and scriptwriters*. Clown & L'enfant.

Further reading

Culpeper, J. (1998), *Exploring the Language of Drama*. London: Routledge

Edgar, D. (2009), *How Plays Work*. Nick Hern Books

Part 3:
Making Connections

Introduction

The coursework element of the English Language and Literature A level course is different in two significant ways from other parts of your study so far. First, coursework allows you to work independently, drafting and editing your writing until you are satisfied with it, rather than responding to set questions under exam conditions. And secondly, it allows you to make an independent choice about the literary and non-literary material you work with. These differences are liberating, but they are also challenging and can feel a little unsettling as you begin your coursework investigation.

The AQA English Language and Literature specification describes your coursework in the following way:

Making Connections

This part of the subject content focuses on language use in different types of text. It is called 'Making Connections' because it requires students to make active connections between a literary text and some non-literary material. The connections must be based either on a chosen theme or on the idea that particular linguistic strategies and features may occur in the different types of material.

It also says this about literary and non-literary material:

For the purposes of this specification, literary texts are defined as those that are drawn from the three main literary genres of prose fiction, poetry and drama.

Texts prescribed for study for the examined units may not be chosen, but further texts by the same authors or from a similar source are acceptable.

The nature of non-literary material to be collected depends entirely on the focus of the task. A wide range of everyday texts and discourses in different genres and modes is possible. The non-literary material needs to qualify on the basis of forming a good source of data for students to use in their investigations.

Making a start

The specification guidance above makes it clear that you are not allowed to do your investigation on any book that you have studied for the examined units. But you may investigate texts by the same author and there is nothing to stop you applying some of the techniques you have learned in studying a set text to another text by the same writer. In fact, that would be a very good use of what you have learned – or are learning, if you start investigating during the course rather than at the end.

For example, if you have enjoyed Arthur Miller's *All My Sons*, which is on the drama list, you could investigate *The Crucible*; if you have enjoyed Shakespeare's *Othello*, you could investigate *Macbeth*; if you have enjoyed Carol Ann Duffy's poetry, you could focus on another of her collections, *The World's Wife*.

Those examples refer to particular writers, but you may also have become interested in particular genres of writing, rather than the work of single authors.

This chapter will help you understand the non-exam assessment (coursework) requirements for A level English Language and Literature. By the end of this chapter you should understand:

- what the English Language and Literature investigation is
- how the investigation should be organized
- how the investigation is assessed.

Chapter 9 will give you some hands-on practical experience of different kinds of possible investigations, using each of the three literary genres of poetry, prose-fiction and drama.

Looking ahead

The ability to study independently and to direct your own research is highly valued by universities. Your investigation will be a practical example of your skills, and you can discuss it in interviews or on application forms.

Link

The World's Wife is referred to in Chapter 5 as an example of a text that overturns traditional perspectives and offers insights into the way gender is represented: we hear from Queen Herod, Mrs Quasimodo and the Kray Sisters.

Key term

Magic realism. A genre of writing in which magic or unreal events impinge upon the representation of an otherwise realistic world.

For example, the prose-fiction texts set for study all involve fantasy elements and, if you wanted to pursue that type of literature, you might look at writers in the **magic realism** tradition, such as Angela Carter. Margaret Atwood's *The Handmaid's Tale* is another example of a set text in a fantasy tradition, termed **dystopian** – foretelling disastrous future events, as a kind of warning. There are many examples of fiction in that tradition, from George Orwell's *1984* to Dave Eggers' *The Circle*, which is all about Internet surveillance.

You do not have to focus on something that has arisen from the set texts you have studied, however. An important aspect of the investigation is that it has to sustain your interest for a considerable amount of time, because doing any research requires planning and working over time. For that reason, it may be better to look for something fresh and new, or think about books that you have been meaning to read and that are nothing to do with the examined set texts. Be aware, though, that any literary text you choose for your investigation needs to be seen as a challenging read: you will not be able to focus on teenage fiction or writing for children. You will need to take advice from your teacher or tutor about the suitability of any text you choose.

Where next?

The investigation isn't just about analysing a piece of literature. It is about comparing literary and non-literary texts on a common theme, or for their use of particular linguistic strategies and features. Having thought a little about your experience of literature on your course so far, you need to turn your attention to the idea of non-literary material.

Looking ahead

Keep a reading diary, listing any books you have read or are planning to read. Make some notes for yourself on what you think of the books.

You will have experienced a wide range of non-literary material in studying the AQA Anthology *Paris*. This collection includes published texts that are classified as non-fiction, such as journalism, letters and memoirs; but there are also texts that never existed as published books, such as pieces of advertising and other promotional material, some in multimodal formats; and there are texts that have more private or personal starting points, such as natural conversation and blogs. There are texts aimed at different audiences, produced at different times, using different modes of communication and with different purposes. This collection therefore gives you a good sense of the scope within the category 'non-literary'.

Just as you are not allowed to use set texts in your coursework, for the same reasons you are not allowed to use the non-literary texts from the Anthology *Paris* as part of your investigation. However, studying the different non-literary genres should have opened your eyes to the possibilities around you for choosing material. Here is a list of some of the non-literary material that we see in everyday life:

- 'old' paper-based media such as newspapers, advertising and magazines
- 'old' sound and visual media such as radio and TV
- 'new' digital media such as websites, blogs, emails, SMS, Internet chat, online games and social media sites
- spoken language of all kinds – spontaneous conversations, speeches, and interviews; these use occupational **registers** such as those of teachers or lawyers, regional dialect and different Englishes, and include male and female speech and spoken rituals such as those at weddings and funerals
- interpersonal communication in the form of letters and greetings cards

- information texts about places or people
- persuasive leaflets and flyers
- other published non-fiction texts such as history texts, science texts, recipe books, books about sport, autobiographies, travel books, books about hobbies and pastimes
- instruction manuals for making or assembling things
- signs and **symbols** of various kinds.

The non-literary category can also include fragments of language that you collect yourself in the form of data. This could consist of a list of examples rather than a continuous text.

> **REMEMBER**
>
> Your non-literary material doesn't have to be extensive. The key factor in its selection is that it enables you to create a good focus for your investigation.

Some investigations suggested in the AQA specification

Some more detailed examples of investigations described below are given in Chapter 9, which adopts a step-by-step approach to the work of investigation – showing how it might work for some specific examples.

A comparison of openings in a novel and an autobiography

The idea of this type of investigation is to compare the job that literary and autobiographical texts have to do at the start. Do they focus on different things? What elements are present, and what is not covered in each? What perspectives are given?

An exploration of real and fictional events

Events in literature have to convince us as readers that they are credible. You saw in Chapter 2 how readers make inferences from their own experiences when they read a piece of fiction. So how are real-world events described in fiction, and how do they compare with the real version? For this type of investigation, you could focus on a particular type of event – e.g. a wedding, a party, a dinner, a journey, a holiday, an occupational setting, a romance, a crime – and compare how examples are treated in a literary text and some non-literary material.

There are various sources for the 'real-life' versions, including factual accounts in autobiographical texts or academic non-fiction, as well as material that you collect yourself. You could, for example, collect the scripted wording of a wedding ceremony or a transcript of how it actually happened, a transcript of talk at a party or dinner, a speaker's description of a journey, a piece of travel writing or a holiday brochure, some examples of occupational register, some published (or unpublished) love letters, some news coverage of a criminal case. There are endless **representations** in literature of real-life events and experiences that could be explored.

There are opportunities here to explore cultural variations in events and experiences too and to access texts written for a more academic purpose. For example, the anthropologist Kate Fox's *Watching the English* describes many 'typically English' events and behaviours, while Eva Hoffman's *Lost in Translation* describes how she had to learn about American society from the perspective of a Polish-Jewish immigrant. Both of these texts are non-fiction, so could be compared with literary **narratives**. Many literary texts focus on the experience

> **REMEMBER**
>
> You will come across many types of non-fiction in the reading you are doing in your other subject areas. Are there any interesting representations in, for example, history, geography, science, or social science books?

Link

In Chapter 2, some of the extracts you analysed are from books that talk about the experience of being an immigrant – for example, *Americanah*, by the award-winning author Chimamanda Ngozi Adichie.

! REMEMBER

Being open-minded means examining your own expectations as well as those in society at large. You are not looking to 'prove' that literary and non-literary texts are the same nor are you looking to prove that they are different. Just report on what you find.

Did you know?

Lancaster University has an Edwardian Postcard Project, where you can learn about the history of postcard writing. There is a link on the website where you can hear an academic, Dr Julia Gillen, who researches **linguistics** from a communication perspective, talking about the collection. Go to http://www.lancaster.ac.uk/fass/projects/EVIIpc/

of immigrants arriving and trying to make sense of a new culture, such as Timothy Mo's *Sour Sweet* or Andrea Levy's *Small Island*.

Representations of particular themes in literary and non-literary sources

A theme goes beyond a particular event and refers to an idea that recurs. The topic of Paris, in the AQA Anthology, is an example of a theme. Literary and non-literary texts might have particular descriptions that you could compare, such as landscape, the weather and seasons, food, specific experiences or emotions. Remember that literary texts include poetry and drama as well as fiction, so you can draw on a wide range of different forms. For example, how does the representation of landscape in a literary text compare with that in a walking guide, or 'literary' weather with a weather forecast? In these comparisons, you are not trying to compare like with like, but to show how language can vary according to different purposes and **contexts**. But be open-minded: you might find that some literary and non-literary texts have more in common than you think. For example, many media texts, such as newspapers and advertisements, make use of the same kind of creative, rule-breaking strategies that you find in texts that we call 'poetic'.

An exploration of the idea of character in literature and in other texts

What do we mean when we talk about a 'character'? The term is used in everyday speech as well as discussion of literary constructions, and in real life we normally mean that someone has a distinctive personality. How is this idea constructed in a literary text, and how is the same idea used in texts such as obituaries, personal ads or social-media profiles, where people are offering pen portraits of themselves or others? What characteristics are included and omitted?

How does storytelling work in different modes?

In Chapter 1, you looked at real stories and stories told in speech and online. You were given a framework for oral storytelling that appears to give spoken narratives a predictable shape. Does this framework work the same way in literary texts, or are there other factors at play? For example, is the book jacket of a literary text the equivalent of the **abstract** we have in spoken stories?

An exploration of the use of non-literary genres within literary texts

Literary texts can sometimes incorporate representations of non-literary texts within their overall narrative. For example, sometimes the characters in a novel send each other letters or postcards, telegrams or memos, SMS or emails, depending on the era in which the novel was written. How are these non-literary texts represented? Are they realistic, or a 'literary' version of the real thing?

An exploration of speech features in literature and in real-world communication

Chapters 1 and 2 looked extensively at aspects of spoken language in real life and in fiction. How do literary texts express the idea of different speakers? What features of real talk are retained, and which are not taken up? How are different varieties of English represented, compared with the real thing?

An exploration of new language in literature and non-literary contexts

Some literary texts – e.g. science fiction – present worlds where forms of language seem very different. This is done in order to construct a sense of an alien world, allowing us to think about alternative realities. Earlier, **dystopian** fiction was mentioned, and there is a long tradition of this type of literature, stretching at least as far back as Jonathan Swift's *Gulliver's Travels*.

But we also have 'new language' in everyday life: 2014 saw the arrival of 'selfie' and 'upcycle' to name just two new coinages. How do new forms of language work in fantasy fiction and in real life? Does new language in real life make us think differently? What are the connections between language and thought? Do we have the kinds of slogans in contemporary society that are used in books such as *1984* and *The Handmaid's Tale*?

What is 'literariness'?

This topic doesn't feature in AQA's specification; there is limited room in official documents, so you shouldn't regard any list, including this one, as definitive. But this topic presents a puzzle that no one has really solved. There is no agreed definition of what literature is or what literary features are. When we think of literary features, this is often with reference to aspects such as **sound symbolism** (**alliteration**, **onomatopoeia**) or **metaphor**. But these features can be found in everyday speech as well as in most media texts, such as newspaper headlines.

An interesting investigation would therefore be to set up a test for readers in which you ask them to read two passages on a similar theme – one from a literary and the other from a non-literary text. Can they spot the difference and what rationale do they give for saying which is which? Another way to investigate the same question would be to focus on a literary text, identify some of its most significant literary features, then try to find examples of those features in the everyday texts that surround us.

> **! REMEMBER**
>
> Your non-fiction data doesn't have to be continuous prose; it can consist of lists of examples. Here are some real political slogans from recent history: *British Jobs for British Workers; Back to Basics; Make Love Not War; Yes We Can; Think Globally, Act Locally.*

> **Research idea**
>
> Go to the website below, where there is a collection of tabloid headlines. Choose a range of headlines that illustrate different forms of creative language play and classify the different language strategies being used. Why do you think the writers chose to use language in this way? Would you call any of these uses 'literary' language? Why/why not? http://www.mcgarvey.co.uk/2007/11/22/best-tabloid-headlines/ ●

Making links

Now that you have a sense of some possibilities, you need to start thinking about making links. A good way to do this is in a group situation, if possible.

Activity

1. In a group, pool your ideas about your wider reading (all the books beyond your set texts) and make two lists: one list for literary texts, and one for non-fiction and other non-literary texts. If you are in any doubt about the classification, look, for example, at how a book is classified on the back cover, or ask your teacher or a librarian.

   Even at this point, just from collecting some titles, interesting questions arise about how different texts work. For example, do literary and non-literary texts have similar, or very different, titles? If you have any of the texts in front of you, are there differences in the ways in which the two categories are sold – in the design work, the author biography, the blurbs – that give you a taster of the story or topic?

2. When you have finished your lists, think about each literary text in terms of its content and its ideas. What events are in the book? What themes? Are there interesting aspects of language in the book? For each text, make some notes. A useful way to do this is to divide up the work and for each person or pair to concentrate on a different text or texts.

   When you pool your findings, you will have many ideas about literary texts that you can take forward.

3. When you have finished your work on literary texts, do the same activity for non-fiction and other non-literary material. This might not be so straightforward, simply because it's harder to recall all the texts that you read (and write) on an everyday basis. Try to include everything, from published books of non-fiction to notes on the fridge door, from online newsfeeds and 'mini-stories' in free newspapers to greetings cards, from emails, SMS, blog and social-media posts to sports reports. These examples are primarily written, so once you have finished this list, go on to examples of spoken language. Try to classify your examples of spoken language into **genres**, such as stories exchanged between friends, news reports, speeches, gossip, shop-counter interactions, family occasions, jokes, talks given in class and so on.

4. Once you have compiled your list of non-literary material, think about what is interesting or distinctive about the items. It might be aspects to do with genre. Perhaps they follow a certain pattern of features; some might be more planned than others; aspects of mode might work differently, with some entirely written, others spoken, but with variations within those broad categories. Some might be more publicly oriented, others more private and individual.

   Before you finish both lists, add in all the examples of literary and non-literary material that have been included in this textbook (leaving out any of the set text extracts).

5. You will now have a wealth of ideas – perhaps too many. Your task now is to see what connections you can make between one literary text and one example of non-literary material.

Your connections don't have to be complicated; in fact, the simpler they are, the better. So an example such as a connection between the way a literary author represents speech (perhaps focusing on fiction or drama) and the features of real speech would be fine.

The next section in this chapter will help you to understand the scope and focus required for this piece of work and how it will be assessed.

What does an investigation look like?

This coursework is not an extended essay. The specification clearly states that it is an independent investigation of 2,500–3,000 words. The piece of writing you complete is a report and there are clear guidelines to help you organize your work.

The title of your investigation is perhaps the most challenging aspect of your coursework, but it does not need to be finalized before you start, as you may refine your ideas and focus as a result of your findings. However, even at an early stage you need to avoid titles that suggest you will be able to prove a hypothesis, because this will not allow you as much scope in terms of your analysis of the texts. Words like 'an exploration of' or 'an analysis of' give you more opportunity to be flexible in the analysis section, where you will gain the majority of your marks; phrases like 'I hope to show that…' tend to lead to narrower, less-reflective analysis sections.

The specification suggests a possible order for the sections of the investigation, as follows (all outlined below): introduction and aims; review; analysis; conclusions; appendix; references. The word counts are given as a guide. There is an overall word count but how you divide that between the sections is up to you.

Introduction and aims (750 words)

In this initial section you need to demonstrate a considered understanding of all texts selected for study. You should explain why you have selected these texts and the decisions you have made about selection of material within the texts (especially how you have narrowed your choice for the literary text). You also need to demonstrate that you understand both texts fully, so a brief synopsis of the whole literary text is required in this section, as well as some contextual background and information about the non-literary choice. When you write about your literary text, don't just tell the story. Certainly explain how the part you have selected is drawn from the larger story, but focus on why this specific extract has been chosen.

Review (300–500 words)

In this section you need to show that you have read some secondary sources, offering a critical understanding of some of the key concepts and ideas you intend to explore in your investigation. For example, if your starting point is a novel that centres on a place such as Amsterdam, finding out everything there is to know about Amsterdam is not as important as understanding how different texts might create **representations** of places.

Remember that English Language and Literature is a joint course that brings together two subjects: it is not simply about literary texts nor is it simply about language as a source of information. Your analytical skills are language-based:

> **!** REMEMBER
>
> Writing a review is not like writing a book or music review. The reason for reviewing material is to say how the writer's ideas are relevant to what you are investigating – in other words, what he or she has said about your topic.

remember the language levels that were covered in the first part of this book. So your secondary sources for the Amsterdam example above could easily be drawn from language study, because there are many textbooks about how to analyse different texts. You should reference any texts carefully in the final section of the investigation.

Analysis (1,250 words)

The analysis of your material is central to the study. This section should have some subheadings showing how your analysis relates to the investigation title. These can be questions or statements, but should reveal a sense of development as the analysis progresses. The specification allows you to discuss the texts separately or together, but be aware that you will be given marks for comparison, so this must be demonstrated whatever your approach. You will need to provide textual evidence for your comments throughout this section.

Conclusions (200–500 words)

This section needs to reflect on your findings and how they link to your investigation title. You need to show that you have reached a conclusion about your analysis of the texts – one that goes beyond repeating your analysis section.

Appendix (no word count)

You need to provide copies of both texts in the forms you have chosen – not the complete novel or collection of poems, just the extracts you have worked with during the investigation.

References (no word count)

Your references should be alphabetical and set out in academic style. Where you have used web-based material, you should also provide the date you accessed the relevant pages.

How the investigation will be assessed

You will be awarded marks for your achievement across a range of Assessment Objectives. These are explained below and, for each one, there are questions you can ask yourself about your study. These are key points that you should keep in mind as you begin thinking about your coursework, because you will then be certain that your investigation has the potential to meet the criteria outlined in the mark scheme.

AO1

This Assessment Objective relates to a number of things. It rewards you for how you go about your study in the sense of how you tackle the area you have chosen (including any references to secondary sources). It rewards you for being able to identify and discuss the language features and patterns you observe in the texts. And finally, it rewards you for your ability to write coherently.

Questions

- Do I explain what I am trying to do in my investigation?

- Do I give examples of language use from the texts?

- Do I write clearly?

AO2

This Assessment Objective rewards you for being able to interpret the aspects of the texts you identify in AO1. Can you build up a picture of how the features relate to each other, to create a whole text that has meaning?

Question

● Do I just label and list features, or do I say what I think they mean and explain how they are being used?

AO3

This Assessment Objective rewards you for showing that you understand the different **contexts** of your texts and how those contexts have shaped the language use.

It shouldn't be difficult for you to gain these marks because the investigation is all about bringing together material from very different contexts.

Questions

● Do I say where each text is from, what it was for, who it was aimed at?
● Do I explore how their different contexts might have shaped their language use?

AO4

This Assessment Objective rewards you for your ability to make connections between the texts. This shouldn't be too difficult as the whole nature of the investigation is exactly that. However, if you analyse each of your texts separately, make sure that you devote some discussion to comparing and contrasting them.

Question

● Where do I discuss in my study how the texts relate to each other?

Some practical considerations

To ensure that there are no disasters with lost data or broken laptops during your coursework, make sure that you have at least two printed copies of both pieces of material in a form that you can work with. Use one for annotation and work, and keep the second for emergencies. You could also email the data to yourself as a safety precaution.

If you have transcribed spoken data, you should also make sure that you keep copies of web addresses or copies of the recordings. First, this will allow you to find it again, and secondly if your data is lost, you will have the date it was accessed as evidence or a recording that you can work from. Don't take the approach that 'this won't happen to me' – lost data is a nightmare for all concerned, so take sensible precautions to avoid it happening to you.

Before you start

Chapter 9 will look at some approaches to investigating literary and non-literary texts – offering some concrete examples and some ideas that could be developed from them. You could work through these within a classroom environment or independently – either approach will allow you to understand more about the process involved in completing an investigation.

Students often find investigations to be very challenging because they only attempt them once, often towards the end of the course, when time is short. A way to make this coursework seem less daunting is to practise the approaches and skills you need for investigating language and literature from the outset. Whilst working through this book you should have completed the many activities offered, and all of these tasks have been preparing you for the coursework, in a sense. If you haven't completed any of these tasks, particularly the research ideas, it would be worthwhile taking the opportunity to complete one or more before you begin thinking about the coursework in more detail, because this will give you a small, structured example of what research means in a practical sense.

You should also review the commentaries on many of the activities at the back of the book, because those that are written in continuous prose will give you a style model for how to write in an analytical way. The more use you make of all of these opportunities, the less likely you are to make mistakes in your 'real' piece of research. Although it is a cliché, practising your skills will improve your performance.

REVIEW YOUR LEARNING

Try answering the following questions:

- Why is the non-exam assessment (coursework) called 'Making Connections'?
- What types of material can you collect?
- What is the word count for the report and what guidance are you given on the sections required?
- How is your investigation assessed?
- What steps can you take to avoid risks and panics?

Further reading

Carter, R. and Goddard, A. (2015), *How To Analyse Texts: A Toolkit for Students of English*. London: Routledge

Themes and linguistic strategies

This chapter looks at the idea of themes and linguistic strategies as starting points for research in more detail – showing you the process of research and the various stages you will need to go through.

Using themes as an idea for comparison is something that you will be familiar with through your study of the AQA Anthology *Paris* and other set texts. But you should also be familiar with taking a language approach to texts of all kinds. The two ideas are not mutually exclusive: a theme is created from language choices and language has to be about something. So the difference here is not absolute, but one of emphasis. It simply means that your starting point may be different in each case.

Introductory section

The introduction of your research needs to show that you have studied a whole literary text. The idea of a 'whole text' means, in the case of a collection of short stories, the whole collection, and in the case of a collection of poems, all the poems in the collection.

But you don't have the luxury of many words in order to get across your knowledge to a reader of your work. Technically, your teacher is the first reader of your work, and then coursework is sampled by an external moderator in order to ensure fairness of marking between different schools and colleges. It is best to think of your reader as someone interested in your research topic but removed from the classroom context, rather than aiming your work at your teacher. This is because you might think your teacher knows everything about your topic so you don't need to explain. Think about an interested reader (or even better, ask a real person to be a reader) and aim your writing at him or her.

So your introduction needs to show your knowledge of a whole text in just 750 words. Clearly, the way *not* to do this is to go through each poem or story (or even one novel) in detail, item by item. What you need to do is briefly summarize the themes and ideas in the literary text and show why you have chosen to focus on the extract or poem that will be your research focus. Part of that explanation also needs to include why you have chosen the non-literary material too. But you don't need to go into as much detail about that material: briefly explaining its **context** will do.

Example 1

How is the theme of journeys represented in literary and non-literary material?

This example will use Larkin's *The Whitsun Weddings* collection of poems and a transcript from a video entitled 'My Favourite Railway Journeys' (made by a student for a media studies project). If we take Larkin's collection as an example of how you might go about using poetry as your literary material, then your first move after reading all the poems could be to summarize the themes in the collection. Summarizing this visually can be helpful, in the form of a diagram like that on the next page.

As outlined in Chapter 8, the specification guidance suggests that you can approach your investigation by either researching a theme or a linguistic strategy. This chapter offers you plenty of ideas and opportunities for practice, and will help you to understand:

- how themes and linguistic strategies can be used as the basis for comparison
- the scope and focus of possible investigations
- the types of non-literary material that it may be useful to collect
- how to transcribe spoken data for analysis
- how to go about analysis
- the role of secondary sources in the investigation.

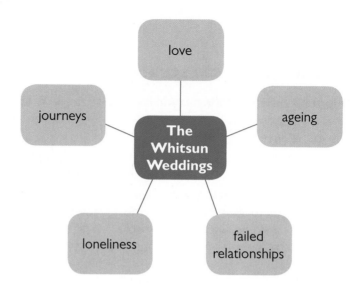

You would need to add the relevant poems to each part of the diagram and there may be further themes to add.

Although your diagram is useful at this early stage of thinking and planning, it might not be a very user-friendly way to present your ideas to your reader. So you would need to set them out in a more essay-like way, as in the following paragraph.

> Philip Larkin's collection of poems, *The Whitsun Weddings*, offers some insight into everyday human events such as train journeys ('The Whitsun Weddings', title poem), renting rooms ('Mr Bleaney'), getting old ('Self's the Man') and emotions such as love ('An Arundel Tomb') and loneliness ('Faith Healing'). Despite the fact that many critics argue that Larkin's poems often deal with unhappiness, *The Whitsun Weddings* has moments of humour as Larkin thinks about his past failed relationships ('Wild Oats'), and some moments of hope through young love ('The Whitsun Weddings'). As well as unhappiness, there are recurring themes throughout the collection such as the passing of time, unsatisfied love, isolation and fear of death.

Once you have mapped out the themes, it is easier to decide which one will provide you with enough material to compare with a non-literary text. The themes of journeys and self-reflection are central to the title poem in the collection ('The Whitsun Weddings') and ideas about travel are plentiful in non-literary texts, so as an initial idea this has plenty of scope. You could choose to compare this poem with a number of texts, such as examples of travel journalism or descriptions in holiday brochures.

However, there are also many examples of journeys and travel which have been described using a different mode. For example, speech presents a very interesting opportunity for research. The data below, collected by a media studies student making a piece of travel journalism, provides a clear point of comparison (the theme of travel) but also some points of contrast (spoken data, accompanied by visual images). You would be able to consider similarities and differences connected with **context**, audience and language use as well as the overall purposes of the literary and non-literary material.

The process of describing how you have selected your extracts forms part of your introduction and this demonstrates your understanding of a method of analysis (AO1). As well as explaining which poem you will focus on, you would need to explain how you reduced the amount of spoken data from a whole programme to a small, useable extract.

As outlined in the introductory chapter, transcribing spoken data is a skill and you need to allow yourself plenty of time to produce a completed transcript. In some ways this method of gathering data seems to be more demanding than choosing other materials, such as a written holiday advertisement or a travel guide, to compare with the poem. The advantage is that there will be many different characteristics for you to explore because of the spoken mode. Also, you will know your data very well by the time you have completed the transcript, which will save you some time when you begin analysing your data.

One of the most obvious differences between the two pieces of data is that they both have very distinct rules about layout. Poems can vary enormously, but visually they are usually set out in **stanzas** and have different layouts from prose texts. Transcripts are also set out differently from a traditional written text. Look at the following transcript of the first few lines of the media studies student's 'My Favourite Railway Journeys' video:

> Narrator: [*background music*] I'm on the train from Barrow [*image of train*] (.) a small town largely overlooked at the bottom of the Lake District (.) near the nuclear power station at Sellafield (.) the power station dominates the landscape (.) and even though I have seen some of the promotional materials [*images of nuclear power station*] (.) the very fact that it spoils the landscape on this beautiful (.) windswept (.) desolate coast [*images of coastline*] makes me sad

Activity

Read the transcript above and make a list of all of the characteristics that differ from a standard written text. What do these features add to the text?

A standard definition of a transcript is 'a written or printed version of material originally presented in another medium'. As outlined in the introductory chapter, the features you include in your transcript depend on what you will be using the text for. The transcript above does not include any information about prosodic features, because this comparison will focus on the theme of journeys. However, if you wanted to explore features such as volume, emphasis or changing intonation, there are some conventions that you can use in the box below.

> Words in CAPITALS mark a section of speech noticeably louder than that surrounding it.
>
> A question mark (?) indicates a rising inflection. It does not necessarily indicate a question.
>
> Pointed arrows (↑↓) indicate a marked rising or falling intonational shift. They are placed immediately before the onset of the shift.
>
> Underlined fragments indicate speaker emphasis.
> (Some transcribers use bold type for this.)

You will encounter different transcription conventions in academic papers, which should not worry you. The most important thing is to be consistent in the symbols you use. The symbols used here are from an academic field called 'Conversation Analysis'.

Extension activity

Go to Lonely Planet's YouTube channel (https://www.youtube.com/user/LonelyPlanet) and select a piece of travel journalism in video format. Transcribe a section and mark the features that you consider important in carrying its meaning (including any prosodic features, music and non-verbal communication).

Does poetry have any equivalent to the features you have marked, or does it communicate its meaning in a completely different way?

Working with transcripts also presents a further challenge in terms of the quantity of data needed; this is dependent on what you are hoping to analyse in the data. The example above is narrated in the main by a single character, so the transcript is fairly dense and contains many features for analysis. In general, if you are dealing with a monologue you will need slightly less speech than you would if the spoken data was a dialogue, with more speakers and frequent short turns.

The extract below represents approximately 1 minute 30 seconds of the programme – which is much shorter than you might imagine. Therefore, it is crucial that you are sensible in terms of the amount of speech you attempt to transcribe for your investigation, because you will be transcribing for extraordinary amounts of time if you are overly ambitious.

Here is the opening of the student's 'My Favourite Railway Journeys' video, continued further:

Narrator: [*background music*] I'm on the train from Barrow [*image of train*] (.) a small town largely overlooked at the bottom of the Lake District (.) near the nuclear power station at Sellafield (.) the power station dominates the landscape (.) and even though I have seen some of the promotional materials [*images of nuclear power station*] (.) the very fact that it spoils the landscape on this beautiful (.) windswept (.) desolate coast [*images of coastline*] makes me sad

[*images of coastline continue for some time without narration*]

Narrator: I was told by a passenger waiting for this train (.) that it is only kept running for the Sellafield workers (.) so without the nuclear power industry (.) I would not be able to make this journey (.) perhaps there's one bonus then [*images of fields in the foreground and power station in the distance*] (4.0) there are many more reasons to visit this area of England but (.) to be honest (.) this is not the type of journey I would recommend if you don't like solitude (.) dramatic weather (.) or towering hills [*narrator gets off the train while talking to camera*]

Platform announcer: platform four (.) platform four (.) all those on the train to Penrith [*inaudible*] Lancaster (.) Preston (.) calling at Manchester Piccadilly (.) Stockport

Narrator: [*speaking on train platform*] luckily (.) I have taken this trip because of all three things (.) it's a nostalgic journey for me because I spent many childhood holidays camping in the Lakes (.) and I am here to meet a family friend (.) hi (.) hello [*addressing figure waiting on platform*]

A further consideration is whether you want to use a transcript of consecutive narration, or take short extracts from different moments in the programme. It is clear that as the extract above ends, the narrator has begun a conversation with a family friend. Although this is part of the video, it doesn't contain any description of the travel itself. Later, she is travelling again, so you could move forward in the narrative and rejoin it later in the journey:

Narrator: we're in Keswick now (.) and we're approaching the town centre (.) which consists of one bustling main street filled with tea shops (.) weary walkers (.) and a ubiquitous Fat Face shop [*visuals of main street looking up the hill, plus music*]

This approach could be repeated until enough data has been collected to compare with your poem. However, remember that although your data is exempted from the overall word count, you won't get more credit for having more data. You need to be able to analyse your data in detail. Therefore a couple of A4 pages of transcription of this type would probably provide you with enough features to compare with the poem 'The Whitsun Weddings'. Below (and on pages 180–181) is the whole poem, which you can also hear being read by Philip Larkin on http://www.youtube.com/watch?v=c9eTF6QNsxA

The Whitsun Weddings

That Whitsun, I was late getting away:
Not till about
One-twenty on the sunlit Saturday
Did my three-quarters-empty train pull out,
All windows down, all cushions hot, all sense
Of being in a hurry gone. We ran
Behind the backs of houses, crossed a street
Of blinding windscreens, smelt the fish-dock; thence
The river's level drifting breadth began,
Where sky and Lincolnshire and water meet.

All afternoon, through the tall heat that slept
For miles inland,
A slow and stopping curve southwards we kept.
Wide farms went by, short-shadowed cattle, and
Canals with floatings of industrial froth;
A hothouse flashed uniquely: hedges dipped
And rose: and now and then a smell of grass
Displaced the reek of buttoned carriage-cloth
Until the next town, new and nondescript,
Approached with acres of dismantled cars.

At first, I didn't notice what a noise
The weddings made
Each station that we stopped at: sun destroys
The interest of what's happening in the shade,
And down the long cool platforms whoops and skirls
I took for porters larking with the mails,
And went on reading. Once we started, though,
We passed them, grinning and pomaded, girls
In parodies of fashion, heels and veils,
All posed irresolutely, watching us go,

As if out on the end of an event
Waving goodbye
To something that survived it. Struck, I leant
More promptly out next time, more curiously,
And saw it all again in different terms:
The fathers with broad belts under their suits
And seamy foreheads; mothers loud and fat;
An uncle shouting smut; and then the perms,
The nylon gloves and jewellery-substitutes,
The lemons, mauves, and olive-ochres that

Marked off the girls unreally from the rest.
Yes, from cafés
And banquet-halls up yards, and bunting-dressed
Coach-party annexes, the wedding-days
Were coming to an end. All down the line
Fresh couples climbed aboard: the rest stood round;
The last confetti and advice were thrown,
And, as we moved, each face seemed to define
Just what it saw departing: children frowned
At something dull; fathers had never known

Success so huge and wholly farcical;
The women shared
The secret like a happy funeral;
While girls, gripping their handbags tighter, stared
At a religious wounding. Free at last,
And loaded with the sum of all they saw,
We hurried towards London, shuffling gouts of steam.
Now fields were building-plots, and poplars cast
Long shadows over major roads, and for
Some fifty minutes, that in time would seem

Just long enough to settle hats and say
I nearly died,
A dozen marriages got under way.
They watched the landscape, sitting side by side
– An Odeon went past, a cooling tower,
And someone running up to bowl – and none
Thought of the others they would never meet
Or how their lives would all contain this hour.
I thought of London spread out in the sun,
Its postal districts packed like squares of wheat:

> There we were aimed. And as we raced across
> Bright knots of rail
> Past standing Pullmans, walls of blackened moss
> Came close, and it was nearly done, this frail
> Travelling coincidence; and what it held
> Stood ready to be loosed with all the power
> That being changed can give. We slowed again,
> And as the tightened brakes took hold, there swelled
> A sense of falling, like an arrow-shower
> Sent out of sight, somewhere becoming rain.

How to begin analysing your data

Selecting your data is perhaps the most creative and interesting aspect of the investigation, and when you have your extracts ready to analyse, you will have a real sense of the potential of your research. However, this is the point where many students find it a challenge to move from thinking about the potential of the data into detailed analysis.

There are many different ways to approach this part of the research process, but students often lose sight of the 'big picture' because they get straight into looking at all of the tiny details of the language features first. Remember that this coursework investigation rewards you for a range of Assessment Objectives, and AO1 – which rewards you for identifying language features – is just one of four objectives. Another objective is your ability to see how meanings are shaped in texts (AO2). This means having a sense of any text as a whole.

You are also rewarded for AO3, which is all about understanding **context**, which means aspects such as audience, purpose, **mode** and **genre**. The remaining Assessment Objective, AO4, which is about connecting texts, forms the basis of what you are doing throughout the study – although you do still have to make connections between the texts in an explicit way.

Start with the big picture

Having selected the theme of journeys, the first question to ask is: How does the idea of a journey function in each text? What is it doing there? This question automatically triggers another question: What is the overall purpose of these two texts that feature journeys?

At this point, you could explore some secondary sources, if you haven't already done so earlier in the research process. These will be books and articles that offer academic insights: in this case, any material about Philip Larkin's poetry and any resources that might help you to analyse a media text. Be prepared to read widely: you could be reading literary criticism, media studies books, articles about humour and articles about travel literature, as well as books that help you analyse language. Some general resources are listed for you at the end of this chapter.

Once you have started thinking about the purpose and audience of the texts, you are really thinking about context. Other aspects of context are genre and mode. Of these, mode in particular – whether something is written for the page, written to be spoken, spoken or multimodal – seems to offer the most potential for saying interesting things about how these texts compare.

Look for language choices

The introductory chapter referred to different language levels that students of English Language and Literature need to be aware of: phonology, lexis and semantics, grammar, pragmatics, and discourse. These can form a helpful checklist for you when you start to look in more detail at the language choices made by the writers and speakers of your texts. But don't be tempted to plough through these areas one by one in great detail; be selective and focus on those aspects that are relevant. For example:

● Discourse refers to different genres, so could be relevant to a discussion of how each text adopts the conventions of its particular genre. For example, the poem has certain features in common with other examples of poetry; the student video has similar features to other pieces of travel journalism. Discourse also includes mode and there are many differences between the texts in their mode of communication.

● Pragmatics refers to the assumptions that lie behind language use and the social knowledge that underlies communication. The Larkin poem refers to newly married couples boarding the London train; the student video makes references to nuclear energy, and to 'the Lakes'.

● Lexis and semantics covers the vocabulary used in the texts and here you might be tempted to assume that just because the narrator in the video is speaking, she is more informal than Larkin. Is that really the case? This language level would also include the study of humour and taboo.

● Phonology might not look very promising as an area of focus, but if you discuss mode, you are automatically thinking about how sounds work in speech and how sounds are represented in writing.

Moving from analysis to writing

Not every detail that you identify in your analysis work will be needed for your written investigation. The investigation length is limited and you have approximately 1,250 words for this section. Therefore, once again you need to make some decisions about what to include: think about which evidence is important in terms of answering the research question.

 Activity

Imagine that the investigation we have been discussing is your coursework. Look back at Chapter 8, where you were given an approximate word count and some advice about the different sections that are needed in an investigation. Re-read the discussion in this chapter and write a plan for what you would cover in each section if you were carrying out this study.

Extension activity

Either:

Carry out this investigation and write it up as a practice for the real thing.

Or:

Choose a poetry collection, identify a theme and collect some non-literary material to compare it with. Then write a plan for what you would cover in your investigation.

Example 2

What linguistic strategies are used to create the idea of a 'character' in literary and non-literary material?

This example will compare prose-fiction with journalism or other non-fiction sources.

This approach has more of a linguistic starting point, because it asks how language choices produce the idea of a character's existence and a character's traits.

The word 'character' comes from ancient Greek (*kharaktār*), where it was the name of a tool used for stamping a mark on an object. You can see from this how it came to refer to a person's **identity**, real or imagined.

In the first part of this book, you focused on many aspects of narrative, including ideas about point of view, different narrators, and how speech and thought are conveyed. You will be able to use all of the skills you acquired in that part of the book in this more independent research work, where you choose your own data.

The idea of looking at how a character is constructed is probably more familiar to you from work in literature, perhaps at GCSE, than it is in language study, although any text you are asked to analyse has a **narrative voice** of some kind. At an earlier stage of your studies, you probably didn't see things in quite that way. However, now you have looked at the idea of non-literary material having not just one perspective, but many – in the AQA Anthology *Paris*, for example – you are in a better position to do justice to the way your chosen non-literary material represents the idea of a person's identity.

Whatever fiction you choose – and there are countless examples you can choose from – your starting point for thinking about how a character is realized in a novel is not so different from the starting point suggested for a collection of poetry. Your first task is to break the fiction down into some ideas about how a character is established. This can be usefully done via a visual representation like that on the next page.

Key term

Narrative voice. The way in which language is used by a writer to construct how a narrator sounds.

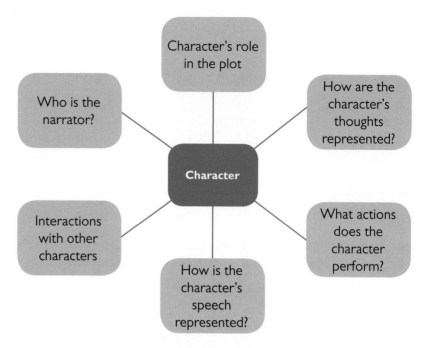

This will help you to offer a resumé of the story (which you have to do in your introduction) in a way that brings you quickly to the focus of your study: how a character is constructed.

Choosing a non-literary source

This is a more complex task for a number of reasons. For a start, there are likely to be some very variable descriptions of real-life people – unless your focus is on a single whole text, such as a biography or autobiography. Variation is not a problem, just something that you need to be aware of. In fact, it can lead to some interesting discussion about the differences between the idea of a literary character and the real-life equivalent.

A novelist is in control of the depiction of character in the same way as individual journalists are when they portray, for example, celebrities or criminals. However, different journalists can have very different perspectives, either because they work for newspapers with different **ideologies** or because times change and the same person is viewed in a different light: think about the ways in which recent high-profile figures, such as Jimmy Savile, Rolf Harris, Stuart Hall and Max Clifford, have been described. Someone in the future looking back at newspaper archives would notice a profound shift in the way these characters were portrayed before and after revelations about their activities.

Sports figures are particularly prone to variable descriptions because of the role they play in public life – often becoming symbols of national identity and achievement. This can be seen in the coverage of the tennis player Andy Murray. If you search his name on the Internet and look for articles written before he won Olympic gold and Wimbledon, he is constructed as a very different character from his post-victory persona. A turning point appeared to come at his most vulnerable moment, when he failed to win Wimbledon in 2012, after which the newspapers started to represent him as a fighter and passionate about his sport. Look at the following headlines, from the coverage at that time.

Key term

Ideology. A set of belief systems, attitudes and values.

> *Daily Express* (article by David Pilditch, 9.7.12): 'Tearful Andy Murray loses Wimbledon but wins over a nation.'

One year later, Murray is a British winner – making tennis history:

> *Daily Telegraph* (article by Paul Hayward, 7.7.13): 'After 77 years, the wait is over'

In the later stories, his 'Britishness' is emphasized and there's a suggestion that he will become part of the establishment. This is clearly the same individual who was represented as morose and Scottish in his early career.

Activity

Choose a well-known figure from a domain of public life, e.g. sport, music, TV, film, politics. Research the ways in which this figure has been portrayed in newspaper articles and online. Are there variations in the depictions or are the opinions and perspectives fairly consistent in their approach?

This discussion of variability in the non-literary texts that you have chosen relates directly to how you introduce your study (see Chapter 8), for it forms part of how you describe your methodology. There is no right or wrong way to approach your text selection, but you must be able to explain what you have done and say why you have done it.

For example, you might want to choose two extracts from a novel where the same character is seen very differently, as part of the way the story works. An example of this would be in *Gone Girl*, where readers are constantly unsettled by twists in the story and uncertainty about whether the different narrators are telling the truth. In this case, it might be a useful comparison to choose two non-literary sources that describe the same real person differently. Or you might decide to focus on the same kind of figure, seen consistently in one way in literary and non-literary material, and explore how that type of figure is treated. For example, there are many literary and non-literary depictions of crime – the latter including many 'true crime' stories in non-fiction books and also journalism about real criminals. Here, each of the sources could be explored via a single extract.

> **! REMEMBER**
>
> Your data doesn't count towards your overall word count, but if you have more data, there is more to cover in your analysis. Try to limit your data and don't take on too much.

Crimes and criminals

As an example of the depiction of a real criminal in the media, complete the following activity – about a GP called Harold Shipman who was discovered to be a mass killer. Dr Shipman killed many of his elderly patients in Hyde, Cheshire, during the 1990s. He was finally convicted in January 2000.

One of the clear contrasts between a **representation** such as this and the way in which a novel might describe a criminal is the use of **mode**.

Activity

Analyse the way in which the following webpage has represented Harold Shipman: http://news.bbc.co.uk/1/hi/in_depth/uk/2000/the_shipman_murders/news_and_reaction/default.stm

- Think about all the different aspects of the representation, not just the lexical items.
- Remember that language levels that were described in the introductory chapter included ideas about different types of **discourse** – different layouts and textual designs – as well as the types of language feature that are found in continuous prose.

How does the main BBC article referred to on the webpage represent Shipman?

A starting point for your analysis is provided below, in the form of a Wordle, which shows the prominence of different language items. Wordle images can help you to see the frequency of key lexical items and this gives a picture of the strongest **semantic fields** in the text. Are these the terms you would have expected to see in an article about a mass killer?

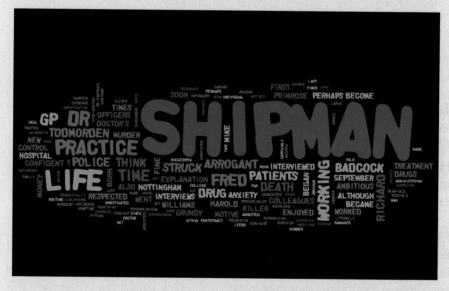

Take the original front page of the 'Shipman Files' website and produce a Wordle from that data. What are the differences in the distribution of the lexical items? What explanations can you offer for these differences?

Many thousands of crime novels feature murderers. That fact is interesting in itself: Why do we enjoy reading about bad people in the first place?

One of the decisions you could make in deciding on your novel is who the narrator of the story is. Crime novels vary considerably in whether we are given an external view of the criminal or whether the story is told partly or wholly from his or her perspective.

There are examples of both types of narration in the work of novelists such as Ruth Rendell (particularly when she is writing as Barbara Vine, who creates a

Link

You worked on the idea of different **narrators** in Chapters 1 and 2.

psychological perspective on her killers) and Ian Rankin. There are also fictional characters, such as Dexter in Jeff Lindsay's novels or Jack Reacher in novels by Lee Child, who are involved in considerable amounts of violence but who are presented as 'good-guy' avengers.

Example 3

What is the difference between the language of drama and everyday speech?

This example will use dramatic dialogue and monologue compared with real language use.

In earlier parts of this book, you have studied many of the language features that characterize spoken language. Here are some examples of that coverage:

- In the introductory chapter, you looked at two of the language levels – phonology and pragmatics – that are particularly related to speech.
- In Chapter 1, you looked at how people tell stories in speech. You worked on the AQA Anthology *Paris*, which illustrates many different modes, including speech.
- In Chapter 2, you looked at how speech is often represented in fiction.
- In Chapter 7, you looked at the constructed nature of dramatic dialogue as part of studying your set drama text.
- Earlier in this chapter, you looked at how even scripted speech (in the student video) relies on aspects of voice and other elements of sound in performance, as well as on images and non-verbal communication.

Therefore you have already learned a lot about how spontaneous spoken language might be very different from the language of drama. You can draw on all this learning and make it count in your investigation.

Hopefully you have also enjoyed studying a drama text. This type of investigation offers you an opportunity to study another work by the same playwright, or to explore a completely different type of play by a new author.

A linguistic focus

Because you now have a broad knowledge of how speech works, you could focus on the language features of interactions and explore their function in real speech and in a drama text. For example:

- How does turn-taking work in real dialogues and how does it work in a drama text of your choice?
- Why does simultaneous speech occur in real dialogues? Is there any equivalent in drama scripts?
- There are many non-fluency features in real speech (false starts, hesitations, back-tracking, errors, unfinished utterances). Are these features ever simulated in dramatic dialogue?
- Real speakers have their own idiolects and dialects. How are ideas about speaker identities used in drama texts?
- How are the many aspects of prosodics and non-verbal behaviour that accompany speech incorporated into drama texts?

It is important to show your recognition of the fact that any drama script becomes something that is performed. A good way to understand what aspects of stage direction mean is to watch your chosen play in performance, if possible. Then you are not simply talking about words on a page.

A thematic focus

Drama texts, like all literary texts, represent issues and questions about human beings. Scripts are not simply lines that enable characters to be realized. The whole script has a larger meaning in its themes and the areas of experience treated. You could explore those issues in a drama text by comparing it with some non-literary material. For example, if you were interested in the fact that a play is about war, or love, or family relationships, or the history of a place or era, or politics, then you would need to focus less on the linguistic features of plays as interactions and more on how the theme has been treated. Of course, you would still need to look at language, whatever approach you take. But in the case of a thematic focus, the non-literary material that you collect would probably need to be different from what would be needed for a purely linguistic approach.

Collecting non-literary material

If your focus is on the interactive features of real speech and on questions of which, if any, features are used in constructing dramatic dialogue, then obviously you need to collect some real speech. This needs some planning and some thinking about, not only because of the practical issues involved, but also some ethical ones.

Collecting real speech means that you will need a method of capturing the talk and a method of saving and storing the recording. You will also need to spend some time transcribing the extracts you choose to work with. We have already discussed some of the practical considerations connected with transcribing data. However, if you choose to work with real spontaneous talk, there are some additional considerations. When you are recording conversations or talk in everyday situations, you must make sure that you ask permission from all of the speakers.

The problem of recording speech that is as close to its natural style as possible is called the **Observer's Paradox**. The linguist William Labov suggested that the aim of researching how people use language in the community is to find out how people talk naturally, when they don't feel observed. And yet the only way to capture that kind of data is to observe them.

This is a problem for people wanting to capture 'real' speech. We need to record data ethically, so speakers must be aware that they are being recorded, but once speakers become aware, they behave differently, and the chance of capturing natural speech is reduced. For the purposes of your data collection, however, you should find that if you record data for long enough periods, the speakers become less aware of the recording device. You can also choose sections from middle or later parts of the recording, therefore minimizing the impact of the recording device.

The Observer's Paradox is not the only consideration you need to think about before you begin collecting your spoken data. In this chapter we also discussed the challenges of transcribing recordings of speech – and clearly this applies to everyday speech as well as speech taken from a TV programme. Practically, you

Key term

Observer's Paradox. The paradox that the only way to collect natural speech is to observe it – but the very act of observation is likely to destroy its naturalness.

need a device to capture the speech, such as your mobile phone, and a way of saving the sound file so that you can listen to it a number of times as you transcribe the talk.

In addition to these practical considerations, you also need to think carefully about the type of spoken data you want to use as your non-literary text. For example, you could record friends talking as a group (as long as you have their permission) or you could choose data that involves fewer ethical considerations, such as a talk on YouTube or a radio conversation, which is already in the public domain. Think about the types of spoken data you could work with and make a list.

The type of talk you need to capture really depends on the kinds of features you want to explore.

Activity

Look at the types of talk below.

a. For each type of talk, suggest the kinds of features you would expect to find in a recording.

b. How might your expected features be compared with those of a drama script?

c. Might any of the following **speech events** actually feature in a drama script?

1. Family dinner-table talk
2. Radio interview
3. YouTube monologue
4. Student common-room chat
5. Spoken ritual, such as a wedding ceremony
6. Job interview
7. Reality TV conversation
8. Parent–child talk at bedtime
9. Speech given in an assembly
10. Talk between strangers at a bus stop

As well as talk in all the forms listed above, new forms of communication have arisen with new technologies. Although these might be composed at a keyboard, some share features with spoken language in that they are interactive, that is, composed in real time. So data such as MSN or Internet chat of another type could be compared with playscripts, and similarities and differences could be identified with a focus either on language features or on themes and topics of discussion.

A thematic approach to a playscript could involve data other than either real speech or online communication. If the play was concerned with, for example, war or a historical theme such as the rise of trade unions, it might be useful to collect some factual data for your non-literary source.

Dramatic and real-world monologues

Monologues offer a distinctive type of study because they are clearly different from interactions. While dialogue of any kind has the give and take of turn-taking, creating a dynamic feel, monologue has to be sustained without many of the features that are offered by listeners, such as **reinforcements** like 'yeah', 'really?', 'mm' or 'I know'.

At the same time, speakers can behave as if they are really talking to someone, for example by using **monitoring features** such as 'Do you know what I mean?'

 Activity

The text below is an extract from one of Alan Bennett's *Talking Heads* monologues.

Compare this literary extract with any of the real-world narratives from Chapter 1. Use any of the theoretical frameworks about storytelling from that chapter to help you in your analysis. Think especially how Bennett represents aspects of real-world speech and storytelling in the literary extract.

Lesley is an aspiring actress. In the first part of the monologue, Lesley describes how she went to a party to say goodbye to a friend who was emigrating. At the party, she meets a man who offers her an audition.

Her Big Chance

Lesley is in her early thirties. She is in her flat. Morning.

… Now my hobby is people. I collect people. So when I saw this interesting-looking man in the corner, next thing is I find myself talking to him. I said 'You look an interesting person. I'm interested in interesting people. Hello'. He said, 'Hello'. I said, 'What do you do?' He said, 'I'm in films'. I said, 'Oh, that's interesting, anything in the pipeline?' He said, 'As a matter of fact, yes', and starts telling me about this project he's involved in making videos for the overseas market, targeted chiefly on West Germany. I said, 'Are you the producer?' He said, 'No, but I'm on the production side, the name's Spud'. I said, 'Spud! That's an interesting name, mine's Lesley'. He said, 'As it happens, Lesley, we've got a problem at the moment. Our main girl has had to drop out because her back's packed in. Are you an actress?' I said, 'Well, Spud, interesting that you should ask because as a matter of fact I am'. He said, 'Will you excuse me one moment, Lesley?' I said, 'Why, Spud, where are you going?' He said, 'I'm going to go away, Lesley, and make one phone call'.

It transpires the director is seeing possible replacements the very next day, at an address in West London. Spud said, 'It's interesting because I'm based in Ealing'. I said, 'Isn't that West London?' He said, 'It is. Where's your stamping ground?' I said, 'Bromley, for my sins'. He said, 'That's a far-ish cry. Why not bed down at my place?' I said, 'Thank you, kind sir, but I didn't fall off the Christmas tree yesterday…'

What is 'literariness' anyway?

So far, the terms 'literary' and 'non-literary' have been used as if their meaning were self-evident. But the terms are, in fact, constantly being disputed. You need to realize that your investigation will by no means be a failure if you don't find differences between literary and non-literary material. Finding similarities is an equally successful outcome, possibly more so. It's tempting to look for differences and find them, if that's your starting point; finding similarities could therefore show how open-minded you have been.

A type of investigation that hasn't been discussed up to now, therefore, is the whole question of 'literariness' itself. What is it, exactly? What are 'literary features'? There are many ways to research this idea and they might involve research methods of a slightly different type from those suggested up to now. For example, you could test out some ideas about literariness (and value judgements about texts) by writing out a literary extract and a non-literary one on a similar theme, and asking people for their responses.

You need to think about the investigation as a genuine opportunity to research questions about the labels we give to texts. After all, these are as much a product of our society as the texts themselves.

REVIEW YOUR LEARNING

Try to answer the following questions:

- What does taking a thematic approach to the investigation involve?
- What does taking a linguistic approach to the investigation involve?
- What are some of the issues to bear in mind when collecting real speech?
- How can visual planning help you in the early stages of the research?
- What skills are you rewarded for in your analysis?
- What is the role of secondary sources in your investigation?

Further reading

The Routledge *Intertext* series contains many individual topic books that will help you to think about texts of different kinds, particularly non-literary material, for example in the following areas:

Technology (e.g. social media, websites, email, SMS)

Region (e.g. the different dialects that people use in real life, not in novels)

Gender (e.g. the way that men and women are represented in texts of all kinds)

Advertising (e.g. the stories that advertisers tell and the linguistic strategies they use)

Newspapers (e.g. the genre of news articles, representations of groups and events)

Magazines (e.g. representations of lifestyles and celebrity figures)

Sport (e.g. sports commentaries, fanzines, reports of sports events)

Politics (e.g. political speeches, posters and campaigns)

War (e.g. media coverage of war, the language of conflict)

Science (e.g. the language of science, how science is viewed in society)

Work (e.g. how work shapes the language we use, different genres of talk)

Go to http://www.routledge.com/books/series/SE0313/ for information on these topic books.

Preparing for assessment

Each of the chapters in this book begins with details about how the learning in that chapter relates to specific assessments and their associated Assessment Objectives. Below is some further practical advice about how to maximize your effectiveness in the different types of assessment that you will face.

Non-exam assessment (coursework)

Make a work schedule

Making a plan to organize how you will go about producing your coursework is essential, because deadlines have to be adhered to.

- If you can trial your ideas as a mini-investigation before you embark on the real thing, it will help you to assess how long things take.

- If you are relying on other people for certain types of information or data, make some clear deadlines and, if things don't work out, change tack or do without their help.

- If you are recording speech, be prepared for the need to make several attempts. Don't be daunted by that idea – studying spoken language can be very rewarding.

Make good use of your teachers

Your teachers are a valuable resource, so don't waste any opportunities to get support and direction from them. They are not there to tell you what to do or to give you answers, but to help you develop your ideas. This means that the more effort you make to arrive at meetings having prepared some plans, the more value you will get from the consultation.

Make notes and organize your material

Keep accurate records of what you read, including where you obtain quotes from, so that you can reference your sources properly. This applies to exam answers as well as to coursework reports. It makes a poor impression if you get academic names wrong or misquote book titles. Remember to include an appendix in your coursework report, containing the material you have collected and analysed.

Exam assessments

Make a plan before you write

Sometimes candidates feel that they should start to write as soon as possible, because they need to use every second for writing rather than thinking. This is a mistake. You need time to make sense of the question, and time to think about how to produce a relevant and well-organized answer. You should aim to produce an answer that groups points together in a coherent way, and that is written concisely – in legible handwriting. Don't let students who write fast and furiously make you feel panicked. Quantity is not the same thing as quality.

Answer the question

Answer the question set, not the question that you would have liked to see. Examiners cannot give you marks unless you do this, even if the points you make are good ones. Only relevant points count. Make sure that you indicate which question you are answering.

Remember that questions come in different types. For example:

- An instruction to analyse a passage requires a text analysis as an answer.
- A question that asks you to discuss an idea requires a discussion essay as an answer.
- If a question asks you to refer to two examples, you need two – if you give one example, you've only done half the job.

In short, make sure that you do what the question asks – in the appropriate way.

Make the best use of open-book opportunities

Open-book exams mean that you don't have to try to remember large chunks of text. They are not opportunities for browsing, however. They enable you to locate key passages and to refresh your memory about events and ideas. Use any book or other material that you are allowed to bring into the exam room, simply as an aid to memory and not as an opportunity to re-read at any length. Remember that you are not allowed to bring annotated material into an exam room – only clean copies are permitted.

Introductory chapter

Page 13. Chatroom dialogue. Natalie said that she was trying to make her 'yeah' sound like a celebration, and that when she said 'yeah man' she meant 'a kind of droning, flat hippy voice like Neil from *The Young Ones*'. Simon said 'yehah' was a 'cowboy cheer'.

Page 15. 'Death of a Naturalist'.

- Examples of onomatopoeia: croaking, slap, plop.

- Examples of alliteration: coarse croaking, chorus, cocked.

- Examples of assonance: the /ɒ/ sound in frogs, cocked, sods, hopped, plop.

Heaney is representing the sounds and movements of the frogs as repulsive and horrifying. Plosive sounds suggest the croaking of the frogs, intensified by the lax vowel /ɒ/ which is produced low in the mouth and at the back. The onomatopoeia of 'slap' and 'plop' symbolizes the wetness of surfaces in contact.

Page 17.

- *All My Sons.* This is the opening scene of the play, and the stage directions describe the non-verbal communication (NVC) of the characters explicitly: they move towards a physical object (a tree that has blown down). The audience see the characters react to the tree's fate, and to each other's state of mind: the characters have to act being 'struck', and 'touched' via their NVC as well as via paralanguage – perhaps a catch or tremor in the voice – and via words. The physical object of the tree links with a tragic aspect of the story that is about to unfold. The audience will come to realize that the tree has a symbolic value.

- *A Streetcar Named Desire.* Aspects of NVC and paralanguage, as specified in the stage directions, suggest some complex tensions between the characters. Stella runs to where Blanche is and her voice is 'joyful'; meanwhile, Blanche first talks faintly to herself to gather some self-control, then speaks later with a kind of false energy. Both characters 'stare' at each other before an embrace that is only 'spasmodic'.

Page 19. Perfume advert. 'Fragrance' and 'perfume' would not have altered the meaning very much. 'Odour' and 'whiff' would have altered the meaning greatly, because both suggest something unpleasant. 'Smell' can be positive or negative, depending on what it is coupled with. The remaining words all have specific connotations: an 'aroma' fills the air; a 'bouquet' suggests something floral; an 'aura' surrounds someone and can have spiritual connotations; and 'redolence' often occurs metaphorically, to mean an indication of something.

Pages 26–27. Speech events. 1. Police caution when making an arrest. 2. Ritual of launching a ship. 3. Train announcement. 4. Opening of a ceremonial speech. 5. Opening of a joke. 6. Voicemail greeting. 7. Satnav (or a passenger navigating the route). 8. Religious ceremony. 9. Parliamentary language. 10. A teacher's lesson. 11. Radio podcast opening. 12. Children's rhyme. 13. Opening of a business phone call. 14. Political speech (John. F. Kennedy's inauguration). 15. Voicemail message. 16. Opening of a story. 17. TV advertisement (for comparethemarket.com), with the words of Aleksandr Orlov, the meerkat puppet. 18. Auctioneer announcing an item for sale. 19. Beginning of a motor race. 20. A bingo caller announcing numbers.

Page 29. Train conversation. The speakers show cohesion in the topics they address, which include: different countries; their respective climates; and the experiences that the speakers and their relatives have had. Cohesive items include: 'Australia', 'Zambia', 'the Middle East', 'India'; 'hot weather', 'air conditioning', 'rainy season', 'monsoon'; 'my granddaughters', 'my niece', 'the youngsters', 'I', 'you'.

On the surface, the speakers appear to align with each other in each contributing an idea about these joint topics, but there are some subtle disagreements. For example, there is an underlying difference of opinion about whether warm weather is a good thing or not, which begins with reference to the weather in Australia – approved of by A but not by B. B's idea of having to stay in and use air conditioning is countered by A's idea that in warm climates fewer clothes are needed. But this argument is countered again by B with the idea that hot weather saps one's energy.

In conclusion, this is an apparently friendly exchange where speakers are engaged in a shared topic, but with some quite strong opposing positions being constructed throughout the talk. This activity should have shown you that conflict doesn't have to involve aggression or even strong arguments – it can work at a very subtle level.

> NOTE: No specific feedback has been provided for any of the Activities in Chapter 1.

Chapter 2

Page 68. First activity. In passage 1 the teller's point of view is more external to the story, compared to passages 2 and 3. You can tell by the use of pronouns. The teller in passage 1 doesn't seem to be an active participant in the story, because he or she doesn't mention him/herself at all. This contrasts with passages 2 and 3, where the tellers mention themselves through the pronoun 'I'.

Page 68. Second activity. *Americanah* is a novel about the story of Ifemelu, a young Nigerian woman who, at one point in her life, leaves her country to go and study in the United States, where she later becomes a successful writer. The author is Chimamanda Ngozi Adichie. She, too, is a young Nigerian woman who, at one point in her life, left her country to go and study in the United States, where she became a successful writer. The novel begins with a description of Princeton, a famous American University, where Adichie stayed for one year.

Page 76.

The narrator in 'Snow' says that snow is 'very, very cold'. This description comes at a point in the story when she has just arrived in America from Zimbabwe, and many of the things that she experiences are new to her. Snow is one of them. In this extract she describes what she sees – snow covering and hiding everything – as well as what she *feels* – snow is very cold.

In 'Fog', some feelings are described, too. But they're not the narrator's own – 'fog cruelly pinching the toes and fingers of his shivering little 'prentice boy on deck', describes how the apprentice boy feels.

Pages 76–77. The first passage allows an insight into Obinze's mind and feelings (he stared, his body went rigid, he wished, he felt), while the second passage presents an external view of Kojo (I don't know what Kojo wants, his eyes have this disappointment in them).

Page 78. First activity.

● Possible answer for indirect speech: He asked me where I was from. I told him that my parents were from Ghana but I was born in Britain.

● Possible answer for NRSA: He asked me about myself, and I told him.

Page 78. Second activity.

The passage describes a situation where a passenger aircraft had to land before reaching its final destination, due to bad weather there. There was a lot of confusion, with passengers wanting to know what was going to happen and being upset because of the disruptions to their plans, and airport staff trying to reassure them.

In this text, speech is reported in a different way. The narrator doesn't indicate it in any way, although you realize when someone is speaking. The sections where speech is reported are:

a) Will someone please… speak to him!

b) Do you realize… to be here!

c) Sir: we have already explained… These things happen.

d) My husband is waiting… This cannot be happening.

We don't know exactly who is speaking, but we can at least guess when the passengers and the airport staff are speaking. In (a), (b), and (d), the speech of some passengers is reported, whereas in (c) it is someone from the airport staff who is trying to calm everybody down. We don't know how many passengers are speaking, but there must be at least two, since one refers to a meeting and the other one to her honeymoon. There may be more, of course.

Page 83.

● There is an example of Direct Thought: 'and what is the use of a book,' thought Alice 'without pictures or conversation?'

● There is also an example of Indirect Thought: she was considering in her own mind… whether the pleasure of making a daisy-chain would be worth the trouble of getting up and picking the daisies.

Both work in exactly the same way as Direct Speech and Indirect Speech, respectively. Remember that with Indirect Speech/Thought the narrator seems to intervene more than he or she does with Direct Speech/Thought – making it seem as though the original words may have been modified slightly.

Chapter 3

Page 89.

● 'House' and 'Beautiful' are joined together and this breaks the language convention of spaces between words. The word order is also unusual, with the adjective 'beautiful' coming after the noun it modifies.

● In the Crown paint advert, language deviates in different ways. The last line looks very different from the rest of the text. It's written in a different font, which looks like handwriting, but painting too. And what exactly is 'a splash of you'? You can't literally 'splash' yourself onto a wall, as if you were made of paint, but you still understand the expression as referring to the idea of making your personal mark.

Page 94. One possibility is that, by making 'eachother' into a single word, the poet wants to convey a sense of being forced together – the couple wanted different things, so ended up in an uncomfortable union. The poem refers to the popular saying 'you can't have your cake and eat it too' and so 'eachother' is one thing, just like 'it' in the original proverb. Of course, you need extra interpretation work to deal with the idea of people eating each other! We'll come back to this last point later on in the chapter.

Page 99. This poem makes use of different kinds of deviation. The most obvious one is graphological deviation. The words are arranged in two columns, in a way that is similar to 'ordnung – unordnung' seen earlier. This is clearly a form of deviation, because texts don't normally have that layout. There are instances of lexical deviation, too: the words *tennis* and *between* are artificially divided. The poem also has no punctuation or capitalization. This breaks grammar rules and so counts as grammatical deviation.

The text plays with meaning. The title of the poem is ambiguous, because both the number 40 and the word 'Love' can refer to different things. The phrase '40-love' is a very common score in tennis, but 'love' also refers to an emotion. The beginning of the poem mentions a middle-aged couple, so it's likely that 40 is their age. In that case, '40 love' may be interpreted as representing a love relationship between 40-year-old people.

The text of the poem supports both interpretations. There are clear references to tennis, but the text doesn't seem to be just about that. The key moment in the poem is when the couple go home. The fact that 'the net is still between them' can't be taken literally – they won't have an actual tennis net in their living room! So the alternative possibility is that the 'net' is a metaphor: it's not an actual net but something that represents, perhaps, a kind of distance or lack of communication between the two partners. So the poem exploits the different possible meanings of tennis terminology in order to talk about something that isn't, really, related to tennis.

Page 101.

1. All three expressions use the idea of movement in one direction (path, steps, road) to talk about objectives or key moments in life. So the underlying metaphor could be:

   LIFE   IS   A JOURNEY

      target   source

2. All three expressions use terms to do with mechanical systems (rusty, crank, process). So the underlying metaphor could be:

   PEOPLE   ARE   MACHINES

      target   source

Page 103.

- The future's x (x = 'bright' and 'orange')
- x wanted y (x = 'I' and 'you'; y = 'one life' and 'another')
- x is y (x = 'yes' and 'if'; y = 'a pleasant country' and 'wintry')

- I ent have no x (x = 'gun' and 'knife')
- I dont need no x to y up yu z (x = 'axe' and 'hammer'; y = 'split' and 'mash'; z = 'syntax' and 'grammar')

Chapter 4

Page 111.

Genre. The article follows typical conventions of travel articles in newspapers: the title introduces the topic; the image provides a cohesive link to the text (illustrating clearly the journey to be taken). The text itself has a chronological discourse, so that the reader can visualize the journey the writer is taking through Paris.

Purpose. This text is clearly to inform – not only about this particular cycle tour around Paris, but also about some of the different sights, events and experiences whilst taking the tour. The article was written by a Paris resident, so this text offers an insider's perspective to the city – 'my favourite route'; 'the waiter is always grumpy; it's part of the folklore'; 'among my favourite stops…'. These personal insights also help to persuade readers that they are getting the inside story.

Audience. The audience is constructed as a discerning traveller, different from 'the riding hordes with their red jackets'. There is assumed shared understanding: 'Velib' is not explained. This helps to develop the relationship between reader and text producer – we join her on her journey through the city.

Page 113.

Structurally, the texts show different discourse features that reflect aspects of mode:

- The website includes links inside the text, allowing the reader to click through the page to other sources. The paper text is linear and so cannot do this.

- The website includes advertising that either has a fixed placement, attached to a page that has agreed to host the charity's appeal, or attached to the digital trail the reader has set up through their own browsing. The paper text is much more fixed and does not show multimodal or intertextual realtionships.

- The website uses images and has a strong personal voice – presenting historical information through a homodiegetic narrator, who offers details about her own experiences and relationships – while the paper text presents a more factual (unattributed) account and formal style, via a heterodiegetic narrator.

- The personal nature of the website account is strengthened by the use of dashes to represent the idea of immediacy in the narrative detail, and by many examples of informality: 'the big ticket items', 'in with the in crowd'. The paper text uses a pun in the title and there is some informality 'higgledy piggledy', 'merely rubbish' but also formality 'tranquil', 'ultimate', 'ominously', 'misfortune'.

Page 116.

The letter follows a conventional structure, with an informal greeting and sign-off. The only French expression which the writer uses is in the final sign-off: 'À bientôt'. The extended metaphor of 'Goldilocks', and the use of adjectives such as 'cozy', 'terrible', 'great', 'delicious', illustrates the extent of the search for the 'perfect' café, somewhere that the writer would feel at home. A traditional, almost picture-postcard version of Paris is presented, where people 'sit and write letters, read the papers and catch up on the latest gossip', which is reflected in the image accompanying the letter. The sense of place is reinforced with tripling: 'sipping, dreaming and listening' and the image of words that 'flutter by on the breeze'.

As this letter is written to a friend, it is personal and affectionate, written in first person to recount her experiences in Paris. There is an absence of polite phatic talk at the beginning, allowing her to focus on the people and places she has encountered. Macleod uses past tense to relay her search for the perfect café, and then writes in present tense so that the reader can experience Paris with her. She even alludes to an imagined future, which reflects the impact that this city has had on her.

Chapter 5

Page 128. The direct speech here reveals the tensions in the Stoners' marriage. The conversation is initiated and led by Edith, and her tone varies between 'casual' at the beginning of this extract, 'sharp' when addressing her daughter, 'indulgent' when first raising the topic, and finally with 'an edge of fear' when William suggests discussing the affair. Her laughter and careful selection of words and phrases aim to unsettle William: 'your little co-ed' and 'little flirtation'. The phrases diminish the significance of the affair, and this is furthered when she does not wait to hear the name of the woman William is having a relationship with.

It is interesting to note that the narrative refers to 'William' but Edith calls him 'Willy'. This usually affectionate nickname is used to ridicule William at this point; 'Willy' does not suggest the gravitas of a mature man.

The writer uses punctuation to capture Edith's careful choice of words: 'Did you think I didn't know about your – little flirtation?' This is echoed by William, and a dash is also used to signal his incomplete utterance: 'It's – '; Edith does not want to hear what William has to say, reinforced with her repetition of negatives at the end of this extract.

Page 130. Williams offers little physical description of Stoner's body, instead focusing on clothing and what this suggests about his character. He wears the same clothes, regardless of climate, perhaps suggesting a lack of interest in clothing, or perhaps indicating a lack of either money or awareness of suitable attire. The noun 'uniform' suggests functionality and a distinct lack of personal identity. Uniforms often indicate group identity, yet here the suggestion that this uniform 'once belonged to someone else' suggests that he does not really belong in a group. Stoner's clothing does not sit comfortably on him: his wrists 'protrude' from the too-short sleeves and his trousers 'rode awkwardly', creating a sense of unease and marking him out as someone who does not belong in his environment.

From such a brief description, we can infer some detail about the awkwardness of this character, perhaps suggesting his inner conflict or his conflict with the society that he finds himself in.

Page 133. The sense of confinement is presented here through key descriptions – 'solid masonry'; 'heavy plank'; 'great iron bars'; 'iron-bound door'; 'brick wall' – illustrating the constricted, oppressive environment which Northup finds himself in. This is reinforced with the lack of light, only glimpsed through the door if opened. Whilst much of the detail is factual ('about twelve feet square'; 'ten or twelve feet high'; 'extended rearward from the house about thirty feet'), Northup's choice of words and phrases expresses his feelings about being incarcerated in such a place ('cell, or vault'; 'wholly destitute of windows'; 'a crazy loft'; 'a farmer's barnyard'). The analogy of the 'barnyard' and 'shed' is emphasized with his reference to slaves as 'human cattle': slaves were held and 'herded' in a manner more suited to livestock than to human beings.

Northup's description of his cell contains some first person pronouns, but is devoid of personal comment. His description of the physical environment in such detail renders this unnecessary; it is difficult to question the factual detail of walls that are 'ten or twelve feet high' and we can fully imagine the restrictions and constraints of a place such as this.

Page 134. The passage begins with a contrast of extremes as we are pitched into the middle of an event that is already unfolding: 'cheers from the distinguished crowd' contrast with 'shouts of the ragged crowd'. There is a clear divide between the 'paying customers and dignitaries' and the 'peasants and the rank and file'. The celebratory atmosphere comes to an abrupt halt with the sudden shift of the wind. Only at this point are we told what the event actually is.

A very strong sense is given of the physical experience of being in the place. Sound symbolism adds to the representation of conflict: the cheers at the start of the extract soon turn to 'shouts', 'screams' and 'muffled thuds of police batons against bodies'. This, coupled with descriptions of the crowd as 'a swirling tide' who 'surged' over the walls creates a wild, frenzied atmosphere. In contrast, Marley himself seems bewildered and disconcerted as he 'darted about, eventually stumbling through an opening', before being 'escorted to safety'.

There is irony in this text, created by the police reaction to the masses swarming the stadium 'for the simple right to hear reggae', particularly as the performer is the 'hero of black freedom fighters everywhere'. Whilst this concert is to celebrate 'the casting off of white colonial tyranny', it is the dignitaries who attend, rather than 'the people'. Looking back at these events and describing how they unfolded enables White to show the racial politics current at that time.

> NOTE: No specific feedback has been provided for any of the Activities in Chapter 6.

Chapter 7

Page 150.

a. Distinctive speech patterns include the following: Ricky uses 'innit' and 'out of ma nut'. He repeats lexical items and uses a lot of negatives: 'no (.) no (.)', 'I don't remember', 'I haven't', 'I don't' which make him sound defensive and which are linked to his self-justifying choices. Joey uses the first person pronoun 'I' and the possessive 'me', as well as the second person pronoun 'you' frequently, which are clearly linked to his motivation for speaking to Ricky and the perceived insult. 'Come on' is also a distinguishing characteristic of Joey's language, as is dialect grammar – 'we was'.

b. Features of 'real' speech. Both speakers use 'look' as a filler and pause frequently throughout their turns because they are thinking as they speak, and because there are heightened emotions across the interaction. The overlap occurs as Ricky attempts to defend himself against Joey's accusation. It is also worth remembering that there is an entertaining element to this exchange, and as the argument develops, the overlap makes for a more 'confrontational' exchange. The repetitions from both speakers also add to the sense of frustration and defensiveness which are important aspects of the exchange. Remember that the visual aspects add a great deal to your interpretation.

c. Power strategies. Given that Joey makes the initial accusation, you would imagine that he is the more powerful speaker with a sense of grievance on his side. However, he mitigates with 'I thought you and me was pals', suggesting regretfulness ('pathos'), and the repetition in the final line also suggests a lack of force and conviction in his challenge to Ricky. He also allows Ricky to overlap him and interrupt, taking control of the turn, and even when Ricky pauses (1.0) he does not attempt to take back the floor. This suggests some hesitancy on his part. However, this may be because of the 'acted' elements of this exchange – perhaps his anger is not genuine and must allow Ricky to complete his defence.

Page 151. Maggie's opening lines contain a number of short, elliptical sentences and evidence of her accent – 'th' parade an' remove'. The incomplete utterance also suggests some of the pragmatic aspects of real speech. The use of punctuation (dashes, question marks, etc.) also represents how the lines could be spoken to indicate 'normal' conversation. The non-verbal communication is clear as Maggie catches sight of herself in the mirror and gasps, followed by a lengthy pause suggesting her reflective, uneasy state of mind.

Brick's whistling adds to the uneasy tension surrounding the couple. Often silence is interpreted as uneasy, but in this case the suspense and disquiet is increased by the contrast with the apparently unperturbed whistling from her husband. This adds to the sense of conflict between the characters even before Maggie's language becomes distressed. The stage directions to Maggie represent her anxious state of mind and her need for emotional comfort from her husband, who is distant and emotionally unresponsive: 'BRICK [coolly]: Know what, Maggie?' as a contrast to her anguish.

Page 154. The conflict in the extract is developed through the use of strong appeals to rationality (logos) from the jurors who want to reach a 'guilty' verdict. The use of lexis, such as 'reasonable', 'obvious' and 'convinced', point to justifications.

Yet, when Juror 8 replies 'No', his lack of a need to justify his point is extremely powerful. He speaks very little in the first half of the exchange, but it is almost because of this that he seems more convincing. The more the other Jurors defend their point of view, the less convincing their reasons seem.

At this point, the emphasis changes and there is a series of lexical choices connected with 'guilt' – which have the effect of making it appear as though Juror 8's simple request 'to talk' is eminently reasonable. Again, his lack of passion contrasts with the emotional intensity of the other Jurors, as he offers minimal responses to a number of questions and remains unflustered in contrast with the urgency and constant challenges of the other characters. It's as if they are performing being rational while he just *is* so.

NOTE: No specific feedback has been provided for any of the Activities in Chapters 8 and 9.

Glossary

Abstract. In Labov's model of narrative structure, the abstract, like the trailer of a film, gives clues to what will follow.

Adjacency. The positioning of elements in an interaction, so that one follows on from another. For example, greetings are nearly always reciprocated.

Adjacency pair. Two elements that are dependent on each other and exist in a pair. For example, a question and an answer.

Affordances. Things that are made possible. For example, a website can be read by many people simultaneously.

Alliteration. The repeated use of the same consonants at the beginnings of words.

Anti-hero. A figure who is not expected to show courage or any other qualities normally ascribed to a hero, but who does so eventually.

Arbitrary. Having no real connection beyond that of social convention.

Assonance. The repetition of vowel sounds in the stressed syllables of different words.

Base text. The original text, which in the case of this specification will be a set text (for A level) or Anthology material (for AS level).

Clause. A clause gives information about people or things (nouns and pronouns) and their states or actions (verbs). Additional information may also be given about the circumstances of the people and their activities.

Cline. A scale or gradient with items placed on it to show how they compare with each other.

Closing. Closing items conclude an interaction. For example, 'bye' or 'see you'.

Coda. The 'wrap up' stage of a narrative, often linking back to the abstract.

Cohesion. The way sentences or utterances join together to form a whole text.

Collocation. The regular occurrence of a word or phrase alongside others.

Commentary. In this specification, a set of analytical comments about a re-creative task.

Common ground. The idea of sharing a perspective with others in an interaction.

Community of practice. A group of people who share understandings, perspectives and forms of language use as a result of meeting regularly over time.

Complication. The twist, or complication that occurs in a narrative.

Concordance line. A line of text from a corpus, showing where the searched item occurred within a sentence or utterance.

Connective. A word that joins elements together, such as 'and' and 'or'. These are also called conjunctions.

Connotation or connotative meaning. The associations that we have for a word or phrase.

Constraints. Overall shaping factors, including both affordances and limitations.

Context. The circumstances of a text, such as when and where it was written, who wrote it and why, the mode and medium of communication, who is reading it now.

Corpus. A collection of searchable language data stored on a computer.

Creative writing. All writing is of course creative to some extent, but this term is frequently used to describe writing that is an individual's original creation. Traditionally, the term referred to literary creations but more recently it has widened to include any type of text.

Critique. A critical analysis that pays attention to all aspects of a text or topic, seeing different perspectives.

Declarative. A clause or sentence that has a statement function.

Deixis. The act of pointing to something by using certain language items. Deictic expressions refer to aspects of space (spatial deixis, for example 'over there'), time (temporal deixis, for example 'yesterday') and person deixis (who is being referred to, for example 'they').

Denotation or denotative meaning. Literal meaning, dictionary meaning in its most basic, factual sense.

Deviation. A form of foregrounding. It is achieved when a piece of language moves away from the normal use of grammar, vocabulary, graphology or meaning.

Direct speech. A form of speech presentation in which the narrator reports some speech by reproducing the exact words uttered by a character, usually enclosed in quotation marks and introduced by a reporting clause.

Discourse. A stretch of language (spoken, written or multimodal) considered in its context of use.

Dystopian. The opposite of 'utopian', which means 'a perfect place'. Dystopian societies are oppressive and full of suffering and misery.

Ellipsis. The omission of elements in a sentence or utterance. For example, 'going to', instead of 'I am going to', when written in a text message.

End-stopped line. A line in a poem which stops at the end of a phrase or a sentence. The opposite of **enjambment**.

Enjambment. This occurs when a line in a poem stops before the end of a sentence, which continues to the next line. The opposite of an **end-stopped line**.

Ethos. In classical Greek rhetoric, ethos is an appeal to authority. For example, by referring to the speaker's credibility.

Evaluation. In Labov's model of storytelling, an assessment of the impact of the narrative events.

External deviation. The way in which a language feature stands out for being used differently from how it is used in texts of different kinds.

False start. Beginning an utterance then stopping and beginning it again.

Filler. A word or speech noise produced by a speaker to create some thinking time. For example, 'um' and 'er'.

Finite verb. A form of the verb that indicates when an action occurred (called 'tense'). For example, she *helps* me (present tense), she *helped* me (past tense).

First person narrator. A narrator who is an active participant in the story and, therefore, mentions him/herself in the narrative. This figure is more usefully described as a **homodiegetic** narrator.

First person pronoun. The pronouns 'I' (singular) and 'we' (plural).

Foregrounding. The capacity of a piece of discourse to make something (words, sentences, or even an entire text) stand out and be noticeable to the reader.

Formal. Designed for use on serious or public occasions where people pay attention to behaviour and appearance.

Framing. The idea that speakers mark their understanding of the context they are in. For example, by smiling or laughing to show that they are being playful.

Free direct speech. A form of direct speech in which the narrator does not use any quotation marks or a reporting clause.

Free indirect speech. A form of indirect speech in which the narrator does not use a reporting clause.

Fricative. A sound that is made by creating a continuous airflow. For example, in the sounds /s/ and /z/. You can see that this term is connected to the word 'friction'.

Genre. In language study, a type of text in any mode which is defined by its purpose, its features, or both. In literary fields, genre tends to refer primarily to the literary genres of prose, poetry and drama, but it can also refer to types of content (for example, crime or romance).

Gothic. The term 'Gothic' refers not just to literature but also to other creative forms, such as painting, architecture, and music. Named after a Germanic tribe called the Goths, a gothic style of fiction includes elements of extreme emotion (such as terror), medieval and dramatic settings, and unnatural events.

Grammar. The structural aspects of language that tie items together. Grammar includes syntax, or word order; and morphology, or the elements added to words to show their grammatical role (such as 'ed' to indicate the past tense of a verb).

Graphological. Relating to the design features of a text.

Graphology. All the visual aspects of textual design, including colour, typeface, layout, images and logos.

Hamartia. Deriving from Greek, this word is used to suggest a tragic weakness or flaw that leads to a protagonist's downfall. Although often identified as a single weakness, it can be more complex than this.

Hero (or heroine). A figure with impressive qualities such as courage and endurance.

Heterodiegetic narrator. A narrator who is not an active participant in the story.

Homodiegetic narrator. A narrator who is an active participant in the story.

Hybrids. Blends of two or more elements. For example, new forms of communication are often seen as having some of the characteristics of both spoken and written language.

Iconic. In semiotics, the term iconic refers to an image that is a picture of its referent, as in a photograph, for example.

Identity. Appearing as a certain kind of person or group member.

Ideology. A set of belief systems, attitudes and values.

Idiolect. An idiolect is the language that is unique to each individual (the language equivalent of fingerprints).

Imperative. A clause or sentence that has a command function.

Indirect speech. A form of speech presentation in which the narrator reports a speech event by integrating the words uttered by a character within the narrative.

Informality. The opposite of formality. An informal context is a relaxed one in which people feel unselfconscious. An informal language style could include slang, regional dialect or other forms of colloquial language that are used within personal relationships and in private settings.

Internal deviation. The way in which a language feature stands out for being used differently from elsewhere in the text.

Intertextual / Intertextuality. The way in which one text echoes or refers to another.

Kinesics. Body movements involved in communication.

Lexis. Lexis refers to the vocabulary of a language.

Limitations. Things that are prevented or restricted. For example, an SMS has no way to convey the subtleties of non-verbal communication (hence the need for emoticons).

Linguistics. The academic study of language, including different languages.

Logos. In classical Greek rhetoric, logos is an appeal to logic, or rationality.

Magic realism. A genre of writing in which magic or unreal events impinge upon the representation of an otherwise realistic world.

Metaphor / Metaphorical. A language strategy for bringing two unrelated ideas together in order to suggest a new way of looking at something. Metaphors are common where something is difficult to understand because it is complex or abstract, so it is compared with something simpler or more concrete.

Minor sentence. A sentence without a main verb.

Mode. Speech and writing are called different modes. Digital communication can draw on both of these modes, so is often called a hybrid form of communication.

Modification. Modifiers add information. For example, adverbs add information to verbs (run *quickly*), and adjectives add information to nouns (a *lovely* day).

Monitoring feature. An element produced by a speaker to check the attention level of the listener. For example, 'you know what I mean?', 'are you with me?'

Multimodal. A multimodal text draws on more than one mode of communication – for example, by using images as well as words.

Narratee. A fictional receiver; the person that the text appears to be aimed at (not the real reader).

Narrative. A social activity in which a teller addresses a listener or a reader and produces a piece of discourse about a story.

Narrative report of a speech act. A form of speech presentation in which the narrator reports a speech event by summarizing its content (without specifying the actual words uttered by the character).

Narrative structure. The stages which a teller would generally follow when telling a story. These typically include *abstract*, *orientation*, *complication*, *resolution* and *coda*.

Narrative voice. The way in which language is used by a writer to construct how a narrator sounds.

Narrator. A fictional 'teller'; the apparent voice of a fictional narrative created by the author.

Natural narratives. A term used in Labov's study of storytelling to label the everyday stories that people tell each other.

Non-finite verb. A form of the verb that doesn't indicate when an action occurred (called 'tense'). For example, in 'exploring the city', the verb element 'exploring' doesn't indicate when the exploration occurred.

Non-verbal communication. Communication that takes place via means that are not language based (such as gesture and facial expression).

Observer's Paradox. The paradox that the only way to collect natural speech is to observe it – but the very act of observation is likely to destroy its naturalness.

Omniscient narrator. An 'all-knowing' figure who can report everything, including the thoughts inside all of the characters' heads.

Onomatopoeia. The way in which some words appear to echo the sounds they describe, such as 'crash' and 'thud'.

Orientation. The setting of a narrative.

Paralanguage. Aspects of an individual's vocal expression such as whispering, laughter, breathiness.

Parallelism. A form of foregrounding. It is achieved when two (or more) pieces of language exhibit similar patterns, without being identical.

Pathos. In classical Greek rhetoric, pathos is an appeal to the emotions.

Personification. Treating an object as if it were a person.

Phonemic alphabet. An alphabet for transcribing general sounds, suitable for a specific language.

Phonetic alphabet. An alphabet designed for transcribing the sounds of all of the world's languages.

Phonetics / Phonology. The study of the sound system. Phonetics refers to the physical production and reception of sound, while phonology is a more abstract idea about all the sounds of a particular language.

Phonological approximation. Writing that tries to reflect pronunciation.

Plosive. A sound that is made by obstructing the airflow and then producing a sudden release of air. For example, in the sounds /b/ and /g/. You can see that this term is connected to the word 'explosion'.

Point of view. The position of the teller in relation to the story.

Positioning. Setting up and maintaining a perspective in an interaction.

Possible world. Everything related to a story that readers accept as possible as a result of their suspension of disbelief.

Pragmatics. Assumptions made about what is meant, or the inferences drawn from what is said or written.

Pre-closing. An item that a speaker will produce to show that he or she wants to close the conversation, for example 'right', 'so', or 'anyway'.

Preposition. A word that typically indicates direction, position, or relationship, such as 'into', 'on', or 'of'.

Prosodics / Prosody. Prosody is the melody that our voices create via prosodic aspects such as rhythm and intonation.

Protagonist. The main character in a story.

Psychological point of view. The feelings and perceptions of the narrator or one of the characters in the story.

Recount. A kind of narrative where the teller attempts to be as neutral as possible.

Re-creative writing. An activity that provides insights about a text by recasting part of it, or by adding new perspectives to it.

Referent. The thing or person being referred to.

Regional variety. A form of a language with its own distinctive features of vocabulary and grammar, used by speakers in a particular geographical region.

Register. A form of specialist language. For example, the language of sport or science.

Reinforcement. A word or speech noise produced by a listener to encourage a speaker to continue. For example, 'really?' or 'mm'.

Reported thought. A form of thought presentation in which the narrator reports the thoughts of a character as if it was speech occurring inside the character's mind and not said aloud.

Reporting clause. A clause used by the narrator when introducing speech. For example, 'she said', 'he murmured'.

Representation. Something that stands in place of something else. Representation is how something *appears* to be, not how it really *is*.

Resolution. How the complication in the narrative gets resolved.

Response cry. A spontaneous cry expressing emotion. For example, surprise, shock or joy.

Rhetoric / Rhetorical. Rhetoric is the study of persuasive language, an area of study dating back to ancient Greece.

Salient. Most important, prominent, or noteworthy.

Semantic field. A group of terms from the same domain. For example, names for food or aspects of computer communication.

Semantics. This refers to the meanings of words and expressions. Semantics can also refer to meaning in a broader sense, i.e. the overall meaning of something.

Semiotics. The study of how signs and symbols work within human communication.

Sonnet. There are different types of sonnet, but a common type is one formed of three quatrains (stanzas with four lines) and one couplet (a stanza with two lines), with a very regular rhyme pattern.

Sound symbolism. The way in which sounds are used to represent ideas. For example, in onomatopoeia – where sounds represent noises. There is no logical connection between the sounds and the ideas they represent.

Source. An alternative term for a base text or original text. Note that in discussing metaphor, this term has a different meaning: it refers to the idea or thing that the target is being compared with.

Spatial point of view. The physical position of the narrator in relation to the events in the story.

Speech event. A spoken interaction of a recognisable type. For example, a lecture or a phone call.

Stanza. A set of lines that are grouped together in a poem and set apart from other lines.

Stereotyping. Assuming that whole groups of people conform to the same, limited, range of characteristics.

Story. A sequence of events that someone considers interesting enough to be the subject of narrative.

Stream of consciousness. A writing technique that attempts to simulate the freewheeling nature of a person's inner thoughts.

Superhero. A hero with superhuman powers.

Suspension of disbelief. The ability of readers to accept the 'world' of a story as possible, without questioning whether it is real or not.

Symbol / Symbolic / Symbolism. A symbol is something that stands for something else, with no logical connection between the items. Symbolic is an adjective meaning 'like a symbol'; symbolism is the process or act of being symbolic.

Synonym / Synonymous. Synonyms are words that have a similar meaning, such as 'help' and 'assist'. If something is synonymous with something else, it has a similar meaning to it.

Target. This has two different meanings. In a metaphor, it refers to the concept being talked about by comparing it with the source. For example, if we say 'love is a drug', the target (the thing you are trying to understand) is love; the source (the thing it's being compared with) is a drug.

But in discussing audiences for writing, 'target' means the person or group being aimed at.

Teller. The person who produces a piece of discourse about a story.

Theme. This has two, related, meanings. In grammar, the theme is the first element in a clause. It says what the clause is about. In more general usage, theme can refers to the topic or subject matter of an entire text.

Thesaurus. A type of dictionary that groups words together on the basis of similar meaning.

Third person narrator. A narrator who is not an active participant in the story and, therefore, does not mention him/herself in the narrative. This figure is more usefully described as a **heterodiegetic narrator**.

Tragedy. In classical Greece, tragedy was a dramatic form that presented human suffering with the idea that it was therapeutic ('cathartic') for an audience to experience and witness. The narrative often involved a character who was impressive but who had a fatal character flaw (for example, too much pride).

Tragic hero. A heroic figure destined for downfall.

Vague completer. A way of completing an utterance that stops it from sounding too abrupt. For example, 'I did the shopping *and stuff*'.

Villain. A stereotypical bad character in stories that have very black and white, simple concepts of 'good' and 'evil'.

Index